American Map

Road Atlas

United States
Canada
Mexico

M000011920

Map Contents

Legend

...NSPORTATION

...TROLLED ACCESS HIGHWAYS
Freeway
Tollway; Toll Booth
Under Construction
Interchange and Exit Number
Rest Area; Service Area
Yellow with facilities; City maps only

...ER HIGHWAYS
Primary Highway
Secondary Highway
Multilane Divided Highway
Primary and Secondary highways only; City maps only
Multilane Divided Highway
State and province maps only
Other Paved Road
State and province maps only
Other Paved Road
City maps only
Unpaved Road
State and province maps only; Check conditions locally
Unpaved Road
City maps only; Check conditions locally

...HWAY MARKERS
Interstate Route
U.S. Route
State or Provincial Route
County or Other Route
Business Route
Trans-Canada Highway
Canadian Provincial Autoroute
Mexican Federal Route

...ER SYMBOLS
Distances along Major Highways
Miles in U.S.; kilometers in Canada and Mexico
Tunnel; Pass
Wayside Stop
City maps only
One-way Street
City maps only
Port of Entry
City maps only
Airport
City maps only
Auto Ferry; Passenger Ferry

RECREATION AND FEATURES OF INTEREST
National Park
National Forest; National Grassland
Other Large Park or Recreation Area
Military Lands
Indian Reservation
Small State Park with
and without Camping
City maps only
Public Campsite
City maps only
Trail
Point of Interest
Visitor Information Center
City maps only
Public Golf Course; Private Golf Course
Professional tournament location; City maps only
Hospital
City maps only
Ski Area
City maps only

CITIES AND TOWNS
National Capital; State or
Provincial Capital
Cities, Towns, and Populated Places
Type size indicates relative importance
Urban Area
State and province maps only
Large Incorporated Cities
City maps only

OTHER MAP FEATURES
JEFFERSON   County Boundary and Name
City maps only
Time Zone Boundary
+ Mt. Olympus   Mountain Peak
7,965   Elevation in Feet
Perennial; Intermittent River

Copyright © 2007
American Map Corporation
www.americanmap.com

Printed in Canada

Cover photo: Glacier National Park, Montana
(Blaine Harrington III/Alamy)

Cartography Copyright by MapQuest, Inc.

© MAPQUEST

Fabulous Drives & Adventures

NORTHWEST

- Glacier National Park, Montana
- North Cascades National Park, Washington
- Wine Country, California

⊙ Going to the Sun Road

Dramatic, mountainous Glacier National Park ranges over a broad and breathtakingly beautiful landscape. High in the mountains of northwestern Montana, dotted with plunging waterfalls, radiant wildflower meadows and swirling turquoise streams, it is celebrated not only for the beauty of its land but also for its abundant wildlife and excellent network of hiking trails.

Start with a trip over Logan Pass on Going-to-the-Sun Road. Aptly named, this amazing 50-mile strip of switchbacked pavement climbs over the spine of the park's mountains and, hugging the cliffs below the Continental Divide, connects two of its most spectacular valleys. Beginning at the east-side village of St Mary, the road skirts the shore of St Mary Lake, a 10-mile body of crystal-clear water. At the head end of the lake, Sun Point offers a smashing view of the lower valley and surrounding peaks.

Soon you plunge into deep forest and begin the long climb to Logan Pass, passing Jackson Glacier. Logan Pass is a stunning place, surrounded by jagged peaks, waterfalls and wildflower meadows. Park rangers offer guided walks in summer. The road then slants down the side of the knife-edged ridge called the Garden Wall to the valley floor, where you follow McDonald Creek through ancient forest and the Trail of the Cedars. Before long, you find yourself along the shores of Lake McDonald, the largest body of water in the park. Going-to-the-Sun Road stops just beyond the west end of Lake McDonald, with a fine overview of the park.

Contacts:
By mail: *Glacier National Park Headquaters, PO Box 128, West Glacier, MT 59936;* **By phone:** *406-888-7800;*
Website: *www.nps.gov/glac*

⊙ The North Cascades Highway

Tucked away in the northwest corner of Washington State, North Cascades National Park is a startlingly beautiful wilderness area of razor-edged summits, massive blue glaciers, primeval forests and hundreds of waterfalls. This park contains more than 300 glaciers – over half the glaciers in the lower 48 states. There is a well-maintained network of hiking trails, but only one main road into the park: the

North Cascades Highway (State Road 20), dubbed "the most scenic mountain drive in Washington."

You can stop at overlooks and trailheads directly on the highway as well as take boating tours of the park's three largest lakes. As you approach the park, the highway follows the magnificent Skagit River. Inside the park boundary is the village of Newhalem. Turn right toward the North Cascades Visitor Center where you can pick up maps and information. Further on, stop at Gorge Creek Falls, one of hundreds of cataracts that tumble down the mountains, and then continue to the little town of Diablo. There are strenuous and moderate hikes from here, or a tugboat ride to Ross Dam. The highway dips south toward Colonial Creek Campground, where the short but steep Thunder Woods Nature Trail takes you on a 1-mile loop into the realm of giant cedars. Drive to the Diablo Lake Overlook for a stunning view. At the Ross Lake Overlook, further on near the park boundary, you'll get a heavenly view of the park's largest lake.

Contacts:
By mail: *North Cascades National Park, 810 State Route 20, Sedro-Woolley, WA 98284-1239;* **By phone:** *360-856-5700;*
Website: *www.nps.gov/noca*

⊙ California Wine Country

North of San Francisco, the Russian River threads through a gorgeous 20-mile valley, watering 3,000 acres of pear orchards and 9,000 acres of vineyards, a lovely mix of redwood forest, wineries, and rolling hills. This is Sonoma County where, along with the more famous Napa Valley, the best vineyards in America are located. About 17 miles long and, at its maximum, 7 miles wide, Sonoma Valley is known as the birthplace of California's wine industry because the first European varietals in America were planted here in 1857.

Much of Santa Rosa, the largest city and county seat, was destroyed in the 1906 earthquake which devastated San Francisco, but the century-old buildings are restored around Historic Railroad Square. More historic buildings surround the 1835 plaza in Sonoma, including the Mission San Francisco Solano. The Wine Exchange of Sonoma on First Street East is the best place to shop for wine in the region. Glen Ellen was the home of the swashbuckling author Jack London, and you can see the cottage where he wrote many of his novels in the nearby State Historic Park.

You can ride the Napa Valley Wine Train or visit famous vineyards such as Robert Mondavi at Oakwood or Beaulieu Vineyard at Rutherford. The Napa Valley Museum at St. Helena has an impressive exhibit on California wine. Take the Skyway Tram to the Sterling Vineyards for a fabulous winery vista. Calistoga, at the northern end of the valley, is famous for its numerous spas offering mud baths and hot mineral pools.

Contacts:
By mail: *Napa Valley Conference and Visitors Bureau, 1310 Napa Towr Center, Napa, CA 94559;* **By phone:** *800-723-6336;*
Website: *www.napavalley.com*

SOUTHWEST

- Tularosa Basin, New Mexico
- Monument Valley, Arizona
- Palos Verdes Peninsula, California

⊙ From White Sands to the Valley of Fires

There's more than a touch of the surreal about the Tularosa Basin in southern New Mexico. Soft silvery gypsum dunes and jagged black lava flows sit side by side at White Sands National Monument and Valley of the Fires Recreation Area. Traces of Indian cultures, ill-fated Spanish missions, pioneer ranches, and a quaint mountain railroad linger in the foothills of nearby mountains.

Begin your tour in Alamogordo. The excellent New Mexico Museum of Space History provides a fascinating look at the region's role in air and space research. The highlight of the region, White Sands National Monument, is 15 miles southwest of town. From the visitor center, take the 16-mile loop drive through the dunes. Interpretive signs and trails tell the story of their formation. These white sands are really a 275-square-mile expanse of fine gypsum washed into the basin from the surrounding mountains.

From Alamogordo take US 54 north to the Valley of Fires Recreation Area, where the stark, sun-blasted landscape of jagged black rocks was created by the 220-square-mile Carrizozo Lava Flow. Or continue east on US 82. This 20-mile scenic drive into the mountains is one of the most dramatic in New Mexico, climbing abruptly from 4,350 feet at Alamogordo to almost 9,000 feet at town of Cloudcroft. Cloudcroft is a popular getaway for picnics, forest walks, and skiing. From here, State Road 244 takes you to Ruidoso via the spectacular Mescalero Apache Reservation.

Contacts:
By mail: *White Sands National Monument, PO Box 1086 Holloman AFB, NM 88330;* **By phone:** *505-679-2599;*
Website: *www.nps.gov/whsa*

⊙ Monument Valley

The 29,817-square mile Navajo Nation is the largest Indian reservation in the country and includes many of Arizona's most interesting parks. Time seems to stand still in this epic landscape, whose stone landmarks and secret canyons are sacred to the people who have called this home for many centuries.

Monument Valley is the crown jewel in the Navajo tribal park system. To reach it, drive north on Highway 89 from Flagstaff and turn east onto Highway 160, passing through Tuba City. When you reach Kayenta, head north 20 miles on Highway 163 to the park. Allow at least two hours to tour the 17-mile unpaved scenic drive into the valley. A tour booklet available at the visitor center identifies 11 scenic overlooks along the drive. Sand Springs, the valley's only water source, offers glimpses of a hogan, corrals, sheep, goats, and local residents dressed in traditional clothing. On the other side of Highway 160, the original 1923 trading post built by Harry Goulding and his wife Mike is now a small museum.

A side tour in Monument Valley will take you into Mystery Valley to view small Anasazi pueblos, but to see the most beautifully preserved cliff dwellings, don't miss little-known Navajo National Monument, 28 miles west of Kayenta. From the small visitor center, the 1/2-mile Sandal Trail leads to an overlook above Betatakin, a spectacular 135-room pueblo built in AD 1250 in a 450-foot high alcove above Tsegi Canyon.

Contacts:
By mail: *Navajo Parks and Recreation Department, PO Box 2520, Window Rock, AZ 86515;* **By phone:** *928-871-6647;*
Website: *www.navajonationparks.org*

⊙ Take the Southern California Coast Road

It takes a little longer to drive down the coast from Los Angeles to San Diego than whizzing down the freeway, but the route is much more interesting. The coastal bluffs of the Palos Verdes peninsula offer some of the loveliest views of the ocean, which can best be enjoyed from the winding Palos Verdes Drive. At Point Vicente Lighthouse and Interpretive Center there are telescopes to view passing whales (December to spring).

A few miles beyond is San Pedro, a former fishing port. Harbor tours run from Ports O'Call Village, and you can visit the maritime museum and Cabrillo Marine Museum. Neighboring Long Beach has several attractions, including the Queen Mary and the Aquarium of the Pacific. At Belmont you can take gondola tours along the canals of the Naples suburb.

Back on the Pacific Coast Highway (Highway 1), you'll pass through the surfer community of Huntington Beach. At Newport Beach, the Balboa peninsula has 6 miles of sandy shore enclosing a harbor filled with yachts, and a paved walkway along the beach for skating, cycling, and strolling. Lovely Laguna Beach is an upscale artists' colony, with a number of arts festivals in summer. At Dana Point Harbor, take a short detour to the historic Mission San Juan Capistrano, famous for the swallows which return every year on St. Joseph's Day. Continuing south, you'll pass several more beaches. Turn off at the Torrey Pines State Reserve to watch hang gliders soar or walk in the woods before reaching the San Diego area.

Contacts:
By mail: *Long Beach Area Convention and Visitors Bureau, One World Trade Center, Third Floor, Long Beach, CA 90831;*
By phone: *800-452-7829;*
Website: *www.visitlongbeach.com*

NORTHEAST

- North Shore, Massachusetts
- Bradywine River Valley, Pennsylvania
- New York State Seaway Trail, New York

⊙ Massachusetts North Shore

The North Shore of Massachusetts is steeped in the maritime heritage of New England, and provides spectacular seashore scenery along with some of the region's finest architecture. For the best ocean views driving

up from Boston, detour off Route 1A at Swampscott and take route 129 to Marblehead, a trove of 18th-century homes.

Next up is Salem – take Route 114 back onto Route 1A and continue north – a wealthy seaport in its day. Drive along 200-year-old Chestnut Street, one of the country's most beautiful thoroughfares. Among the town's his-

toric sites and museums are those that tell the story of the famous witch trials of the 1690s. At Beverly, on the other side of the Danvers River, pick up Route 127 and meander along the south coast of Cape Ann. Continue into Gloucester, Massachusetts' oldest fishing port, dating from 1623. Continue along Route 127A to Rockport.

Drive around the rocky northern tip of Cape Ann on Route 127 and continue via Route 126 to Route 133 north and the village of Essex. Its single main street is lined with antiques shops. Ipswich, 6 miles north, is one of the oldest coastal settlements, founded in 1633. Turn down leafy Argilla Road to reach Crane's Beach, a popular swimming spot. Continuing on Route 1A, pass through the towns of Rowley and Newbury, where hay is still harvested in dome-shaped stacks as it was centuries ago. At Newburyport, many Georgian and Federal homes have been lovingly preserved. Crossing into New Hampshire, it's a 19-mile drive to Portsmouth.

Contacts:
By mail: *Massachusetts Office of Travel and Tourism, 10 Park Plaza, Suite 4510, Boston, MA 02116;* **By phone:** *800-227-6277;*
Website: *www.massvacation.com*

⊖ The Brandywine River Valley

An easy 20-minute drive southeast of Philadelphia leads to a valley of old homesteads, hamlets, and quiet country roads, with a strong history of 19th-century American industry. Heading out of the city on Route 1, you'll come to the valley of the Brandywine River, which twists through 20 miles of rolling hills and estates. The river is really no more than a creek where two east and west branches meet at Chadds Ford. The scenery inspired painter N.C. Wyeth and his descendants to settle here, and the Brandywine River Museum has an outstanding collection of Wyeth paintings. You can follow a pretty river walk to historic John Chads House, or visit Chadds Ford Winery. A few minutes' away, near the quiet town of Kennett Square, is beautiful Longwood Gardens, with elaborate fountains, lakes, and greenhouses, and the Phillips Mushroom Museum.

Hop on Route 52 south, stopping just 30 miles south of Philadelphia and 6 miles north of Wilmington, Delaware at the Winterthur Museum and Gardens. The former home of Henry Francis du Pont, it houses the nation's largest collection of early American decorative arts, set in a mansion on 1,000 superbly landscaped acres. Continue south on Route 52, turning left on Route 141 for the Hagley Museum and Library, built beside the Brandywine on the original site of the 1802 du Pont mills. Today it is an outdoor museum dedicated to America's economic and techno-

logical heritage. Overlooking the river is Eleutherian Mills, the 1803 Georgian-style mansion that housed five generations of du Ponts.

For more du Pont grandeur, continue on Route 141 to Nemours Mansion and Gardens. The Louis XVI-style estate of Alfred I. du Pont displays art and antiques, dating from the 15th century. The Brandywine eventually joins the Delaware River at Wilmington. The city offers a wealth of historical and cultural sites, including the Delaware Art Museum and the Rockwood Museum and Gardens.

Contacts:
By mail: *Brandywine Conference and Visitors Bureau, One Beaver Valley Road, Chadds Ford, PA 19317;* **By phone:** *610-565-3679;*
Website: *www.brandywinecountry.org*

⊖ New York State Seaway Trail

New York's "North Coast" encompasses the easternmost of the Great Lakes, Lake Ontario, source of one of the world's great rivers, the St. Lawrence. From here the Thousand Islands archipelago extends eastward for some 35 miles of the river. This route follows part of the longer New York State Seaway Trail, a 454-mile scenic drive. The area is rich in early American historical sites and recreation facilities.

From Oswego, on the shores of Lake Ontario, head north along the lakeshore on Route 104 to the resort town of Sackets Harbor. The Seaway Trail Discovery Center has exhibits and information on the trail. A few miles inland, Watertown is the headquarters of several whitewater rafting companies. Head out toward Cape Vincent on Route 12E through Brownville and past Chaumont Bay, the largest freshwater bay in the world. Northwest of Three Mile Bay, turn off Route 12E onto Route 6 to the tip of Cape Vincent. The 1854 Tibbetts Point Lighthouse stands where the St. Lawrence River flows out of Lake Ontario.

Follow Route 12E along the banks of the St. Lawrence to Clayton, a one-time shipbuilding and lumbering. One of the region's most impressive museums is the Antique Boat Museum. Further east, the Thousand Islands International Bridge crosses to Wellesley Island State Park. From Alexandria Bay, you can take a water taxi to see Boldt Castle on Heart Island. Continue north on Routes 12 and 37 to reach the Frederic Remington Art Museum in Ogdensburg. The artist is renowned for his paintings and bronzes of Western figures. At Massena, you can watch the cargo vessels navigating the Eisenhower Locks from an observation deck. The visitor center has exhibits on the St. Lawrence Seaway. The route ends at Hogansburg, on the St. Regis Indian Reservation, where the Akwesasne Cultural Museum has thousands of artifacts.

Contacts:
By mail: *Seaway Trail, Inc., PO Box 660, Sackets Harbor, NY 13685;*
By phone: *800-732-9298;*
Website: *www.seawaytrail.com*

MIDWEST

■ Black Hills, South Dakota
■ Ozark Mountains, Arkansas

⊖ Around the Black Hills of South Dakota

In the semi-arid country west of the Missouri River, the rolling prairie abruptly gives way to the rugged Badlands and the beautiful Black Hills. Within easy driving distance of Rapid City, South Dakota, on the eastern edge of the Black Hills, are some extraordinary natural and cultural features of this region. The most famous attraction of the Black Hills is Mount Rushmore National Memorial, near Keystone via Highways 16 and 244. Nearby, you can visit the even larger memorial to the Lakota warrior Crazy Horse, being carved out of Thunderhead Mountain.

The dramatic Iron Mountain Road leads through tunnels and over picturesque bridges to Wind Cave National Park. On the surface, the park is a sanctuary of rolling grasslands and ponderosa forest snuggled against the foot of the Black Hills. Below ground, with more than 75 miles of explored passages, it's the third longest cave in the United States and one

of the most complex "maze caves" in the world. The cave's most conspicuous feature is the wind that streams in and out of its narrow mouth, sometimes as fast as 70 mph. It's a cave of remarkable beauty, with rare boxwork calcite and other delicate formations. The park is also full of wildlife, which can be seen from Highway 87 which winds through the forest and grasslands.

If you're in the mood for more underground adventures, Jewel Cave National Monument is about 35 miles west of Wind Cave. Slightly smaller, it has beautiful formations that justify its fanciful name. Devil's Tower National Monument, an 865-foot column of volcanic rock near Sundance, Wyoming, lies northwest of the Black Hills.

Contacts:
By mail: *Mount Rushmore National Memorial, 13000 Highway 244, Building 31, Suite 1, Keystone, SD 57751;* **By phone:** *605-574-3171;*
Website: *www.nps.gov/moru*

⊙ Paddling Through the Ozark Mountains

Rising to 2,800 feet, the Ozarks stretch from southern Missouri into Arkansas. One of the few elevated regions between the Appalachians and Rocky Mountains, it is a meeting place of eastern forests and western prairie. Forests of oak and hickory interspersed with sun-dappled glades stand atop ancient limestone cliffs. Below the surface, thousands of caves have been carved out of the limestone by rainwater. Springs gush from the rocks. In fact, the largest concentration of springs in the world are found in the Ozarks.

The Buffalo National River tumbles down the north face of the Boston Mountains, the most rugged section of the Ozarks, before crossing the Springfield Plateau and emptying into the White River, a journey of 150 miles The Buffalo's location in northwest Arkansas, within a two-hour drive of Little Rock, makes it both accessible and remote. Boating, fishing, and hiking are the main activities here. Canoe rentals and outfitting are available in many locations, and float trips can be arranged for almost any duration.

Although the park is set up for boaters, those who enjoy driving can find access to many sites of interest. Fourteen campgrounds are accessible by car. The Tyler Bend Visitor Center, midway in the park off Highway 65, and ranger stations at other locations offer interpretive programs, Ozark craft and folk music, guided hikes, and canoe floats. Also within the park are the Indian Rockhouse, one of the largest prehistoric bluff shelters in the Ozarks, and the Rush Mining District ghost town. At the Ozark Folk Center in Mountain View, southeast of the river on Highway 14, artisans demonstrate traditional crafts and music and highlight the region's culture and history.

Contacts:
By mail: *Buffalo National River, 402 N Walnut, Suite 136, Harrison, AR 72601;* **By phone:** *870-439-2502;*
Website: *www.nps.gov/buff*

SOUTHEAST

- Shenandoah National Park, Virginia
- Civil Rights Trail, Alabama
- Savannah, Georgia

⊙ Virginia's Heavenly Skyline Drive

Situated in Virginia's Blue Ridge Mountains, Shenandoah National Park is a long, narrow corridor of ridges and valleys clothed in dense forest and laced with leaping streams and waterfalls. Running along the backbone of the mountains is Skyline Drive, a 105-mile scenic highway that serves as the park's main thoroughfare.

Upon leaving Highway 340 at Front Royal you will enter a shady green tunnel of hardwoods. The pavement curves around the hills, then sprawls into a breathtaking overlook above the Shenandoah Valley. Dickey Ridge Visitor Center provides an introduction to Shenandoah's history.

By mile 21, you will be nearing an elevation of 3,400 feet and from Hogback Overlook on a clear day, you can count several bends in the Shenandoah River meandering through the verdant valley. At Thornton Gap, Highway 211 crosses Skyline Drive. You can hike to Mary's Rock for a panoramic view. Continuing south, the rocky visage of Stony Man appears above the drive around milepost 39. At 3,680 feet, Skyland Resort is the highest point on Skyline Drive; trails to the summit start from here. Continuing south, Big Meadows marks the halfway point. Loft Mountain is the southernmost campground along the route. From here you slowly descend to the terminus of Skyline Drive at Rockfish Gap, where you can continue your odyssey on the Blue Ridge Parkway to the Great Smoky Mountains National Park.

Contacts:
By mail: *Shenandoah National Park, 3655 U.S. Highway, 211 East, Luray, VA 22835-9036;* **By phone:** *540-999-3500;*
Website: *www.nps.gov/shen*

⊙ Alabama's Civil Rights Trail

Many of Alabama's Civil Rights landmarks can be seen in its central plains. Downtown Birmingham has poignant reminders of the bitter struggles of the 1960s. Striking sculptures in Kelly Ingram Park portray the demonstrations that took place here. West of the park, Alabama's largest statue of Dr. Martin Luther King, Jr. faces the Sixteenth Street Baptists Church, where four young girls were killed by a racist bombing. Nearby, the Birmingham Civil Rights Institute contains moving exhibits that show how African-Americans were treated under local segregation laws.

The state capital, Montgomery, lies 91 miles south via Interstate 65. Most landmarks here predate the Civil War, such as the State Capitol, an 1851 Greek Revival structure. Walk a block west for the red brick Dexter Avenue King Memorial Church, where 25-year-old King organized the Montgomery Bus Boycott in 1955 that launched the Civil Rights Movement. A block behind the church is the Civil Rights Memorial, where a sheet of water flows over the names of 40 civil rights martyrs. Nearby, the Rosa Parks Museum tells the moving story of the black seamstress who refused to give up her seat on the bus to a white man; her arrest sparked the bus boycott that brought worldwide attention to the cause.

The 51-mile route west along US 80 was the site of the Selma-to-Montgomery march for voting rights in 1965. There are photos in Selma's National Voting Rights Museum. South of Montgomery, about halfway to Mobile, Monroeville is the hometown of Harper Lee, whose novel *To Kill a Mockingbird* is one of the strongest portrayals of the segregated south.

Contacts:
By mail: *Alabama Bureau of Tourism & Travel, 401 Adams Avenue, Suite 126, PO Box 4927, Montgomery, AL 36103-4927;* **By phone:** *334-242-4169;*
Website: *www.touralabama.org*

⊙ From the New South to the Old South

The bold skyscraper city of Atlanta is called the "capital of the New South," but a half-day's drive brings you to Savannah, Georgia's oldest city and one of the most charming in the Old South. About 16 miles south of Atlanta via Interstate 75 and Georgia Highway 54 is Jonesboro. Where Margaret Mitchell drew inspiration for her epic *Gone with the Wind*. Several antebellum homes still remain in the town.

Continue southeast on I-75 to Macon. The Georgia Music Hall of Fame honors Macon-born musicians Otis Redding, Little Richard, and the Allman Brothers, along with other home-grown stars who found fame. You can also visit Hay House, a stunning 1859 Italian Renaissance palazzo.

Interstate 16 takes you to the coastal city of Savannah, founded in 1733. Today, 21 of its original 24 public squares have been refurbished, forming the nucleus of Savannah's Historic District – one of the largest, loveliest urban National Historic Landmark districts in the country, covering a 2 1/2-mile radius. Each square has a distinctive character, defined by the structures that encompass it, whether a towering cathedral, a Confederacy statue, or an ornate fountain. These excel in Savannah's most characteristic details: fancy ironwork and Spanish moss. Many are ringed by Greek Revival mansions. Other highlights include the Telfair Museum of Art, the Owens-Thomas House, and Wright Square.

Contacts:
By mail: *Savannah Tourist Information, 101 East Bay Street, Savannah, GA 31401;* **By phone:** *877-282-6624;*
Website: *www.savannah-visit.com*

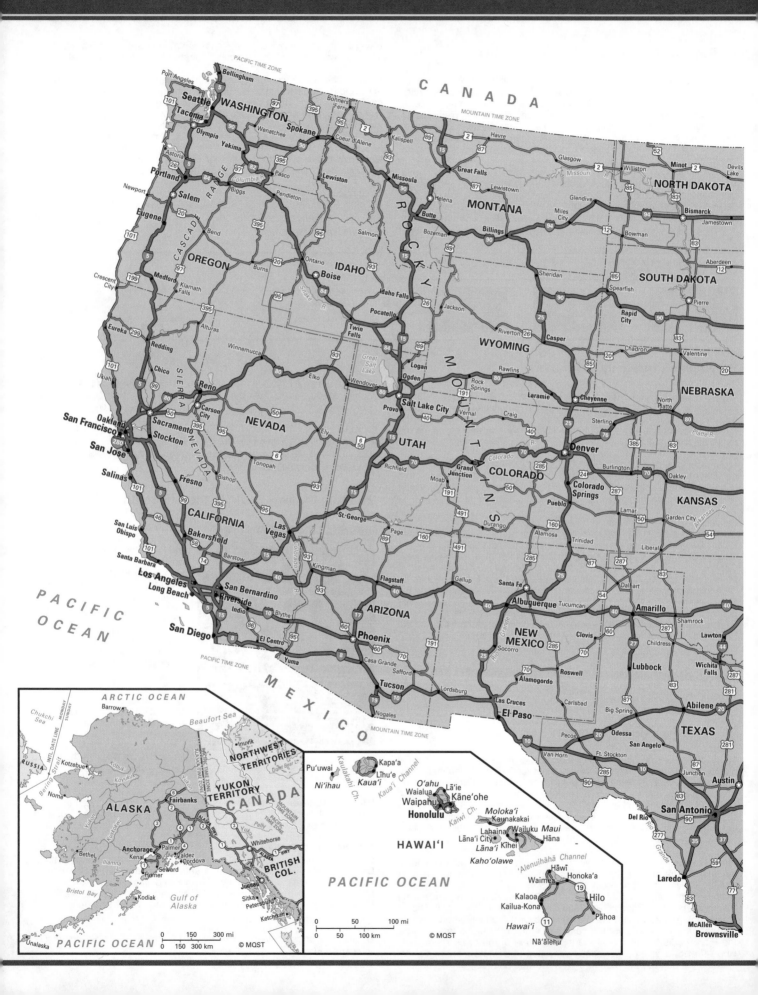

CENTRAL TIME ZONE

L. of the Woods

C A N A D A

EASTERN TIME ZONE

MAINE

Van Buren
Houlton
Calais
Bangor

L. Superior

Grand Portage

Sault Ste. Marie

International Falls

Grand Forks
Fargo
Bemidji
Duluth
Ironwood
Grand Marais

MINNESOTA

Willmar
St. Paul
Minneapolis
Watertown

WISCONSIN

Rhinelander
Iron Mountain
Green Bay
Eau Claire
Stevens Point

MICHIGAN

Alpena
Traverse City
Mackinaw City
Ludington

L. Michigan

L. Huron

Sioux Falls
Albert Lea
Mason City
La Crosse
Madison
Milwaukee
Manitowoc

Grand Rapids
Lansing
Jackson
Flint
Bay City
Port Huron

L. Ontario

Rochester
Syracuse
Watertown
Burlington

VT.
N.H.
Montpelier
Concord
Lebanon
Rutland
Portland
Portsmouth

Yankton
Sioux City
Waterloo
Dubuque
Rockford

IOWA

Cedar Rapids
Des Moines
Davenport
Joliet
Chicago

Benton Harbor
South Bend
Ft. Wayne
Lima
Toledo

Detroit
L. Erie
Cleveland
Erie
Buffalo

Binghamton
Elmira

NEW YORK

Albany
Pittsfield
Springfield

MASS.
Boston
Providence
New Bedford
Provincetown

CONN.
New Haven
Hartford
New London
R.I.

Omaha
Lincoln
St. Joseph

Ottumwa
Burlington
Peoria
Bloomington

ILLINOIS
Springfield
Champaign

INDIANA
Indianapolis
Dayton
Terre Haute

Mansfield

OHIO
Columbus
Akron
Youngstown
Pittsburgh
Wheeling

PA.
Du Bois
Williamsport
Scranton
Harrisburg
Johnstown

Warren
Newark
N.J.
Allentown
Trenton
Philadelphia
New York
Atlantic City

Topeka
Kansas City

MISSOURI
Jefferson City
St. Louis

Mt. Vernon
Louisville
Evansville
Owensboro

KENTUCKY
Frankfort
Lexington
Cincinnati
Huntington
Charleston

WEST VIRGINIA
Parkersburg
Morgantown
Cumberland
Frederick
Winchester
Staunton

MD.
Baltimore
Washington, D.C.
Annapolis
Dover
DEL.
Wilmington
Salisbury

Salina
Concordia

Springfield
Poplar Bluff
Cairo
Paducah

Clarksville
Nashville
Bowling Green
London

Bristol
Beckley
Roanoke

VA.
Lynchburg
Petersburg
Danville

Richmond
Hampton
Norfolk

Wichita
Blackwell
Joplin

ARKANSAS
Fayetteville
Jonesboro
Jackson

TENN.
Memphis
Huntsville
Chattanooga
Knoxville
Asheville
Greenville

Winston-Salem
Greensboro
Durham
Raleigh
New Bern

N.C.
Charlotte
Spartanburg
Fayetteville

APPALACHIAN

Tulsa
Muskogee

OKLAHOMA
Oklahoma City
Ft. Smith

Little Rock

Tupelo
Columbus

MISSISSIPPI
Jackson
Meridian

ALABAMA
Birmingham
Montgomery
Columbus

GEORGIA
Atlanta
Macon
Augusta

Columbia
Florence

S.C.
Myrtle Beach
Charleston
Wilmington

ATLANTIC OCEAN

Sherman
Paris
Texarkana
El Dorado
Winona

LOUISIANA
Shreveport
Monroe
Natchez
Alexandria
Hattiesburg

Dothan
Albany
Waycross

Savannah
Brunswick

Dallas
Ft. Worth
Tyler
Lufkin

Baton Rouge
Lafayette
Houma
New Orleans
Biloxi
Mobile
Pensacola
Panama City
Tallahassee

Jacksonville

Lake City

FLORIDA
Ocala
Daytona Beach
Orlando

Waco
Beaumont
Lake Charles

Houston
Galveston

Victoria

Corpus Christi

Gulf of Mexico

CENTRAL TIME ZONE

Tampa
St. Petersburg
Ft. Pierce
W. Palm Beach
Ft. Lauderdale
Miami
Ft. Myers
Naples
L. Okeechobee
EVERGLADES PKWY

Key West

EASTERN TIME ZONE

1 inch represents 195 miles
or 314 kilometers
(1:12,350,000)

MI   100   200   300
100   200   300   KM

© MapQuest, Inc.

BORDER CROSSING

CANADA

U.S. citizens entering Canada from the U.S. are required to present passports or proof of U.S. citizenship accompanied by photo identification. U.S. citizens entering from a third country must have a valid passport. Visas are not required for U.S. citizens entering from the U.S. for stays of up to 180 days. Naturalized citizens should travel with their naturalization certificates. Alien permanent residents of the U.S. must present their Alien Registration Cards. Individuals under the age of 18 and travelling alone should carry a letter from a parent or legal guardian authorizing their travel in Canada.

U.S. driver's licenses are valid in Canada, and U.S. citizens do not need to obtain an international driver's license. Proof of auto insurance, however, is required.

For additional information, consult http://travel.state.gov/tips_canada.html before you travel.

UNITED STATES (FROM CANADA)

Canadian citizens entering the U.S. are required to demonstrate proof of their citizenship, normally with a photo identification accompanied by a valid birth certificate or citizenship card. Passports or visas are not required for visits lasting less than six months; for visits exceeding six months, they are mandatory. Individuals under the age of 18 and travelling alone should carry notarized documentation, signed by both parents, authorizing their travel.

Canadian driver's licenses are valid in the U.S. for one year, and automobiles may enter free of payment or duty fees. Drivers need only provide customs officials with proof of vehicle registration, ownership, and insurance.

Before you travel, find out about any road construction or road closures. You can find this information on individual state transportation websites. A full list of these websites can be found at www.fhwa.dot.gov/webstate.htm.

In addition, 511 is a nationwide telephone number that provides current information about road conditions. A list of active 511 locations can be found at www.fhwa.dot.gov/trafficinfo/511.htm.

Distances in chart are in miles. To convert miles to kilometers, multiply the distance in miles by 1.609. Example: New York, NY to Boston, MA = 215 miles or 346 kilometers (215 x 1.609)	ALBANY, NY	ALBUQUERQUE, NM	AMARILLO, TX	ATLANTA, GA	BALTIMORE, MD	BILLINGS, MT	BIRMINGHAM, AL	BISMARCK, ND	BOISE, ID	BOSTON, MA	BUFFALO, NY	CHARLESTON, SC	CHARLESTON, WV	CHARLOTTE, NC	CHEYENNE, WY	CHICAGO, IL	CINCINNATI, OH	CLEVELAND, OH	COLUMBUS, OH	DALLAS, TX	DENVER, CO	DES MOINES, IA	DETROIT, MI	EL PASO, TX	HARTFORD, CT	HOUSTON, TX	INDIANAPOLIS, IN	JACKSON, MS	JACKSONVILLE, FL	KANSAS CITY, MO	LAS VEGAS, NV
ALBANY, NY		2095	1811	1010	333	2083	1093	1675	2526	172	292	913	634	771	1789	832	730	484	621	1680	1833	1155	571	2326	111	1768	795	1331	1094	1282	2586
ALBUQUERQUE, NM	2095		286	1490	1902	991	1274	1333	966	2240	1808	1793	1568	1649	538	1352	1409	1619	1476	754	438	1091	1608	263	2139	994	1298	1157	1837	894	578
AMARILLO, TX	1811	286		1206	1618	988	991	1398	1266	1957	1524	1510	1285	1365	534	1069	1126	1335	1192	470	434	808	1324	438	1855	711	1014	874	1517	610	864
ATLANTA, GA	1010	1490	1206		679	1889	150	1559	2218	1100	910	317	503	238	1482	717	476	726	577	792	1403	967	735	1437	998	800	531	386	344	801	2067
BALTIMORE, MD	333	1902	1618	679		1959	795	1551	2401	422	370	583	352	441	1665	708	521	377	420	1399	1690	1031	532	2045	321	1470	600	1032	763	1087	2445
BILLINGS, MT	2083	991	988	1889	1959		1839	413	626	2254	1796	2157	1755	2012	455	1246	1552	1597	1608	1433	554	1007	1534	1255	2153	1673	1432	1836	2237	1088	965
BIRMINGHAM, AL	1093	1274	991	150	795	1839		1509	2170	1215	909	466	578	389	1434	667	475	725	576	647	1356	919	734	1292	1114	678	481	241	494	753	1852
BISMARCK, ND	1675	1333	1398	1559	1551	413	1509		1039	1846	1388	1749	1347	1604	594	838	1144	1189	1200	1342	693	675	1126	1597	1745	1582	1024	1548	1906	801	1378
BOISE, ID	2526	966	1266	2218	2401	626	2170	1039		2697	2239	2520	2182	2375	737	1708	1969	2040	2036	1711	833	1369	1977	1206	2595	1952	1852	2115	2566	1376	760
BOSTON, MA	172	2240	1957	1100	422	2254	1215	1846	2697		462	1003	741	861	1961	1003	862	654	760	1819	2004	1326	741	2465	102	1890	940	1453	1184	1427	2757
BUFFALO, NY	292	1808	1524	910	370	1796	909	1388	2239	462		899	431	695	1502	545	442	197	333	1393	1546	868	277	2039	401	1513	508	1134	1080	995	2299
CHARLESTON, SC	913	1793	1510	317	583	2157	466	1749	2520	1003	899		468	204	1783	907	622	724	637	1109	1705	1204	879	1754	901	1110	721	703	238	1102	2371
CHARLESTON, WV	634	1568	1285	503	352	1755	578	1347	2182	741	431	468		265	1445	506	209	255	168	1072	1367	802	410	1718	639	1192	320	816	649	764	2122
CHARLOTTE, NC	771	1649	1365	238	441	2012	389	1604	2375	861	695	204	265		1637	761	476	520	433	1031	1559	1057	675	1677	760	1041	575	625	385	956	2225
CHEYENNE, WY	1789	538	534	1482	1665	455	1434	594	737	1961	1502	1783	1445	1637		972	1233	1304	1300	979	100	633	1241	801	1859	1220	1115	1382	1829	640	843
CHICAGO, IL	832	1352	1069	717	708	1246	667	838	1708	1003	545	907	506	761	972		302	346	359	936	1015	337	283	1543	901	1108	184	750	1065	532	1768
CINCINNATI, OH	730	1409	1126	476	521	1552	475	1144	1969	862	442	622	209	476	1233	302		253	105	958	1200	599	261	1605	760	1079	116	700	803	597	1955
CLEVELAND, OH	484	1619	1335	726	377	1597	725	1189	2040	654	197	724	255	520	1304	346	253		144	1208	1347	669	171	1854	570	1328	319	950	904	806	2100
COLUMBUS, OH	621	1476	1192	577	420	1608	576	1200	2036	760	333	637	168	433	1300	359	105	144		1059	1266	665	192	1706	659	1179	176	801	818	663	2021
DALLAS, TX	1680	754	470	792	1399	1433	647	1342	1711	1819	1393	1109	1072	1031	979	936	958	1208	1059		887	752	1218	647	1717	241	913	406	1049	554	1331
DENVER, CO	1833	438	434	1403	1690	554	1356	693	833	2004	1546	1705	1367	1559	100	1015	1200	1347	1266	887		676	1284	701	1903	1127	1088	1290	1751	603	756
DES MOINES, IA	1155	1091	808	967	1031	1007	919	675	1369	1326	868	1204	802	1057	633	337	599	669	665	752	676		606	1283	1225	992	481	931	1315	194	1429
DETROIT, MI	571	1608	1324	735	532	1534	734	1126	1977	741	277	879	410	675	1241	283	261	171	192	1218	1284	606		1799	679	1338	318	960	1060	795	2037
EL PASO, TX	2326	263	438	1437	2045	1255	1292	1597	1206	2465	2039	1754	1718	1677	801	1543	1605	1854	1706	647	701	1283	1799		2364	758	1489	1051	1642	1085	717
HARTFORD, CT	111	2139	1855	998	321	2153	1114	1745	2595	102	401	901	639	760	1859	901	760	570	659	1717	1903	1225	679	2364		1788	839	1351	1082	1326	2655
HOUSTON, TX	1768	994	711	800	1470	1673	678	1582	1952	1890	1513	1110	1192	1041	1220	1108	1079	1328	1179	241	1127	992	1338	758	1788		1033	445	884	795	1474
INDIANAPOLIS, IN	795	1298	1014	531	600	1432	481	1024	1852	940	508	721	320	575	1115	184	116	319	176	913	1088	481	318	1489	839	1033		675	879	485	1843
JACKSON, MS	1331	1157	874	386	1032	1836	241	1548	2115	1453	1134	703	816	625	1382	750	700	950	801	406	1290	931	960	1051	1351	445	675		598	747	1735
JACKSONVILLE, FL	1094	1837	1517	344	763	2237	494	1906	2566	1184	1080	238	649	385	1829	1065	803	904	818	1049	1751	1315	1060	1642	1082	884	879	598		1148	2415
KANSAS CITY, MO	1282	894	610	801	1087	1088	753	801	1376	1427	995	1102	764	956	640	532	597	806	663	554	603	194	795	1085	1326	795	485	747	1148		1358
LAS VEGAS, NV	2586	578	864	2067	2445	965	1852	1378	760	2757	2299	2371	2122	2225	843	1768	1955	2100	2021	1331	756	1429	2037	717	2655	1474	1843	1735	2415	1358	
LITTLE ROCK, AR	1354	900	617	528	1072	1530	381	1183	1808	1493	1066	900	745	754	1076	662	632	882	733	327	984	567	891	974	1391	447	587	269	873	382	1478
LOS ANGELES, CA	2859	806	1092	2237	2705	1239	2092	1702	1033	3046	2572	2554	2374	2453	1116	2042	2215	2374	2281	1446	1029	1703	2310	801	2944	1558	2104	1851	2441	1632	274
LOUISVILLE, KY	832	1320	1036	419	602	1547	369	1139	1933	964	545	610	251	464	1197	299	106	356	207	852	1118	595	366	1499	862	972	112	594	766	516	1874
MEMPHIS, TN	1214	1033	750	389	933	1625	241	1337	1954	1353	927	760	606	614	1217	539	493	742	594	466	1116	720	752	1112	1251	586	464	211	733	536	1611
MIAMI, FL	1439	2155	1834	661	1109	2554	812	2224	2883	1529	1425	583	994	730	2147	1382	1141	1250	1163	1367	2069	1632	1401	1959	1427	1201	1196	915	345	1466	2733
MILWAUKEE, WI	929	1426	1142	813	805	1175	763	767	1748	1100	642	1003	601	857	1012	89	398	443	454	1010	1055	378	380	1617	999	1193	279	835	1160	573	1808
MINNEAPOLIS, MN	1245	1339	1055	1129	1121	839	1079	431	1465	1417	958	1319	918	1173	881	409	714	760	771	999	924	246	697	1530	1315	1240	596	1151	1477	441	1677
MOBILE, AL	1344	1344	1106	332	1013	2019	258	1765	2302	1433	1165	642	837	572	1570	923	731	981	832	639	1478	1115	991	1231	1332	473	737	187	410	930	1922
MONTPELIER, VT	167	2226	1943	1193	516	2219	1308	1811	2661	178	423	1096	834	954	1925	967	861	615	752	1811	1969	1291	690	2458	195	1983	927	1546	1277	1413	2722
MONTREAL, QC	230	2172	1888	1241	564	2093	1289	1685	2535	313	397	1145	822	1003	1799	841	815	588	725	1772	1843	1165	564	2363	338	1892	872	1514	1325	1359	2596
NASHVILLE, TN	1003	1248	965	242	716	1648	194	1315	1976	1136	716	543	395	397	1240	474	281	531	382	681	1162	725	541	1328	1034	801	287	423	589	559	1826
NEW ORLEANS, LA	1440	1276	993	473	1142	1955	351	1734	2234	1563	1254	783	926	713	1502	935	820	1070	921	525	1409	1117	1079	1118	1461	360	826	185	556	932	1854
NEW YORK, NY	151	2015	1731	869	192	2049	985	1641	2491	215	400	773	515	631	1755	797	636	466	535	1589	1799	1121	622	2235	115	1660	715	1223	953	1202	2552
NORFOLK, VA	570	1970	1686	558	239	2141	708	1733	2584	660	573	437	415	319	1847	890	624	559	604	1350	1782	1213	714	1996	558	1360	735	944	617	1179	2537
OKLAHOMA CITY, OK	1549	546	262	944	1354	1227	729	1136	1506	1694	1262	1248	1022	1102	773	807	863	1073	930	209	681	546	1062	737	1593	449	752	612	1291	348	1124
OMAHA, NE	1292	973	726	989	1168	904	941	616	1234	1463	1005	1290	952	1144	497	474	736	806	802	669	541	136	743	1236	1362	910	618	935	1336	188	1294
ORLANDO, FL	1235	1934	1613	440	904	2333	591	2003	2662	1324	1221	379	790	525	1926	1161	920	1045	958	1146	1847	1411	1180	1738	1223	980	975	694	141	1245	2512
PHILADELPHIA, PA	223	1954	1671	782	104	2019	897	1611	2462	321	414	685	454	543	1725	768	576	437	474	1501	1744	1091	592	2147	219	1572	655	1135	866	1141	2500
PHOENIX, AZ	2561	466	753	1868	2366	1199	1723	1662	993	2706	2274	2184	2035	2107	1004	1819	1876	2085	1942	1077	904	1558	2074	432	2605	1188	1764	1482	2072	1360	285
PITTSBURGH, PA	485	1670	1386	676	246	1719	763	1311	2161	592	217	642	217	438	1425	467	292	136	190	1246	1460	791	292	1893	491	1366	370	988	822	857	2215
PORTLAND, ME	270	2338	2054	1197	520	2352	1313	1944	2795	107	560	1101	839	959	2059	1101	960	751	858	1917	2102	1424	838	2563	199	1988	1038	1550	1281	1525	2855
PORTLAND, OR	2954	1395	1695	2647	2830	889	2599	1301	432	3126	2667	2948	2610	2802	1166	2137	2398	2469	2464	2140	1261	1798	2405	1767	3024	2381	2280	2544	2994	1805	1188
RALEIGH, NC	639	1782	1499	396	309	2110	547	1702	2495	729	642	279	313	158	1758	861	522	568	482	1189	1680	1157	724	1834	627	1198	639	783	460	1077	2360
RAPID CITY, SD	1750	841	837	1511	1626	379	1463	320	930	1921	1463	1824	1422	1678	305	913	1219	1264	1275	1077	404	629	1201	1105	1820	1318	1101	1458	1859	710	1035
RENO, NV	2747	1020	1306	2440	2623	960	2392	1372	430	2919	2460	2741	2403	2595	959	1930	2191	2262	2257	1933	1054	1591	2198	1315	2817	2072	2073	2337	2787	1598	442
RICHMOND, VA	482	1876	1593	527	152	2053	678	1645	2496	572	485	428	322	289	1760	802	530	471	517	1309	1688	1126	627	1955	471	1330	641	914	609	1085	2444
ST. LOUIS, MO	1036	1051	767	549	841	1341	501	1053	1628	1181	749	850	512	704	892	294	350	560	417	635	855	436	549	1242	1080	863	239	505	896	252	1610
SALT LAKE CITY, UT	2224	624	964	1916	2100	548	1868	960	342	2395	1936	2218	1880	2072	436	1406	1667	1738	1734	1410	531	1067	1675	864	2293	1650	1549	1813	2264	1074	417
SAN ANTONIO, TX	1953	818	513	1000	1671	1500	878	1599	1761	2092	1665	1310	1344	1241	1046	1270	1231	1481	1332	271	946	1009	1490	556	1990	200	1186	644	1084	812	1272
SAN DIEGO, CA	2919	825	1111	2166	2724	1302	2021	1765	1096	3065	2632	2483	2393	2405	1179	2105	2234	2437	2300	1375	1092	1766	2373	730	2963	1487	2122	1780	2370	1695	337
SAN FRANCISCO, CA	2964	1111	1397	2618	2840	1176	2472	1749	646	3135	2677	2934	2620	2759	1176	2146	2407	2478	2474	1827	1271	1807	2415	1181	3034	1938	2290	2232	2822	1814	575
SEATTLE, WA	2899	1463	1763	2705	2775	816	2657	1229	500	3070	2612	2973	2571	2827	1234	2062	2368	2413	2424	2208	1329	1822	2350	1944	2969	2449	2249	2612	3052	1872	1256
TAMPA, FL	1290	1949	1628	455	960	2348	606	2018	2677	1380	1276	434	845	581	1941	1176	935	1101	1036	1161	1862	1426	1194	1753	1278	995	990	709	196	1259	2526
TORONTO, ON	400	1841	1557	958	565	1762	958	1354	2204	570	106	1006	537	802	1468	510	484	303	440	1441	1512	834	233	2032	509	1561	541	1183	1187	1028	2265
VANCOUVER, BC	3032	1597	1897	2838	2908	949	2791	1362	633	3204	2745	3106	2705	2960	1368	2196	2501	2547	2558	2342	1463	1956	2483	2087	3102	2583	2383	2746	3186	2007	1390
WASHINGTON, DC	369	1896	1612	636	38	1953	758	1545	2395	458	384	539	346	397	1659	701	517	370	416	1362	1686	1025	526	2008	357	1433	596	996	720	1083	2441
WICHITA, KS	1471	707	423	989	1276	1067	838	934	1346	1616	1184	1291	953	1145	613	728	7856	995	852	367	521	390	984	898	1515	608	674	771	1337	192	1276

LITTLE ROCK, AR	LOS ANGELES, CA	LOUISVILLE, KY	MEMPHIS, TN	MIAMI, FL	MILWAUKEE, WI	MINNEAPOLIS, MN	MOBILE, AL	MONTPELIER, VT	MONTREAL, QC	NASHVILLE, TN	NEW ORLEANS, LA	NEW YORK, NY	NORFOLK, VA	OKLAHOMA CITY, OK	OMAHA, NE	ORLANDO, FL	PHILADELPHIA, PA	PHOENIX, AZ	PITTSBURGH, PA	PORTLAND, ME	PORTLAND, OR	RALEIGH, NC	RAPID CITY, SD	RENO, NV	RICHMOND, VA	ST. LOUIS, MO	SALT LAKE CITY, UT	SAN ANTONIO, TX	SAN DIEGO, CA	SAN FRANCISCO, CA	SEATTLE, WA	TAMPA, FL	TORONTO, ON	VANCOUVER, BC	WASHINGTON,DC	WICHITA, KS
1354	2859	832	1214	1439	929	1245	1344	167	230	1003	1440	151	151	1549	1292	1235	223	2561	485	270	2954	639	1750	2747	482	1036	2224	1953	2919	2964	2899	1290	400	3032	369	1471
900	806	1320	1033	2155	1426	1339	1344	2226	2172	1248	1276	2015	2015	546	973	1934	1954	466	1670	2338	1395	1782	841	1020	1876	1051	624	818	825	1111	1463	1949	1841	1597	1896	707
617	1092	1036	750	1834	1142	1055	1106	1943	1888	965	993	1731	1731	262	726	1613	1671	753	1386	2054	1695	1499	837	1306	1593	767	964	513	1111	1397	1763	1628	1557	1897	1612	423
528	2237	419	389	661	813	1129	332	1193	1241	242	473	869	869	944	989	440	782	1868	676	1197	2647	396	1511	2440	527	549	1916	1000	2166	2618	2705	455	958	2838	636	989
1072	2705	602	933	1109	805	1121	1013	516	564	716	1142	192	192	1354	1168	904	104	2366	246	520	2830	309	1626	2623	152	841	2100	1671	2724	2840	2775	960	565	2908	38	1276
1530	1239	1547	1625	2554	1175	839	2019	2219	2093	1648	1955	2049	2049	1227	904	2333	2019	1199	1719	2352	889	2110	379	960	2053	1341	548	1500	1302	1176	816	2348	1762	949	1953	1067
381	2092	369	241	812	763	1079	258	1308	1289	194	351	985	985	729	941	591	897	1723	763	1313	2599	547	1463	2392	678	501	1868	878	2021	2472	2657	606	958	2791	758	838
1183	1702	1139	1337	2224	767	431	1765	1811	1685	1315	1734	1641	1641	1136	616	2003	1611	1662	1311	1944	1301	1702	320	1372	1645	1053	960	1599	1765	1749	1229	2018	1354	1362	1545	934
1808	1033	1933	1954	2883	1748	1465	2302	2661	2535	1976	2234	2491	2491	1506	1234	2662	2462	993	2161	2795	432	2495	930	430	2496	1628	342	1761	1096	646	500	2677	2204	633	2395	1346
1493	3046	964	1353	1529	1100	1417	1433	178	313	1136	1563	215	215	1694	1463	1324	321	2706	592	107	3126	729	1921	2919	572	1181	2395	2092	3065	3135	3070	1380	570	3204	458	1616
1066	2572	545	927	1425	642	958	1165	423	397	716	1254	400	400	1262	1005	1221	414	2274	217	560	2667	642	1463	2460	485	749	1936	1665	2632	2677	2612	1276	106	2745	384	1184
900	2554	610	760	583	1003	1319	642	1096	1145	543	783	773	773	1248	1290	379	685	2184	642	1101	2948	279	1824	2741	428	850	2218	1310	2483	2934	2973	434	1006	3106	539	1291
745	2374	251	606	994	601	918	837	834	822	395	926	515	515	1022	952	790	454	2035	217	839	2610	313	1422	2403	322	512	1880	1344	2393	2620	2571	845	537	2705	346	953
754	2453	464	614	730	857	1173	572	954	1003	397	713	631	631	1102	1144	525	543	2107	438	959	2802	158	1678	2595	289	704	2072	1241	2405	2759	2827	581	802	2960	397	1145
1076	1116	1197	1217	2147	1012	881	1570	1925	1799	1240	1502	1755	1755	773	497	1926	1725	1004	1425	2059	1166	1758	305	959	1760	892	436	1046	1179	1176	1234	1941	1468	1368	1659	613
662	2042	299	539	1382	89	409	923	967	841	474	935	797	797	807	474	1161	768	1819	467	1101	2137	861	913	1930	802	294	1406	1270	2105	2146	2062	1176	510	2196	701	728
632	2215	106	493	1141	398	714	731	861	815	281	820	636	636	863	736	920	576	1876	292	960	2398	522	1219	2191	530	350	1667	1231	2234	2407	2368	935	484	2501	517	785
882	2374	356	742	1250	443	760	981	615	588	531	1070	466	466	1073	806	1045	437	2085	136	751	2469	568	1264	2262	471	560	1738	1481	2437	2478	2413	1101	303	2547	370	995
733	2281	207	594	1163	454	771	832	752	725	382	921	535	535	930	802	958	474	1942	190	858	2464	482	1275	2257	517	417	1734	1332	2300	2474	2424	1036	440	2558	416	852
327	1446	852	466	1367	1010	999	639	1811	1772	681	525	1589	1589	209	669	1146	1501	1077	1246	1917	2140	1189	1077	1933	1309	635	1410	271	1375	1827	2208	1161	1441	2342	1362	367
984	1029	1118	1116	2069	1055	924	1478	1969	1843	1162	1409	1799	1799	681	541	1847	1744	904	1460	2102	1261	1680	404	1054	1688	855	531	946	1092	1271	1329	1862	1512	1463	1686	521
567	1703	595	720	1632	378	246	1115	1291	1165	725	1117	1121	1121	546	136	1411	1091	1558	791	1424	1798	1157	629	1591	1126	436	1067	1009	1766	1807	1822	1426	834	1956	1025	390
891	2310	366	752	1401	380	697	991	690	564	541	1079	622	622	1062	743	1180	592	2074	292	838	2405	724	1201	2198	627	549	1675	1490	2373	2415	2350	1194	233	2483	526	984
974	801	1499	1112	1959	1617	1530	1231	2458	2363	1328	1118	2235	2235	737	1236	1738	2147	432	1893	2563	1767	1834	1105	1315	1955	1242	864	556	730	1181	1944	1753	2032	2087	2008	898
1391	2944	862	1251	1427	999	1315	1332	195	338	1034	1461	115	115	1593	1362	1223	219	2605	491	199	3024	627	1820	2817	471	1080	2293	1990	2963	3034	2969	1278	509	3102	357	1515
447	1558	972	586	1201	1193	1240	473	1983	1892	801	360	1660	1660	449	910	980	1572	1188	1366	1988	2381	1198	1318	2072	1330	863	1650	200	1487	1938	2449	995	1561	2583	1433	608
587	2104	112	464	1196	279	596	737	927	872	287	826	715	715	752	618	975	655	1764	370	1038	2280	639	1101	2073	641	239	1549	1186	2122	2290	2249	990	541	2383	596	674
269	1851	594	211	915	835	1151	187	1546	1514	423	185	1223	1223	612	935	694	1135	1482	988	1550	2544	783	1458	2337	914	505	1813	644	1780	2232	2612	709	1183	2746	996	771
873	2441	766	733	345	1160	1477	410	1277	1325	589	556	953	953	1291	1336	141	866	2072	822	1281	2994	460	1859	2787	609	896	2264	1084	2370	2822	3052	196	1187	3186	720	1337
382	1632	516	536	1466	573	441	930	1413	1359	559	932	1202	1202	348	188	1245	1141	1360	857	1525	1805	1077	710	1598	1085	252	1074	812	1695	1814	1872	1259	1028	2007	1083	192
1478	274	1874	1611	2733	1808	1677	1922	2722	2596	1826	1854	2552	2552	1124	1294	2512	2500	285	2215	2855	1188	2360	1035	442	2444	1610	417	1272	337	575	1256	2526	2265	1390	2441	1276
	1706	526	140	1190	747	814	457	1485	1446	355	455	1262	1262	355	570	969	1175	1367	920	1590	2237	889	1093	2030	983	416	1507	600	1703	2012	2305	984	1115	2439	1036	464
1706		2126	1839	2759	2082	1951	2031	2995	2869	2054	1917	2820	2820	1352	1567	2538	2760	369	2476	3144	971	2588	1309	519	2682	1856	691	1356	124	385	1148	2553	2538	1291	2702	1513
526	2126		386	1084	394	711	625	963	920	175	714	739	739	774	704	863	678	1786	394	1062	2362	564	1215	2155	572	264	1631	1125	2144	2372	2364	878	589	2497	596	705
140	1839	386		1051	624	940	395	1345	1306	215	396	1123	1123	487	724	830	1035	1500	780	1451	2382	749	1247	2175	843	294	1652	739	1841	2144	2440	845	975	2574	896	597
1190	2759	1084	1051		1478	1794	727	1622	1671	907	874	1299	1299	1609	1654	232	1211	2390	1167	1627	3312	805	2176	3105	954	1214	2581	1401	2688	3140	3370	274	1532	3504	1065	1655
747	2082	394	624	1478		337	1019	1064	939	569	1020	894	894	880	514	1257	865	1892	564	1198	2063	956	842	1970	899	367	1446	1343	2145	2186	1991	1272	607	2124	799	769
814	1951	711	940	1794	337		1335	1381	1255	886	1337	1211	1211	793	383	1573	1181	1805	881	1515	1727	1273	606	1839	1216	621	1315	1257	2014	2055	1654	1588	924	1788	1115	637
457	2031	625	395	727	1019	1335		1526	1575	450	146	1203	1203	799	1119	506	1115	1662	1019	1531	2731	730	1641	2545	861	688	2000	673	1960	2411	2799	521	1214	2933	970	958
1485	2995	963	1345	1622	1064	1381	1526		138	1134	1656	310	310	1680	1428	1417	414	2693	685	196	3090	822	1886	2883	665	1167	2359	2084	3051	3099	3034	1473	457	3168	551	1602
1446	2869	920	1306	1671	939	1255	1575	138		1094	1632	383	383	1625	1300	1466	454	2637	607	282	2963	871	1758	2756	714	1112	2232	2043	2931	2972	2907	1522	330	3041	600	1547
355	2054	175	215	907	569	886	450	1134	1094		539	906	906	703	747	686	818	1715	569	1234	2405	532	1269	2198	626	307	1675	954	2056	2360	2463	701	764	2597	679	748
455	1917	714	396	874	1020	1337	146	1656	1632	539		1332	1332	731	1121	653	1245	1548	1108	1660	2663	871	1643	2431	1002	690	1932	560	1846	2298	2731	668	1302	2865	1106	890
1262	2820	739	1123	1299	894	1211	1203	310	383	906	1332		430	1469	1258	1094	91	2481	367	313	2920	499	1716	2713	342	956	2189	1861	2839	2929	2864	1150	507	2998	228	1391
1076	2776	666	937	962	987	1303	891	753	801	720	1032	430		1424	1350	758	342	2436	428	757	3012	179	1808	2805	91	927	2282	1560	2725	3022	2957	814	747	3090	196	1368
355	1352	774	487	1609	880	793	799	1680	1625	703	731	1469	1424		463	1388	1408	1012	1124	1792	1934	1237	871	1727	1331	505	1204	466	1370	1657	2002	1403	1295	2136	1350	161
570	1567	704	724	1654	514	383	1119	1428	1300	747	1121	1258	1350	463		1433	1228	1440	928	1561	1662	1265	525	1455	1263	440	932	927	1630	1672	1719	1448	971	1853	1162	307
969	2538	863	830	232	1257	1573	506	1417	1466	686	653	1094	758	1388	1433		1006	2169	963	1422	3091	601	1955	2884	750	993	2360	1180	2467	2918	3149	82	1327	3283	860	1434
1175	2760	678	1035	1211	865	1181	1115	414	454	818	1245	91	342	1408	1228	1006		2420	306	419	2890	411	1686	2683	254	895	2160	1774	2779	2900	2835	1062	522	2968	140	1330
1367	369	1786	1500	2390	1892	1805	1662	2693	2637	1715	1548	2481	2436	1012	1440	2169	2420		2136	2804	1335	2249	1308	883	2343	1517	651	987	358	750	1513	2184	2307	1655	2362	1173
920	2476	394	780	1167	564	881	1019	685	607	569	1108	367	428	1124	928	963	306	2136		690	2590	497	1386	2383	341	611	1859	1519	2494	2599	2534	1019	321	2668	240	1046
1590	3144	1062	1451	1627	1198	1515	1531	196	282	1234	1660	313	757	1792	1561	1422	419	2804	690		3223	827	2019	3016	670	1279	2493	2189	3162	3233	3168	1478	668	3301	556	1714
2237	971	2362	2382	3312	2063	1727	2731	3090	2963	2405	2663	2920	3012	1934	1662	3091	2890	1335	2590	3223		2923	1268	578	2925	2057	771	2322	1093	638	170	3106	2633	313	2824	1775
889	2588	564	749	805	956	1273	730	822	871	532	871	499	179	1237	1265	601	411	2249	497	827	2923		1777	2716	157	825	2193	1398	2563	2894	2926	656	820	3060	265	1266
1093	1309	1215	1247	2176	842	606	1641	1886	1758	1269	1643	1716	1808	871	525	1955	1686	1308	1386	2019	1268	1777		1151	1720	963	628	1335	1372	1368	1195	1970	1429	1328	1620	712
2030	519	2155	2175	3105	1970	1839	2545	2883	2756	2198	2431	2713	2805	1727	1455	2884	2683	883	2383	3016	578	2716	1151		2718	1850	524	1870	642	217	755	2899	2426	898	2617	1568
983	2682	572	843	954	899	1216	861	665	714	626	1002	342	91	1331	1263	750	254	2343	341	670	2925	157	1720	2718		834	2194	1530	2684	2934	2869	805	660	3003	108	1274
416	1856	264	294	1214	367	621	688	1167	1112	307	690	956	927	505	440	993	895	1517	611	1279	2057	825	963	1850	834		1326	968	1875	2066	2125	1008	782	2259	837	441
1507	691	1631	1652	2581	1446	1315	2000	2359	2232	1675	1932	2189	2282	1204	932	2360	2160	651	1859	2493	771	2193	628	524	2194	1326		1419	754	740	839	2375	1902	973	2094	1044
600	1356	1125	739	1401	1343	1257	673	2084	2043	954	560	1861	1560	466	927	1180	1774	987	1519	2189	2322	1398	1335	1870	1530	968	1419		1285	1737	2275	1195	1714	2410	1635	624
1703	124	2144	1841	2688	2145	2014	1960	3051	2931	2056	1846	2839	2725	1370	1630	2467	2779	358	2494	3162	1093	2563	1372	642	2684	1875	754	1285		508	1271	2481	2601	1414	2720	1531
2012	385	2372	2144	3140	2186	2055	2411	3099	2972	2360	2298	2929	3022	1657	1672	2918	2900	750	2599	3233	638	2894	1368	217	2934	2066	740	1737	508		816	2933	2643	958	2834	1784
2305	1148	2364	2440	3370	1991	1654	2799	3034	2907	2463	2731	2864	2957	2002	1719	3149	2835	1513	2534	3168	170	2926	1195	755	2869	2125	839	2275	1271	816		3164	2577	140	2769	1843
984	2553	878	845	274	1272	1588	521	1473	1522	701	668	1150	814	1403	1448	82	1062	2184	1019	1478	3106	656	1970	2899	805	1008	2375	1195	2481	2933	3164		1383	3297	916	1448
1115	2538	589	975	1532	607	924	1214	457	330	764	1302	507	747	1295	971	1327	522	2307	321	668	2633	820	1429	2426	660	782	1902	1714	2601	2643	2577	1383		2711	563	1217
2439	1291	2497	2574	3504	2124	1788	2933	3168	3041	2597	2865	2998	3090	2136	1853	3283	2968	1655	2668	3301	313	3060	1328	898	3003	2259	973	2410	1414	958	140	3297	2711		2902	1977
1036	2702	596	896	1065	799	1115	970	551	600	679	1106	228	196	1350	1162	860	140	2362	240	556	2824	265	1620	2617	108	837	2094	1635	2720	2834	2769	916	563	2902		1272
464	1513	705	597	1655	769	637	958	1602	1547	748	890	1391	1368	161	307	1434	1330	1173	1046	1714	1775	1266	712	1568	1274	441	1044	624	1531	1784	1843	1448	1217	1977	1272	

BORDER CROSSING

MEXICO

U.S. citizens entering Mexico are required to present passports or proof of U.S. citizenship accompanied by photo identification. Visas are not required for stays of up to 180 days. Naturalized citizens should travel with their naturalization certificates, and alien permanent residents must present their Alien Registration Cards. Individuals under the age of 18 traveling alone, with one parent, or with other adults must carry notarized parental authorization or valid custodial documents.

In addition, all U.S. citizens visiting for up to 180 days must procure a tourist card, obtainable from Mexican consulates, tourism offices, and border crossing points, which must be surrendered upon departure. However, tourist cards are not needed for visits shorter than 72 hours to cities along the Mexico/U.S. border.

U.S. driver's licenses are valid in Mexico.

Visitors who wish to drive beyond the Baja California Peninsula or the Border Zone (extending approximately 25 km into Mexico) must obtain a temporary import permit for their vehicles. Permits may be obtained from a Mexican Customs Office at border crossing points as long as the original and two copies of the following documents bearing the driver's name are provided: passport/proof of U.S. citizenship, tourist card, vehicle registration, driver's license, and a major international credit card for use in paying the prevailing fee. Permits are valid for 180 days, and they must be surrendered upon final departure from Mexico.

All visitors driving in Mexico should be aware that U.S. auto insurance policies are not valid and that buying short-term tourist insurance is virtually mandatory. Many U.S. insurance companies sell Mexican auto insurance. American Automobile Association (for members only) and Sanborn's Mexico Insurance (800.638.9423) are popular companies with offices at most U.S. border crossings.

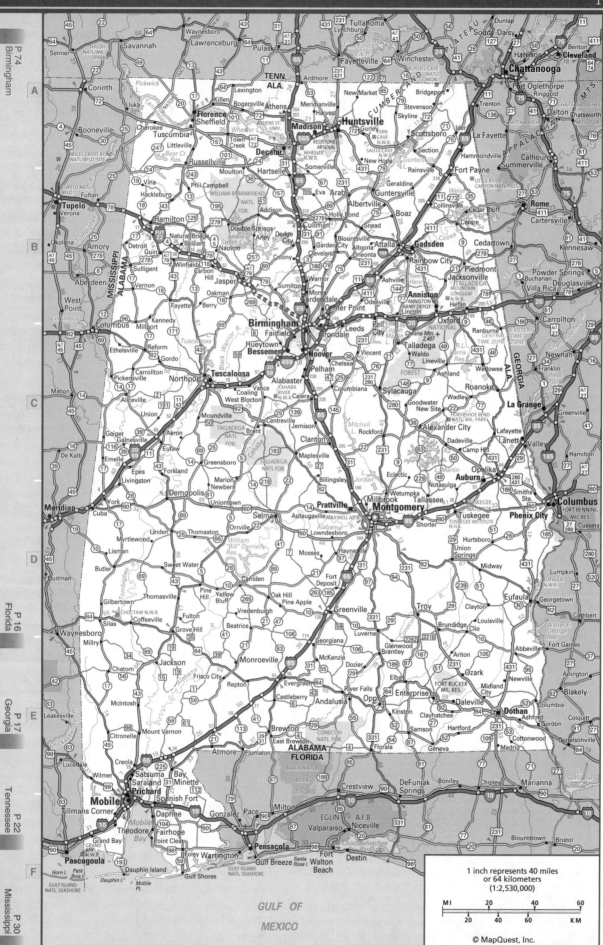

1 inch represents 40 miles
or 64 kilometers
(1:2,530,000)

MI 20 40 60

20 40 60 KM

© MapQuest, Inc.

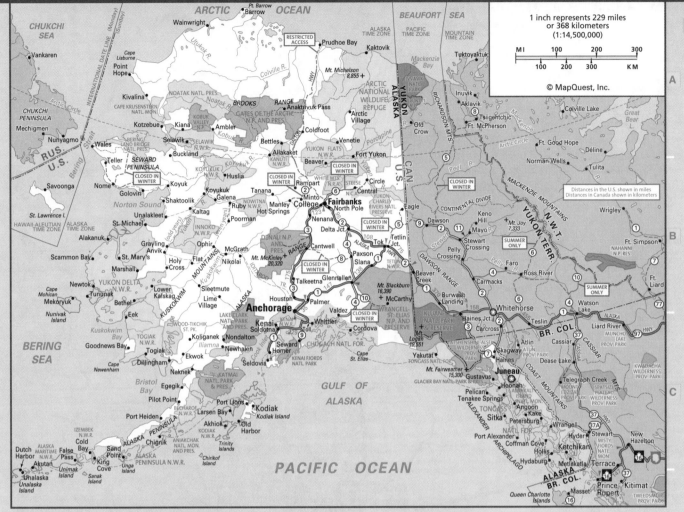

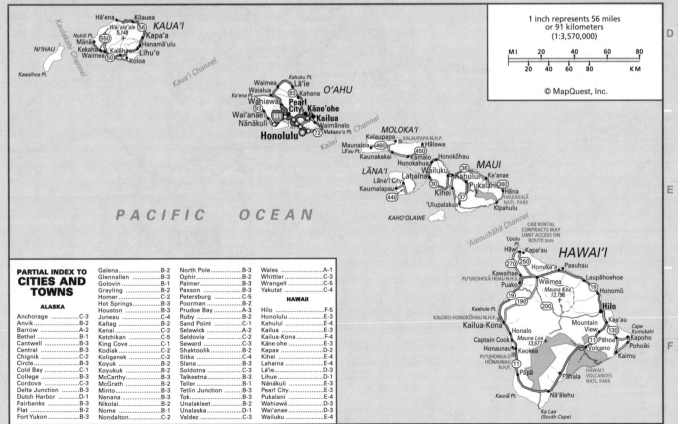

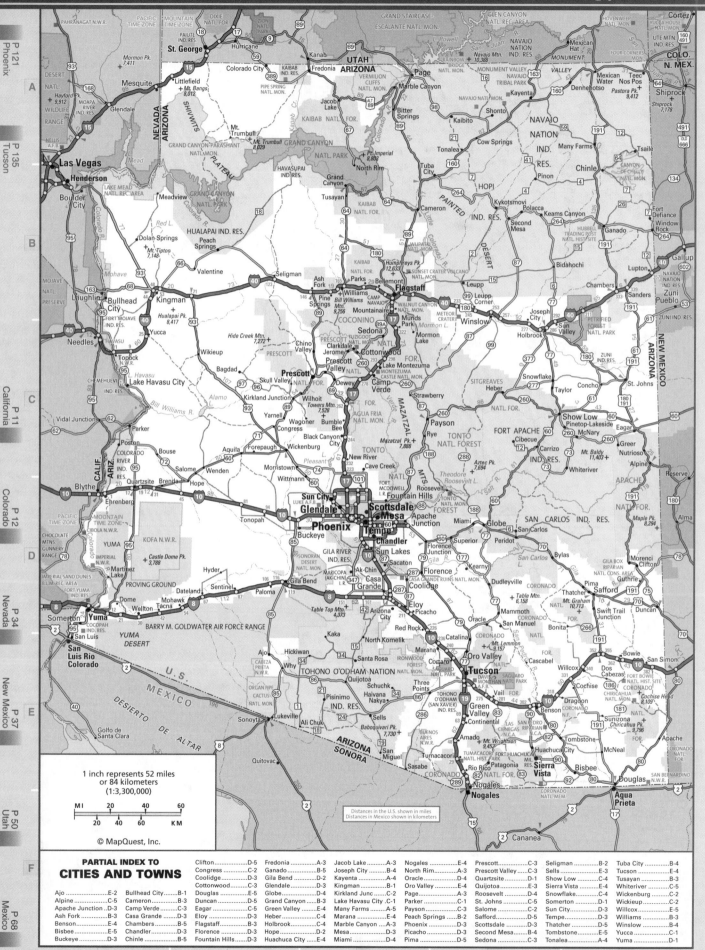

PARTIAL INDEX TO
CITIES AND TOWNS

1 inch represents 52 miles
or 84 kilometers
(1:3,300,000)

MI 20 40 60

KM 20 40 60

© MapQuest, Inc.

P 121 Phoenix
P 135 Tucson
P 11 California
P 12 Colorado
P 34 Nevada
P 37 New Mexico
P 50 Utah
P 68 Mexico

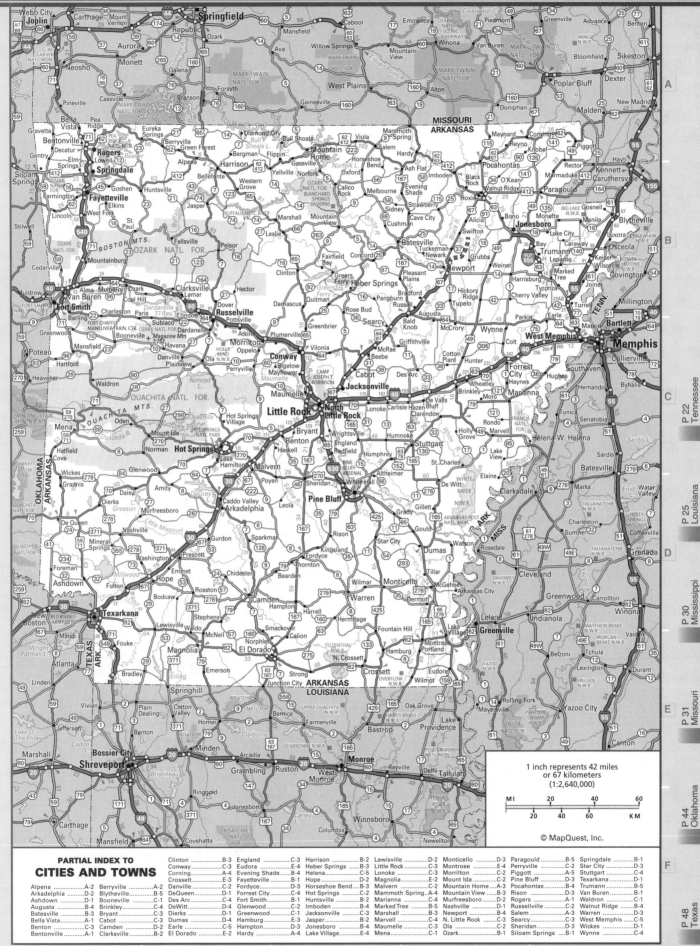

1 inch represents 42 miles
or 67 kilometers
(1:2,640,000)

© MapQuest, Inc.

P 22 Tennessee
P 25 Louisiana
P 30 Mississippi
P 31 Missouri
P 44 Oklahoma
P 48 Texas

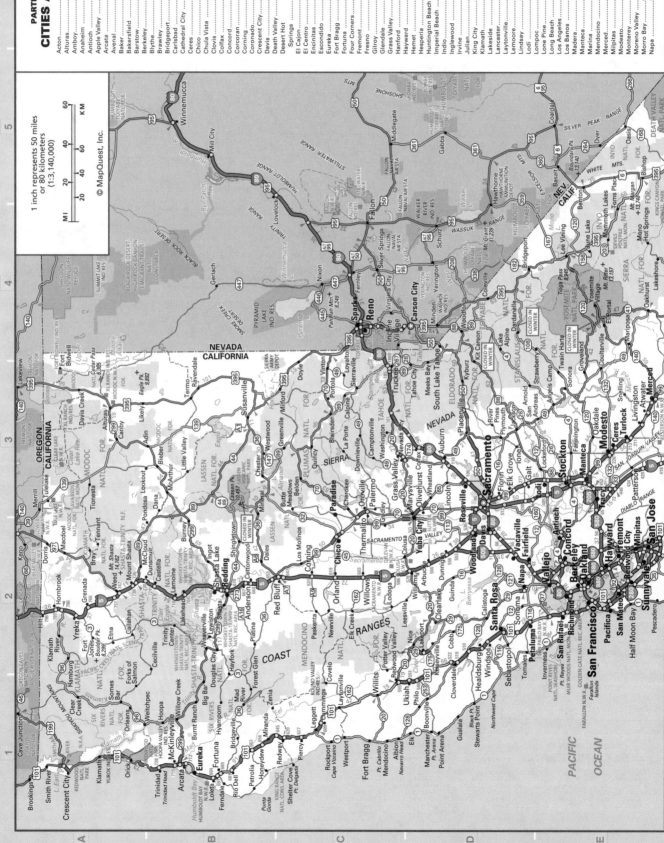

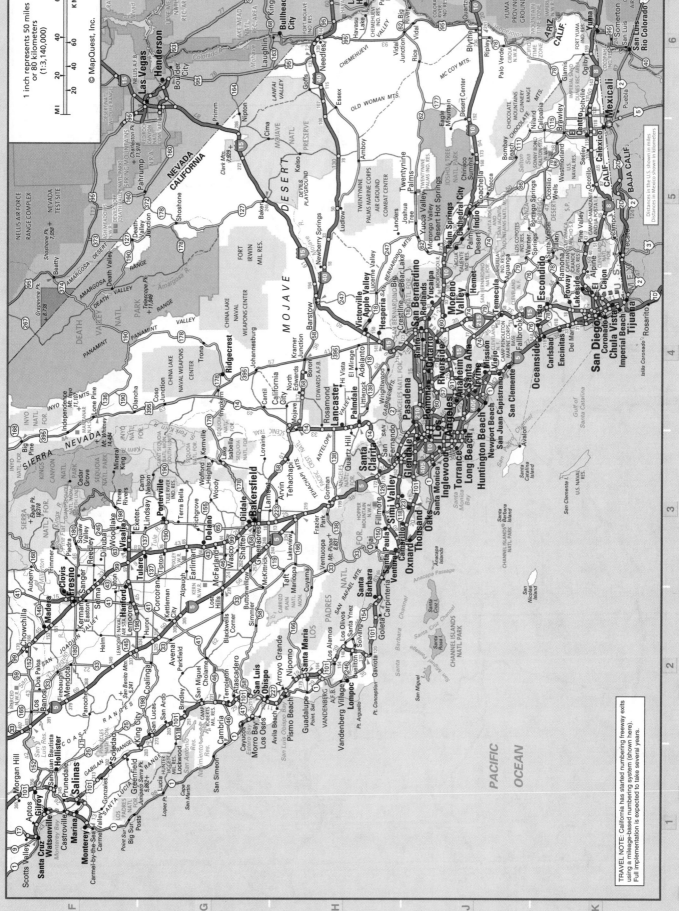

1 inch represents 50 miles
or 80 kilometers
(1:3,140,000)
© MapQuest, Inc.

TRAVEL NOTE: California has started numbering freeway exits
using a mileage-based numbering system (shown here).
Full implementation is expected to take several years.

Distances in the U.S. shown in miles
Distances in Mexico shown in kilometers

P 98   Los Angeles
P 130   San Diego
P 8   Arizona
P 10   California North
P 34   Nevada
P 68   Mexico

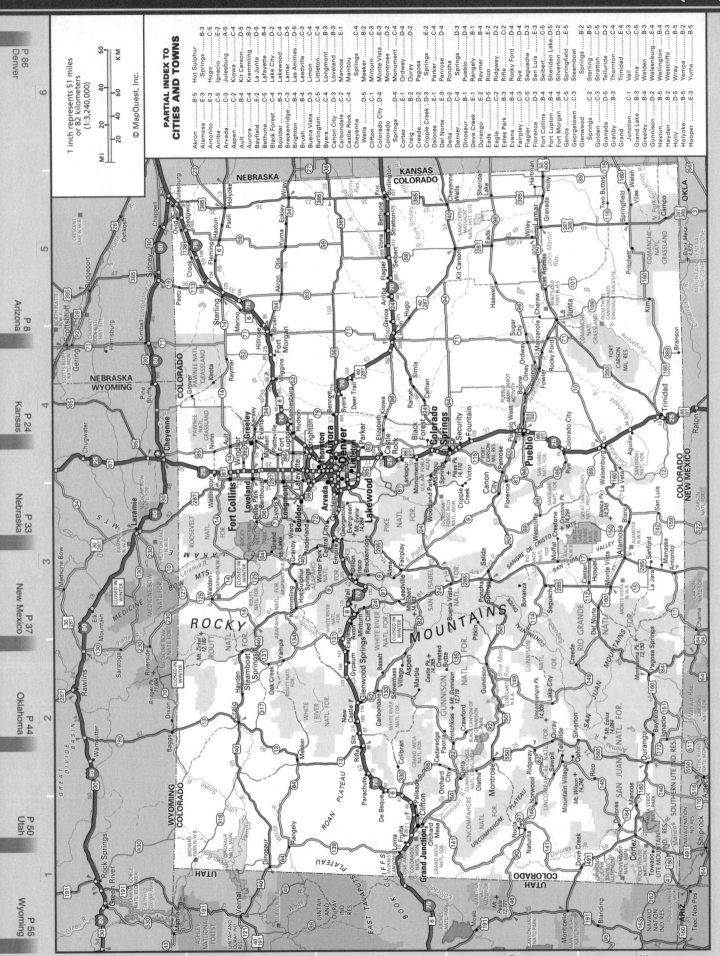

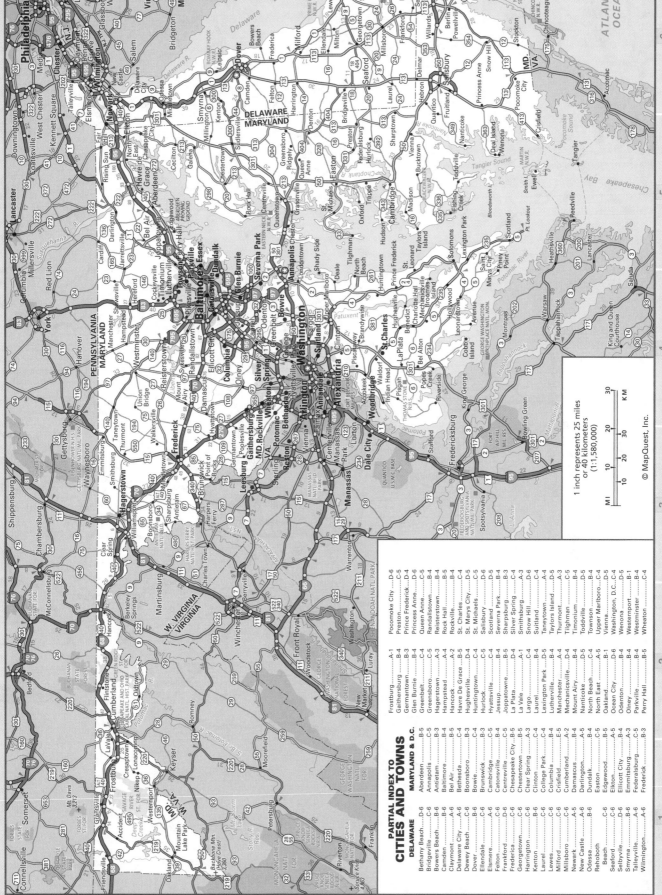

P 72 Baltimore

P 137 Washington, D.C.

P 36 New Jersey

P 46 Pennsylvania

P 52 Virginia

P 52 West Virginia

PARTIAL INDEX TO CITIES AND TOWNS

DELAWARE

SCALE: 1 inch represents 25 miles or 40 kilometers (1:1,580,000)

© MapQuest, Inc.

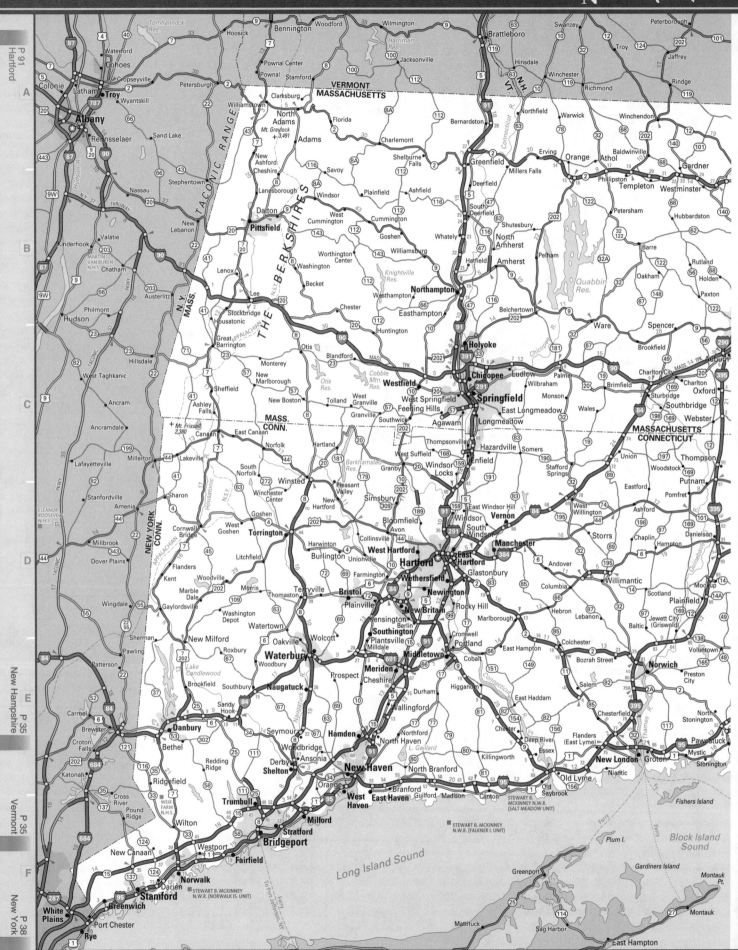

P 91
Hartford

P 35
New Hampshire

P 35
Vermont

P 38
New York

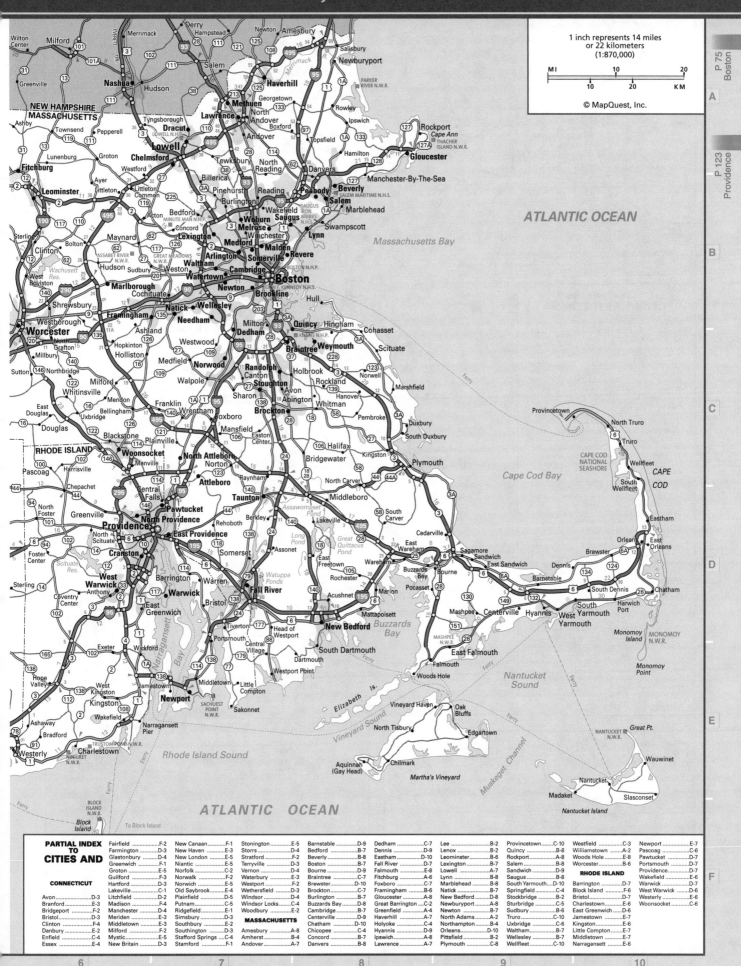

N

1 inch represents 48 miles
or 77 kilometers
(1:3,020,000)

MI	20	40	60
20	40	60	KM

© MapQuest, Inc.

PARTIAL INDEX TO CITIES AND TOWNS

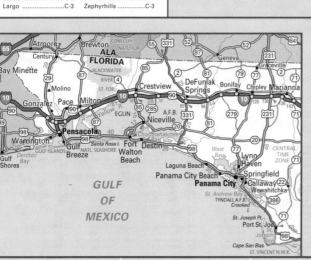

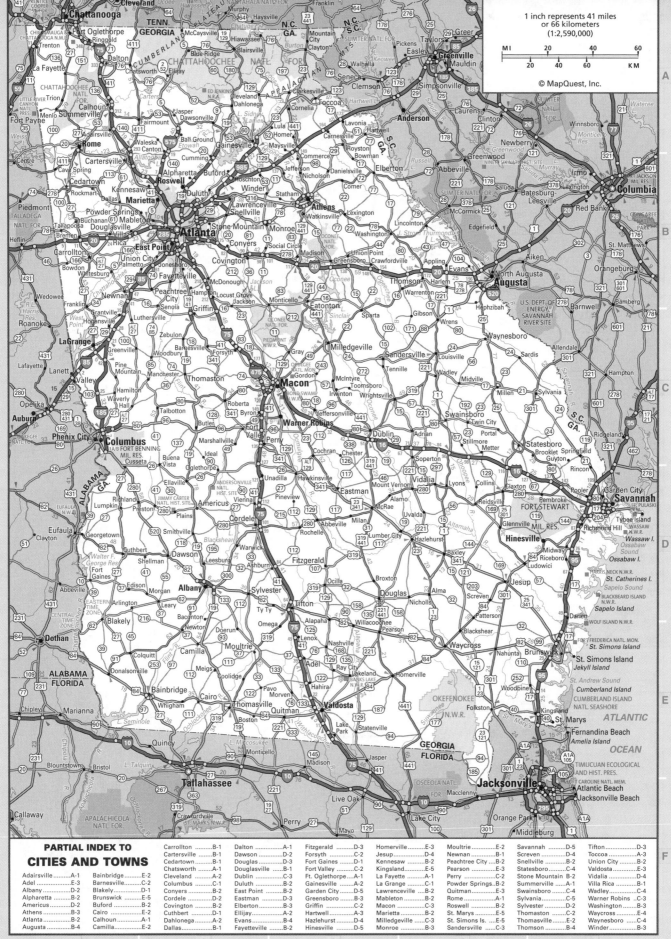

P 71
Atlanta

P 6
Alabama

P 16
Florida

P 22
Tennessee

P 40
South Carolina

P 40
North Carolina

1 inch represents 41 miles
or 66 kilometers
(1:2,590,000)

© MapQuest, Inc.

PARTIAL INDEX TO
CITIES AND TOWNS

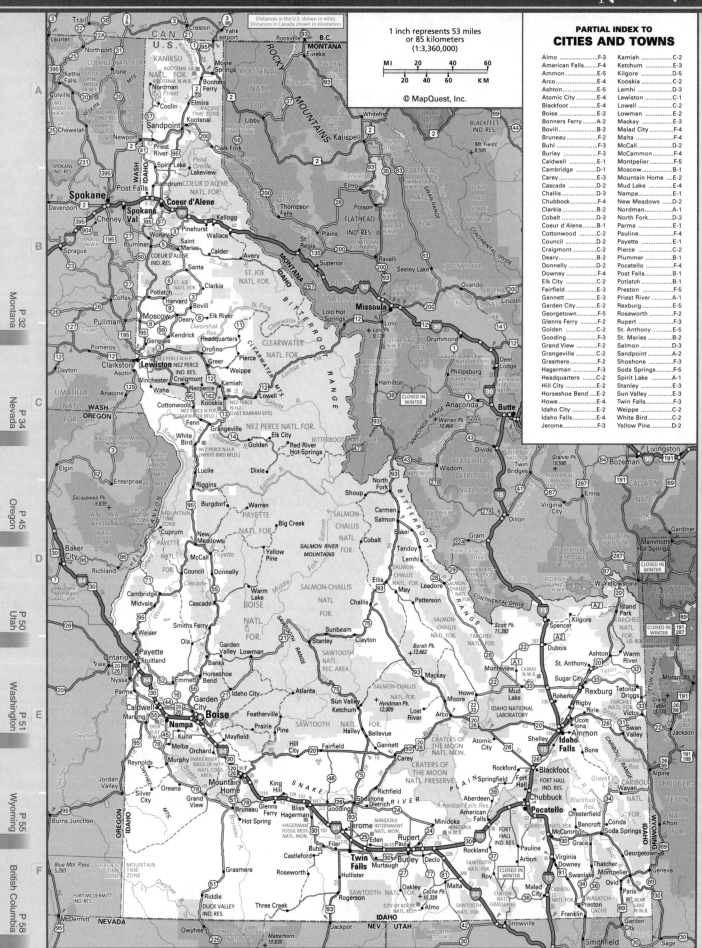

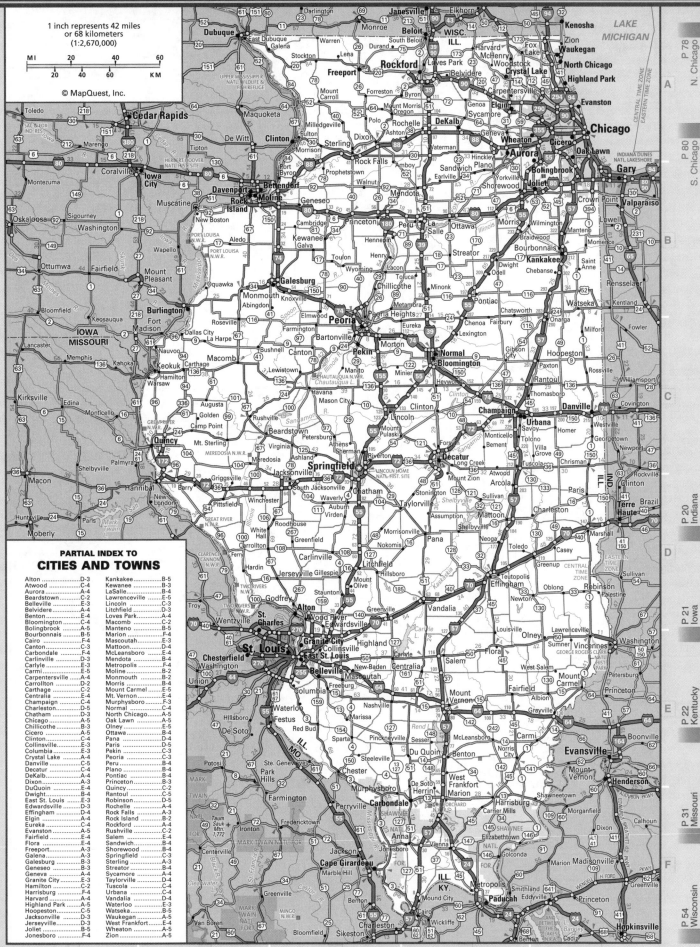

P 79
Gary

P 94
Indianapolis

P 19
Illinois

P 22
Kentucky

P 28
Michigan

P 43
Ohio

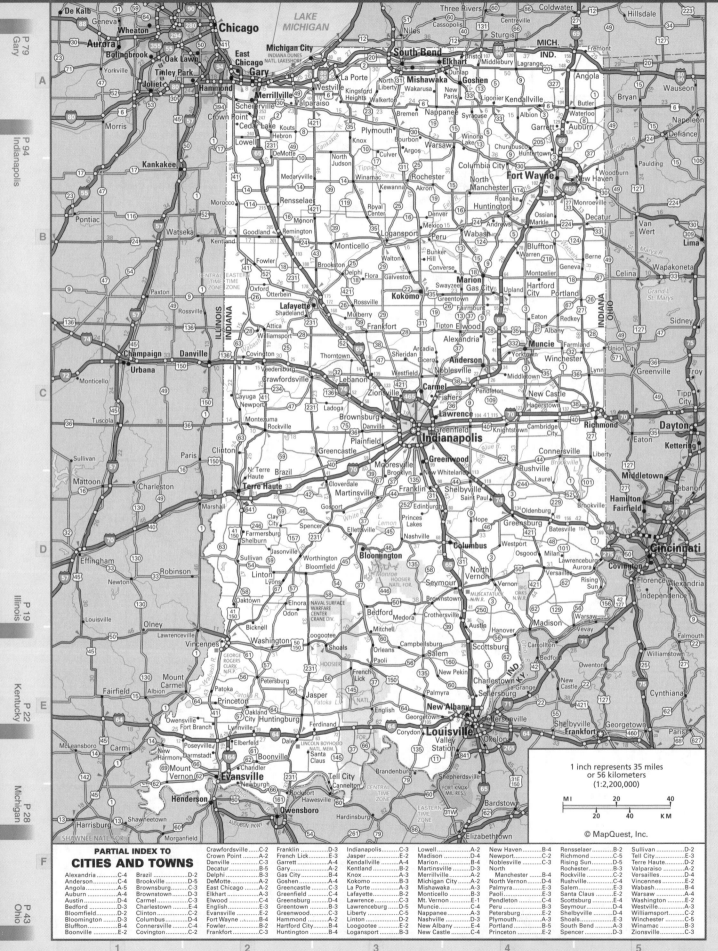

1 inch represents 35 miles
or 56 kilometers
(1:2,200,000)

MI   20   40

KM   20   40

© MapQuest, Inc.

PARTIAL INDEX TO CITIES AND TOWNS						
Alexandria........C-4	Brazil............D-2	Franklin............D-3	Indianapolis.......C-3	Lowell..............A-2	New Haven........B-4	Rensselaer........B-2	Sullivan............D-2
Anderson.........C-4	Brookville.......D-5	French Lick......E-3	Jasper.............E-2	Madison............D-4	Newport...........C-2	Richmond..........C-5	Tell City...........E-3
Angola............A-5	Brownsburg.....C-3	Garrett............A-4	Kendallville.......A-4	Marion.............B-4	Noblesville........C-3	Rising Sun.........D-5	Terre Haute.......D-2
Auburn............A-4	Brownstown.....D-3	Gary...............A-2	Kentland..........B-2	Martinsville.......D-3	North	Rochester..........B-3	Valparaiso.........A-2
Austin.............D-4	Carmel...........C-3	Gas City..........B-4	Knox..............A-3	Merrillville........A-2	Manchester.....B-4	Rockville...........C-2	Versailles..........D-4
Bedford...........D-4	Charlestown.....E-4	Goshen............A-4	Kokomo...........B-3	Michigan City.....A-2	North Vernon.....D-4	Rushville...........C-4	Vincennes.........E-2
Bloomfield........D-2	Clinton...........C-2	Greencastle......C-3	La Porte...........A-3	Mishawaka........A-3	Palmyra...........E-3	Salem..............D-4	Wabash............B-4
Bloomington......D-3	Columbus........D-4	Greenfield........C-4	Lafayette..........C-2	Monticello.........B-3	Paoli..............E-3	Santa Claus.......E-2	Warsaw............A-4
Bluffton...........B-4	Connersville.....C-4	Greensburg......D-4	Lawrence.........C-3	Mt. Vernon........E-1	Pendleton.........C-4	Scottsburg.........D-4	Washington........E-2
Boonville.........E-2	Covington........C-2	Greentown........B-3	Lawrenceburg....D-5	Muncie............B-4	Peru..............B-3	Seymour...........D-4	Westville...........A-3
	Crawfordsville...C-2	Greenwood.......C-3	Liberty............C-5	Nappanee.........A-3	Petersburg........E-2	Shelbyville........D-4	Williamsport......C-2
	Crown Point.....A-2	Hammond.........A-2	Linton.............D-2	Nashville..........D-3	Plymouth..........A-3	Shoals.............E-3	Winchester........B-5
	Danville..........C-3	Hartford City.....B-4	Logootee.........E-2	New Albany........E-4	Portland...........B-5	South Bend........A-3	Winamac..........B-3
	Decatur..........B-5	Huntington........B-4	Logansport.......B-3	New Castle........C-4	Princeton..........E-2	Spencer...........D-3	Zionsville..........C-3
	DeMotte.........A-2						
	East Chicago....A-3						
	Elkhart...........A-4						
	Elwood...........C-4						
	English...........E-3						
	Evansville.......E-2						
	Fort Wayne......B-4						
	Fowler...........B-2						
	Frankfort........C-3						

1   2   3   4   5

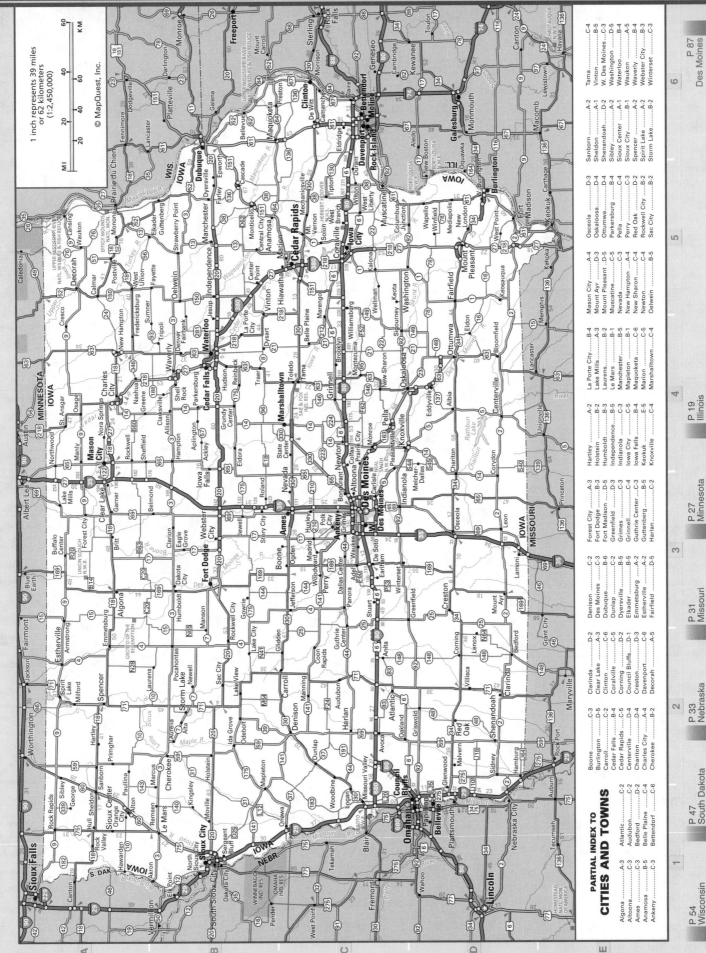

P 87
Des Moines

P 19
Illinois

P 27
Minnesota

P 31
Missouri

P 33
Nebraska

P 47
South Dakota

P 54
Wisconsin

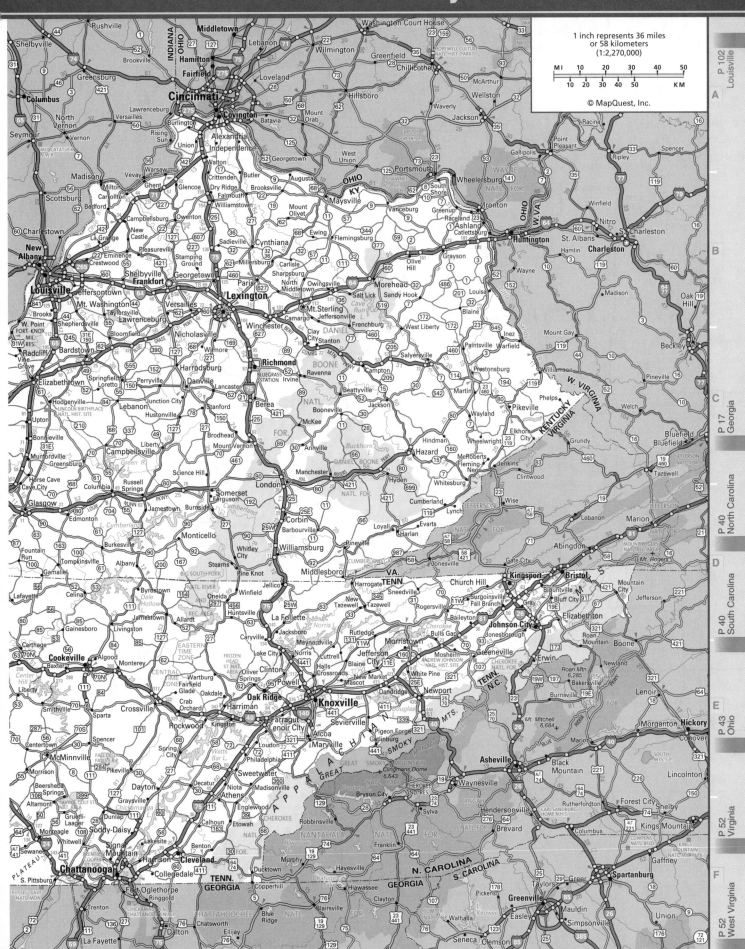

P 102 Louisville
P 17 Georgia
P 40 North Carolina
P 40 South Carolina
P 43 Ohio
P 52 Virginia
P 52 West Virginia

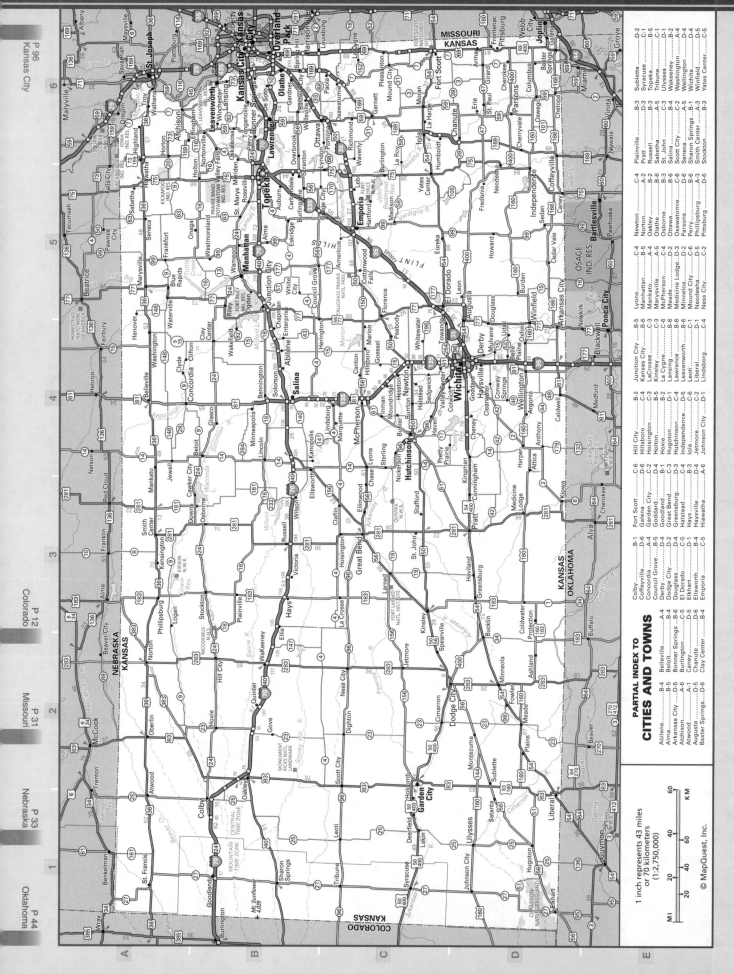

PARTIAL INDEX TO
CITIES AND TOWNS

Abilene	B-4	Fort Scott	C-6	Junction City	B-5	Newton	C-4	Sublette	B-3
Alma	B-5	Galena	D-6	Kansas City	D-6	Norton	A-2	Syracuse	A-2
Arkansas City	C-5	Garden City	A-4	Kinsley	C-3	Oakley	A-3	Topeka	B-5
Atchison	B-6	Goddard	C-4	La Crosse	C-3	Olathe	B-6	Tribune	A-3
Atwood	A-6	Goodland	B-1	Lansing	B-6	Osborne	C-4	Ulysses	A-5
Augusta	D-5	Great Bend	C-3	Lawrence	D-5	Ottawa	A-6	Wakeeney	B-2
Baxter Springs	D-6	Greensburg	C-4	Leavenworth	D-5	Parsons	D-6	Washington	A-4
Colby	C-6	Halstead	D-1	Leoti	C-2	Perry	D-6	Wellington	D-4
Coffeyville	D-6	Hays	B-3	Liberal	D-1	Pittsburg	D-5	Wichita	B-1
Concordia	C-2	Haysville	B-4	Lindsborg	C-4	Plainville	B-3	Winfield	B-1
Council Grove	D-2	Hiawatha	B-4	Lyons	B-5	Pratt	A-2	Yates Center	C-5
Derby	D-4	Hill City	C-6	Manhattan	A-1	Russell	B-2		
Dodge City	D-4	Hillsboro	D-6	Mankato	C-3	Sabetha	B-5		
Douglass	D-4	Hoisington	C-2	Marysville	A-5	St. John	B-3		
El Dorado	C-5	Holton	C-4	McPherson	C-6	Scott City	A-6		
Elkhart	B-3	Hoxie	B-1	Meade	D-2	Seneca	D-6		
Ellsworth	B-4	Hugoton	D-1	Medicine Lodge	B-6	Sharon Springs	A-3		
Emporia	C-5	Hutchinson	D-3	Minneola	B-6	Smith Center	C-2		
		Independence	D-5	Mound City	D-6	Stockton	D-6		
		Iola	B-3	Neodesha	D-5				
		Jetmore	B-4	Ness City	C-4				
		Johnson City	A-6						

1 inch represents 43 miles
or 70 kilometers
(1:2,750,000)

MI 0 20 40 60
KM 0 20 40 60

© MapQuest, Inc.

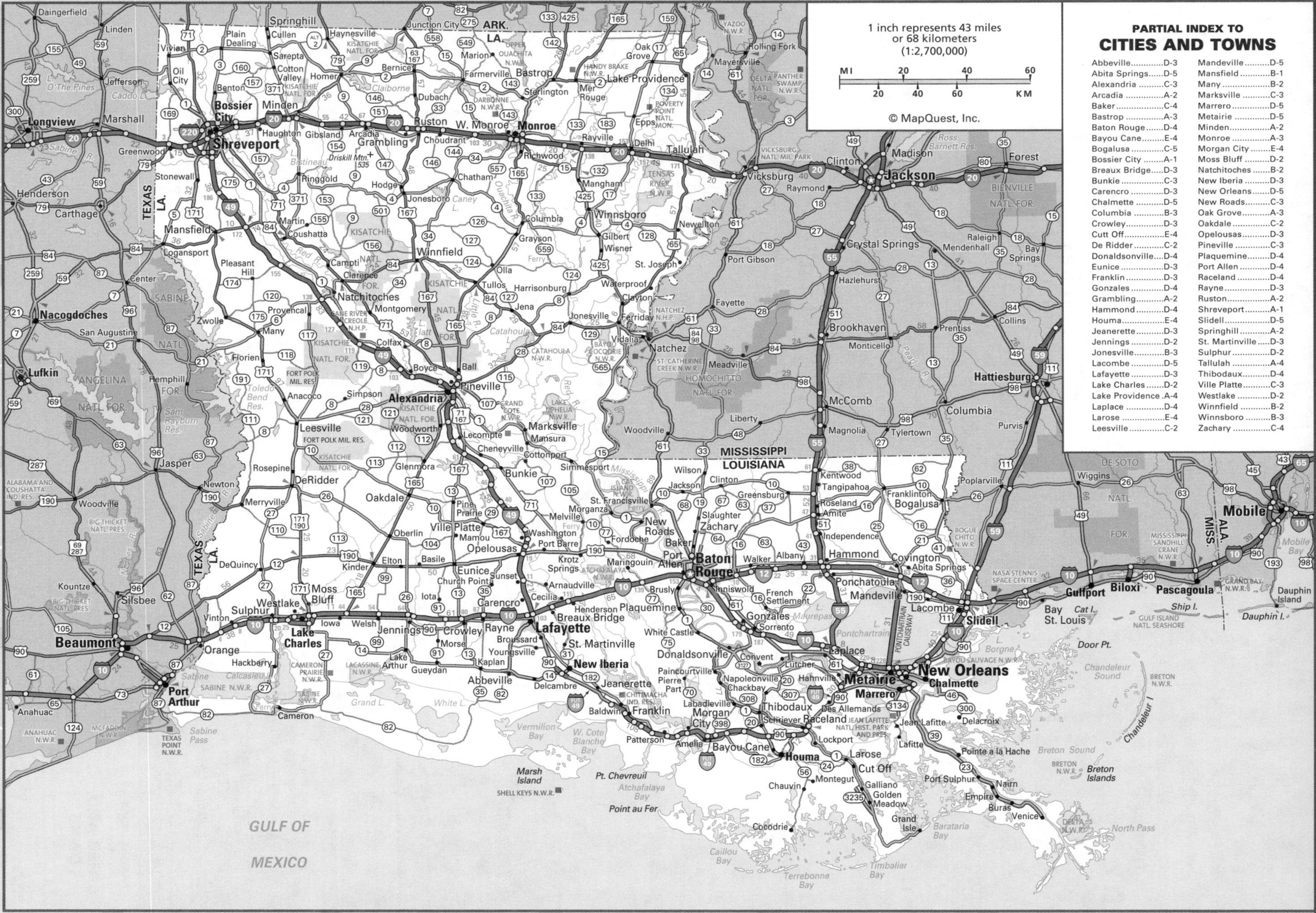

N

1 inch represents 43 miles
or 68 kilometers
(1:2,700,000)

© MapQuest, Inc.

KM
MI

GULF OF MEXICO

ALA. / MISS.

Mobile

MISSISSIPPI

LOUISIANA

TEXAS

ARK. / LA.

New Orleans

Baton Rouge

Shreveport

Bossier City

Lafayette

Lake Charles

Alexandria

Monroe

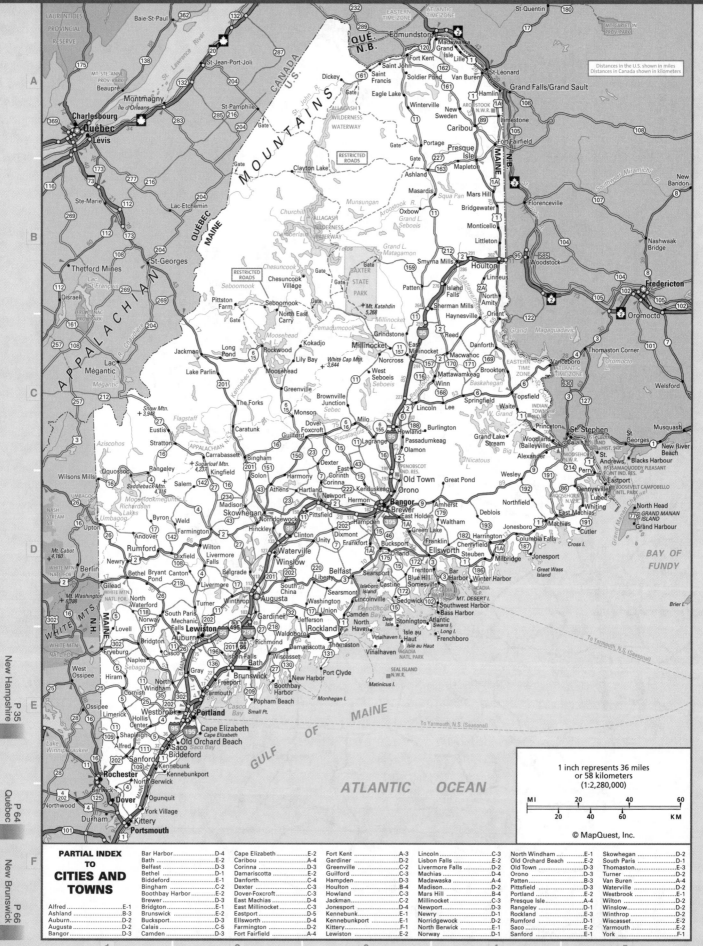

Distances in the U.S. shown in miles
Distances in Canada shown in kilometers

1 inch represents 36 miles
or 58 kilometers
(1:2,280,000)

© MapQuest, Inc.

ATLANTIC OCEAN

GULF OF MAINE

BAY OF FUNDY

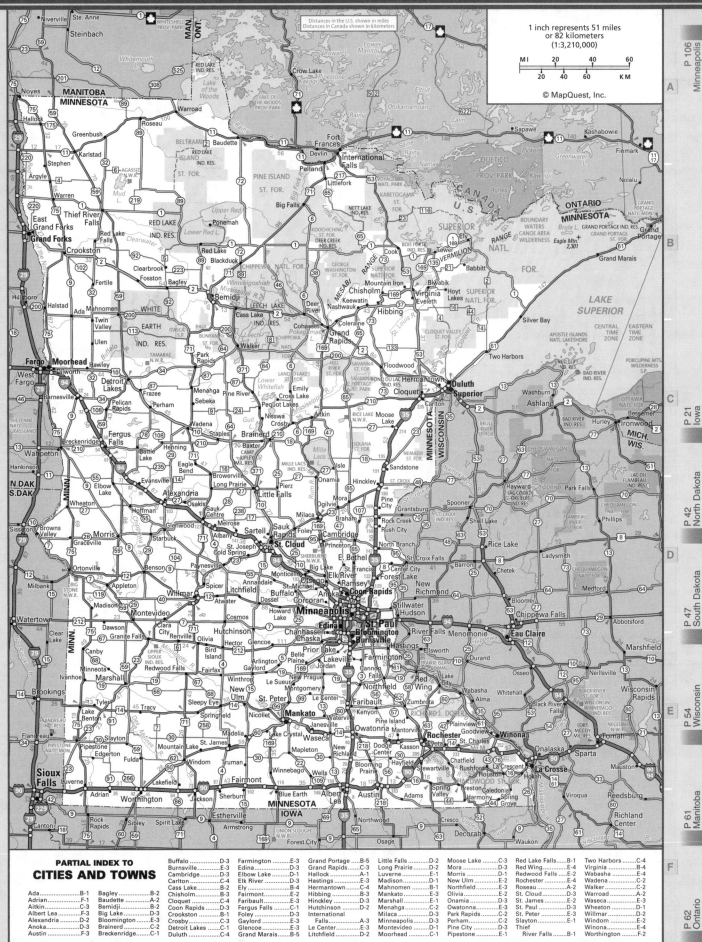

Distances in the U.S. shown in miles
Distances in Canada shown in kilometers

1 inch represents 51 miles
or 82 kilometers
(1:3,210,000)

© MapQuest, Inc.

PARTIAL INDEX TO
CITIES AND TOWNS

P 106 Minneapolis
P 21 Iowa
P 42 North Dakota
P 47 South Dakota
P 54 Wisconsin
P 61 Manitoba
P 62 Ontario

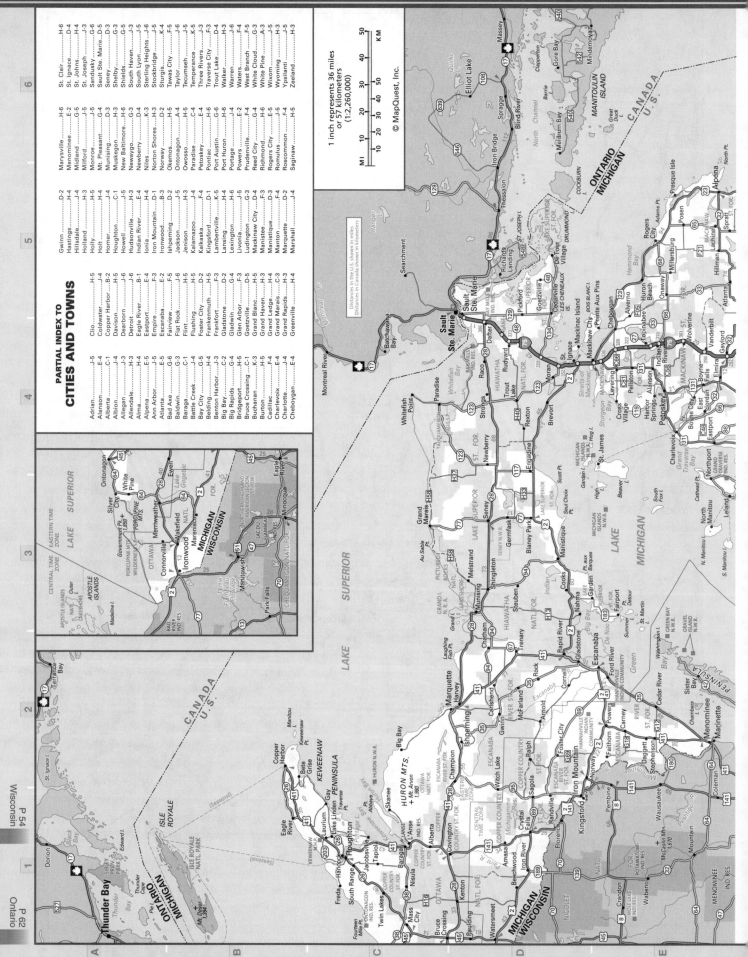

PARTIAL INDEX TO
CITIES AND TOWNS

Adrian	J-5
Alanson	E-4
Alberta	C-1
Albion	J-4
Allegan	J-3
Allendale	H-3
Alma	H-4
Alpena	E-5
Ann Arbor	J-5
Atlanta	E-5
Bad Axe	G-6
Baldwin	G-3
Baraga	C-1
Battle Creek	J-4
Bay City	G-5
Belding	H-4
Benton Harbor	J-3
Big Bay	C-2
Big Rapids	H-4
Bridgeport	H-5
Bruce Crossing	C-1
Buchanan	K-3
Cadillac	F-4
Charlevoix	E-4
Charlotte	J-4
Cheboygan	E-4

Clio	H-5
Coldwater	J-4
Copper Harbor	B-2
Davison	H-5
Dearborn	J-6
Detroit	J-6
Eagle River	B-1
Eastport	F-3
Escanaba	E-2
Fairview	F-5
Flat Rock	J-6
Flint	H-5
Flushing	H-5
Foster City	D-2
Frankfort	F-3
Frankenmuth	H-5
Gladstone	D-2
Gladwin	G-4
Glen Arbor	F-3
Goetzville	D-5
Grand Blanc	H-5
Grand Haven	H-3
Grand Ledge	H-4
Grand Marais	C-3
Grand Rapids	H-3
Greenville	E-4

Gwinn	D-2
Hastings	J-4
Hillsdale	J-4
Holland	H-3
Holt	H-4
Holly	H-5
Homer	J-4
Houghton	C-1
Hudsonville	H-3
Howell	H-5
Ionia	H-4
Iron Mountain	D-1
Ironwood	B-3
Ishpeming	D-2
Jackson	H-5
Jenison	H-3
Kalamazoo	J-3
Kalkaska	F-4
Kingsford	D-1
Lambertville	K-5
Lansing	H-4
Lexington	H-6
Livonia	J-5
Ludington	G-3
Mackinaw City	D-4
Manistee	F-3
Manistique	D-3
Manton	F-4
Marquette	D-2
Marshall	J-4

Marysville	H-6
Menominee	E-2
Midland	G-5
Milford	J-5
Monroe	J-5
Mt. Pleasant	G-4
Munising	D-3
Muskegon	H-3
New Baltimore	H-6
Newaygo	G-3
Newberry	D-3
New Baltimore	H-6
Niles	K-3
Norton Shores	H-3
Norway	D-1
Okemos	H-4
Ontonagon	B-3
Owosso	A-4
Paradise	H-4
Petoskey	C-4
Pontiac	E-4
Port Austin	J-5
Port Huron	G-6
Portage	H-6
Powers	J-4
Prudenville	E-2
Reed City	F-4
Richmond	G-4
Rogers City	H-6
Romulus	E-5
Roscommon	J-5
Saginaw	D-2

St. Clair	H-6
St. Ignace	D-4
St. Johns	H-4
St. Joseph	J-3
Sandusky	G-6
Sault Ste. Marie	D-5
Seney	D-3
Shelby	G-3
Shields	G-5
South Haven	J-3
South Lyon	J-5
Sterling Heights	J-6
Stockbridge	J-4
Sturgis	K-4
Tawas City	F-5
Taylor	J-5
Tecumseh	K-5
Temperance	K-5
Three Rivers	J-3
Traverse City	F-4
Trout Lake	D-4
Walker	H-3
Warren	J-6
Waters	F-4
West Branch	F-5
White Cloud	A-3
White Pine	A-3
Wixom	J-5
Wyoming	H-3
Ypsilanti	J-5
Zeeland	H-3

1 inch represents 36 miles
or 57 kilometers
(1:2,260,000)

© MapQuest, Inc.

Distances in the U.S. shown in miles
Distances in Canada shown in kilometers

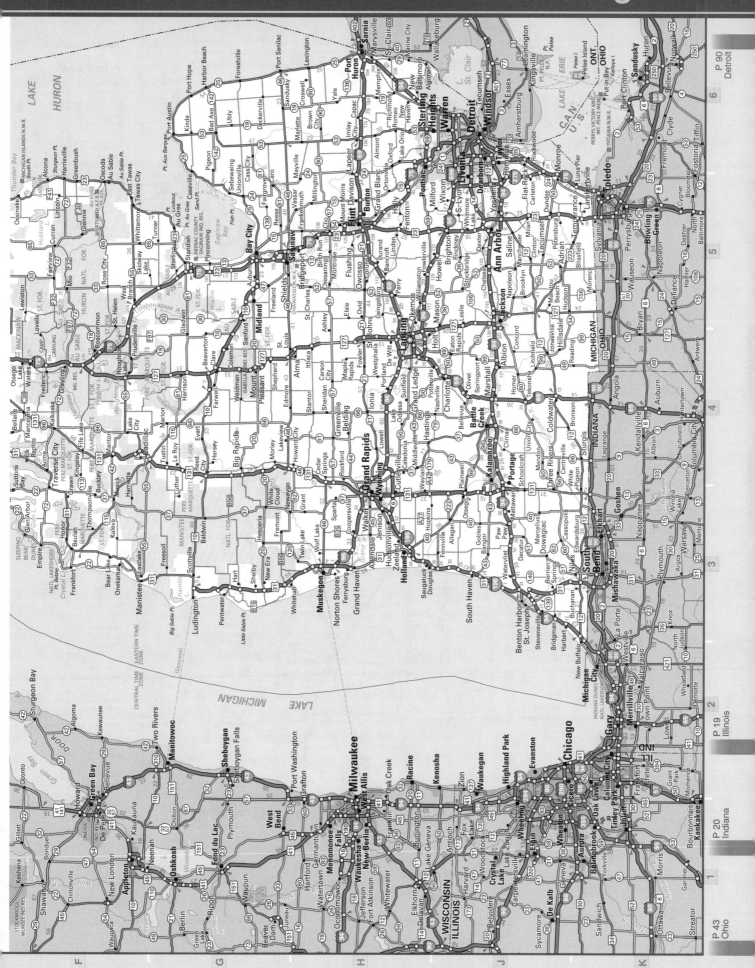

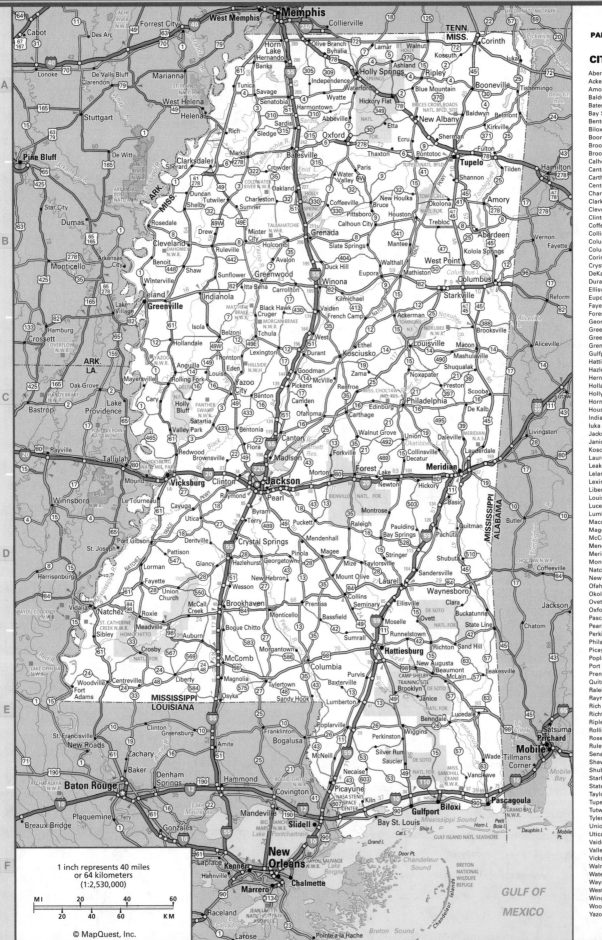

1 inch represents 40 miles
or 64 kilometers
(1:2,530,000)

MI 20   40   60
KM 20   40   60

© MapQuest, Inc.

GULF OF MEXICO

PARTIAL INDEX TO CITIES AND

Aberdeen B-4
Ackerman B-3
Amory B-4
Baldwyn A-4
Batesville A-3
Bay Springs D-3
Bentonia C-2
Biloxi...............F-4
Booneville A-4
Brookhaven D-2
Brooklyn E-3
Calhoun City B-3
Canton C-3
Carthage C-3
Centreville E-1
Charleston B-3
Clarksdale B-2
Cleveland B-2
Clinton D-2
Coffeeville B-3
Collins D-3
Columbia E-3
Columbus.............B-4
Corinth A-4
Crystal Springs......D-2
DeKalb C-4
Durant C-3
Ellisville D-3
Eupora B-3
Fayette D-1
Forest C-3
Georgetown D-2
Greenville B-2
Greenwood B-2
Grenada B-3
Gulfport F-4
Hattiesburg E-3
Hazlehurst D-2
Hernando A-3
Hollandale C-2
Holly Springs A-3
Horn Lake A-3
Houston B-4
Indianola B-2
Iuka A-4
Jackson D-2
Janice E-4
Kosciusko C-3
Laurel D-3
Leakesville E-4
Leland B-2
Lexington C-3
Liberty E-2
Louisville C-4
Lucedale E-4
Lumberton E-3
Macon C-4
Magee D-3
McComb E-2
Mendenhall D-3
Meridian C-4
Monticello D-2
Natchez D-1
New Albany A-4
Ofahoma C-3
Okolona B-4
Ovett D-4
Oxford A-3
Pascagoula F-4
Pearl D-2
Perkinston E-4
Philadelphia C-4
Picayune E-3
Poplarville E-3
Port Gibson D-2
Prentiss D-3
Quitman D-4
Raleigh D-3
Raymond D-2
Rich A-2
Richton E-4
Ripley A-4
Rolling Fork C-2
Rosedale B-2
Ruleville B-2
Senatobia A-3
Shaw B-2
Shubuta D-4
Starkville B-4
State Line D-4
Taylorsville D-3
Tupelo A-4
Tutwiler B-2
Tylertown E-2
Union C-4
Utica................D-2
Vaiden B-3
Valley Park C-2
Vicksburg D-2
Walnut A-4
Water Valley B-3
Waynesboro D-4
West Point B-4
Winona B-3
Woodville E-1
Yazoo City C-2

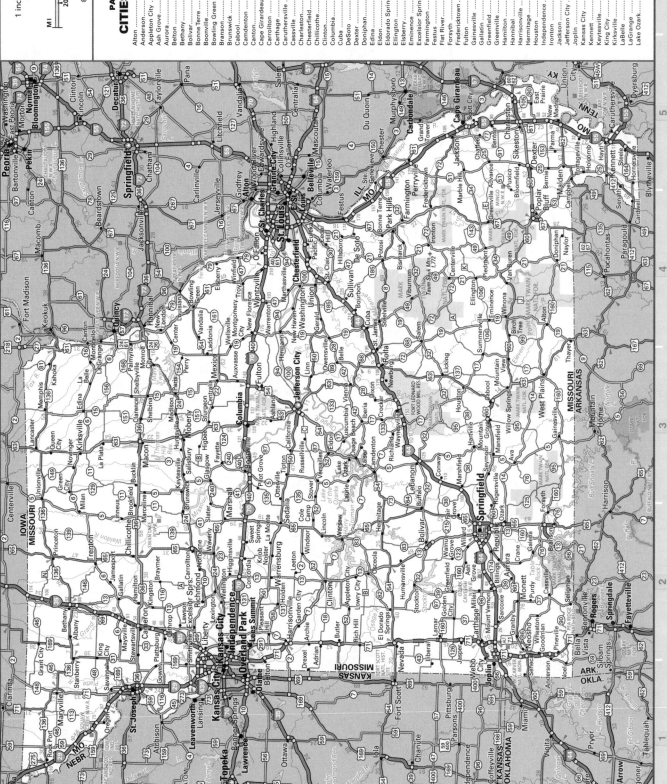

1 inch represents 50 miles
or 80 kilometers
(1:3,150,000)

© MapQuest, Inc.

PARTIAL INDEX TO CITIES AND TOWNS

Alton	A-4	Lancaster	E-4	Monett	D-2	Warrensburg	C-3
Anderson	D-2	LaPlata	E-2	Monroe City	A-3	Warrenton	B-4
Appleton City	C-2	Lebanon	D-3	Montgomery City	B-4	Warsaw	C-3
Ash Grove	D-2	Liberty	B-2	Mountain Grove	E-5	Washington	B-4
Aurora	D-2	Licking	D-3	Neosho	D-2	Waynesville	D-4
Belton	B-4	Louisiana	A-4	Nevada	C-2	Webb City	D-2
Bethany	A-2	Macon	B-3	New Madrid	D-4	Wentzville	B-4
Bolivar	D-2	Madison	B-3	O'Fallon	B-4	West Plains	E-3
Bonne Terre	B-4	Malden	E-5	Owensville	C-4	Willow Springs	A-3
Boonville	C-3	Marshall	B-2	Ozark	D-2	Winona	C-3
Bowling Green	B-4	Marshfield	D-3	Paris	B-3		
Branson	D-2	Maryville	A-1	Perryville	C-4		
Brunswick	B-2	Memphis	A-3	Piedmont	D-4		
Camdenton	C-3	Mexico	D-2	Poplar Bluff	D-4		
Canton	A-4	Moberly	C-3	Potosi	E-5		
Cape Girardeau	D-5	Monett	D-2	Princeton	A-2		
Carrollton	B-2			Republic	A-3		
Carthage	D-2			Richland	D-4		
Caruthersville	E-5			Richmond	C-3		
Cassville	D-2			Rock Port	A-1		
Charleston	D-5			Rolla	C-3		
Chesterfield	C-4			St. James	B-2		
Chillicothe	B-2			St. Joseph	B-1		
Clinton	C-2			St. Louis	D-4		
Columbia	B-3			Salem	A-1		
Cuba	C-4			Savannah	C-2		
Dexter	E-5			Sedalia	B-3		
Doniphan	E-4			Shelbina	D-5		
Edina	A-3			Sikeston	A-2		
Eldorado Springs	C-2			Springfield	D-4		
Ellington	D-4			Stanberry	A-3		
Elsberry	B-4			Sullivan	D-3		
Eminence	D-4			Summersville	C-4		
Excelsior Springs	B-2			Trenton	A-2		
Farmington	C-4			Union	B-4		
Festus	C-4			Unionville	D-4		
Flat River	C-4			Vandalia	D-5		
Forsyth	E-2			Versailles	D-3		
Fredericktown	D-4			Vienna	D-4		
Fulton	C-3						
Gainesville	E-3						
Gallatin	A-2						
Greenfield	D-2						
Greenville	A-4						
Hamilton	B-2						
Hannibal	B-4						
Harrisonville	C-2						
Hermitage	D-3						
Houston	D-5						
Independence	B-2						
Ironton	D-4						
Jackson	D-5						
Jefferson City	C-3						
Joplin	B-1						
Kansas City	E-5						
Kennett	B-3						
Keytesville	C-4						
King City	D-2						
Kirksville	A-3						
LaBelle	A-4						
LaGrange	C-3						
Lake Ozark	D-4						

P 96 Kansas City
P 128 St. Louis
P 9 Arkansas
P 19 Illinois
P 21 Iowa
P 22 Tennessee
P 24 Kansas
P 33 Nebraska
P 44 Oklahoma

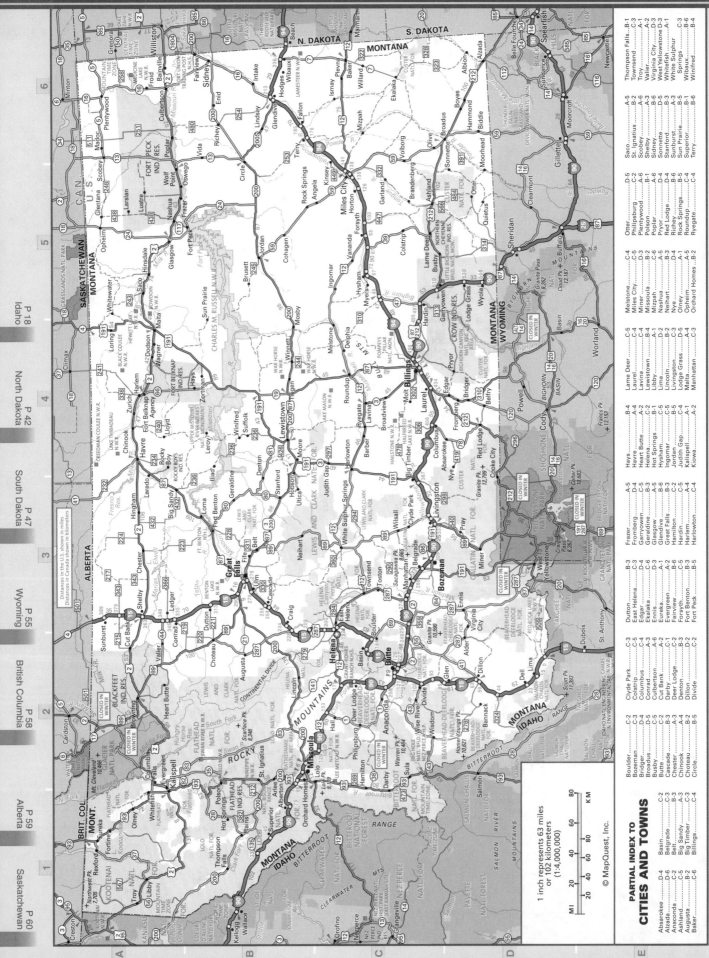

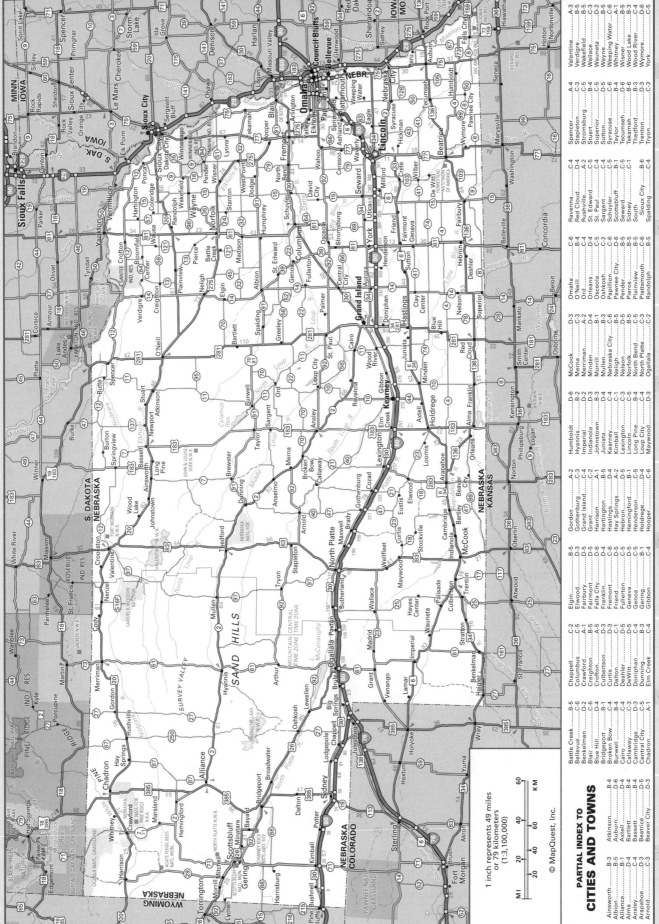

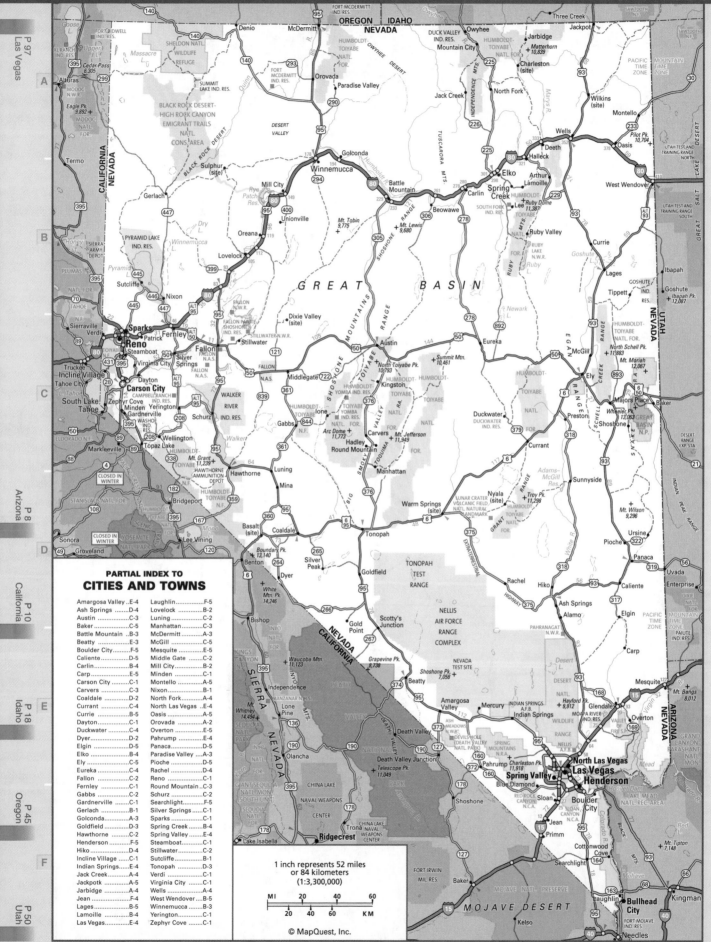

1 inch represents 52 miles
or 84 kilometers
(1:3,300,000)

MI   20   40   60

20   40   60   KM

© MapQuest, Inc.

P 97 Las Vegas
P 8 Arizona
P 10 California
P 18 Idaho
P 45 Oregon
P 50 Utah

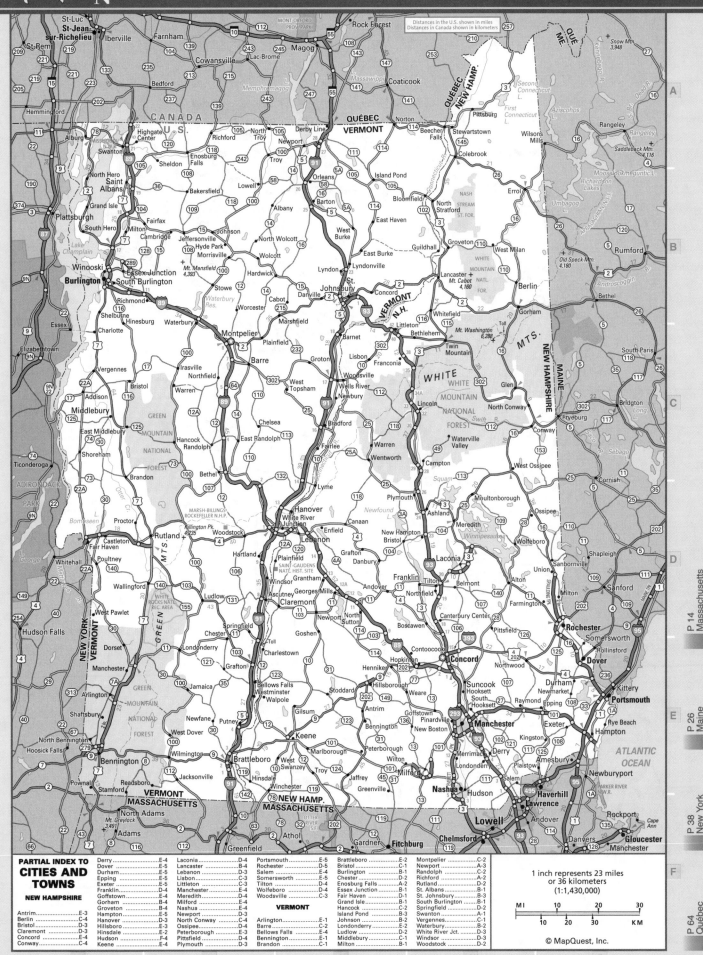

Distances in the U.S. shown in miles
Distances in Canada shown in kilometers

PARTIAL INDEX TO CITIES AND TOWNS

NEW HAMPSHIRE

1 inch represents 23 miles
or 36 kilometers
(1:1,430,000)

© MapQuest, Inc.

P 14 Massachusetts
P 26 Maine
P 38 New York
P 64 Québec

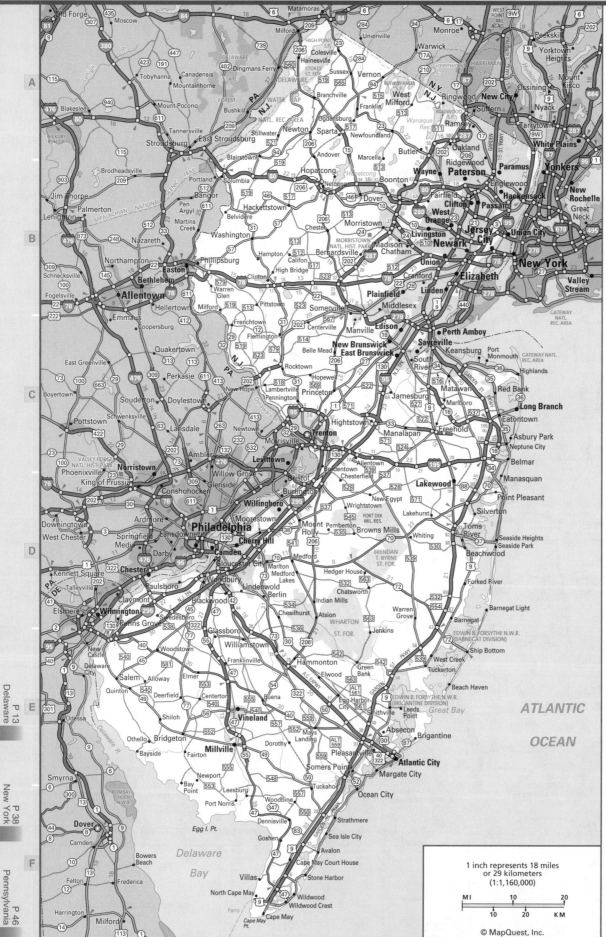

PARTIAL INDEX TO
CITIES AND TOWNS

Absecon E-3
Asbury Park C-4
Atlantic City E-3
Avalon F-3
Bay Point E-2
Beach Haven E-4
Beachwood D-4
Belmar C-4
Berlin D-2
Bernardsville B-3
Blackwood D-2
Boonton B-3
Bridgeton E-2
Brigantine E-3
Browns Mills D-3
Buena E-2
Burlington D-2
Butler A-3
Camden D-2
Cape May F-2
Chatham B-3
Cherry Hill D-2
Clifton B-4
Cranford B-3
Dover B-3
East Brunswick C-3
East Orange B-4
Eatontown C-4
Edison C-3
Elizabeth B-4
Englewood B-4
Fairfield B-3
Freehold C-4
Glassboro E-2
Gloucester City D-2
Green Bank E-3
Hackensack B-4
Hackettstown B-2
Hainesville A-2
Hammonton E-2
Highlands C-4
Hightstown C-3
Hopatcong B-3
Jamesburg C-3
Jersey City B-4
Keansburg C-4
Lakewood D-4
Linden B-4
Lindenwold D-2
Livingston B-3
Long Branch C-4
Madison B-3
Manalapan C-3
Manasquan D-4
Manville C-3
Margate City E-3
Marlboro C-4
Matawan C-4
Middlesex B-3
Millville E-2
Moorestown D-2
Morristown B-3
Mount Holly D-2
New Brunswick C-3
Newark B-4
Newton A-3
Oakland A-4
Ocean City F-3
Paramus B-4
Passaic B-4
Paterson B-4
Paulsboro D-2
Perth Amboy C-4
Phillipsburg B-2
Plainfield B-4
Pleasantville E-3
Point Pleasant D-4
Princeton C-3
Red Bank C-4
Ridgewood A-4
Salem E-1
Sayreville C-3
Seaside Heights D-4
Ship Bottom E-4
Silverton D-4
Somers Point E-3
Somerville B-3
South River C-3
Sparta A-3
Stone Harbor F-3
Toms River D-4
Trenton C-3
Union B-4
Union City B-4
Vernon A-3
Villas F-2
Vineland E-2
Warren Grove D-3
Washington B-2
Wayne B-4
West Milford A-3
Wildwood F-3
Williamstown E-2
Willingboro D-2
Woodbury D-2

1 inch represents 18 miles
or 29 kilometers
(1:1,160,000)

© MapQuest, Inc.

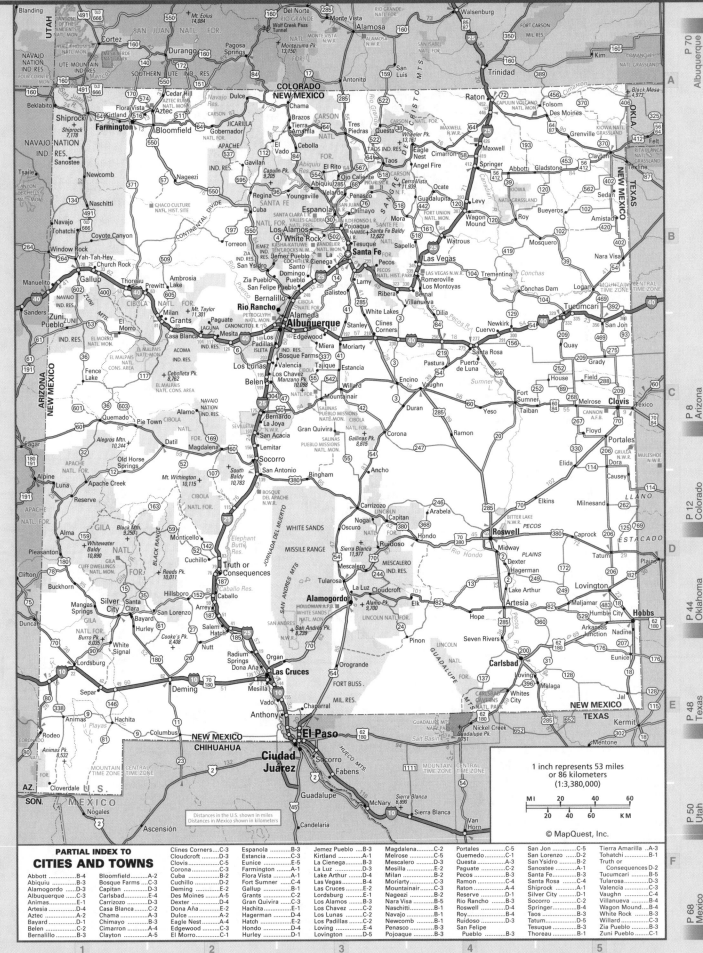

1 inch represents 53 miles
or 86 kilometers
(1:3,380,000)

MI   20   40   60
20   40   60   KM

© MapQuest, Inc.

Distances in the U.S. shown in miles
Distances in Mexico shown in kilometers

PARTIAL INDEX TO
CITIES AND TOWNS

P 70 Albuquerque
P 8 Arizona
P 12 Colorado
P 44 Oklahoma
P 48 Texas
P 50 Utah
P 68 Mexico

Left margin: P 76 Buffalo · A · P 112 New York City · B · P 125 Rochester · C · D · P 36 New Jersey · E · P 46 Pennsylvania · P 62 Ontario · F

1 inch represents 27 miles or 43 kilometers (1:1,700,000)

© MapQuest, Inc.

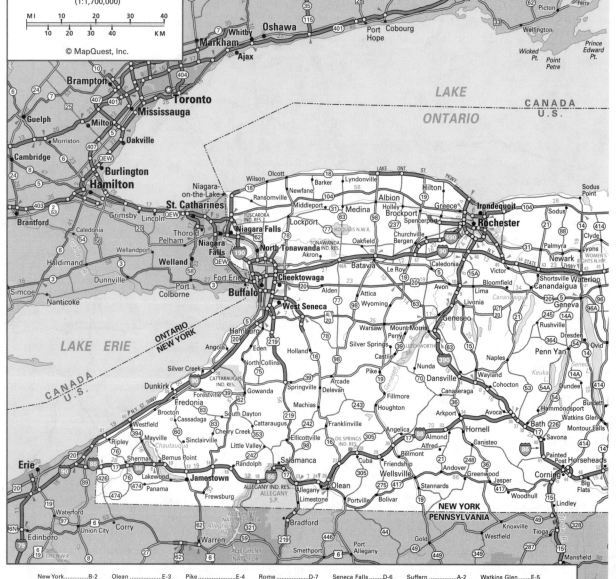

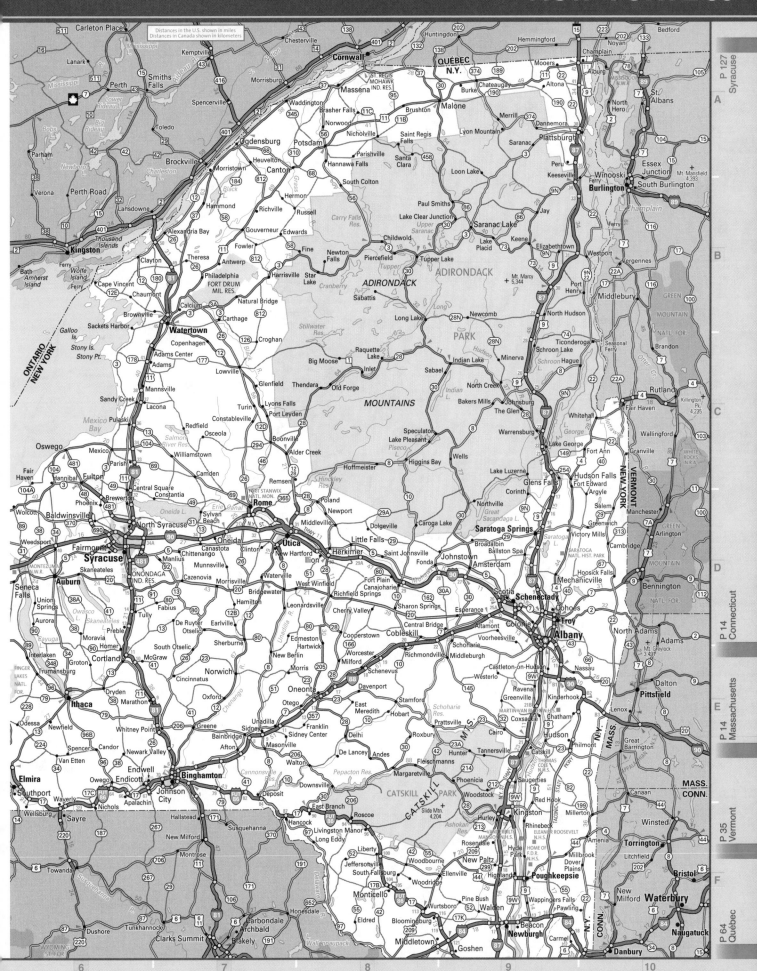

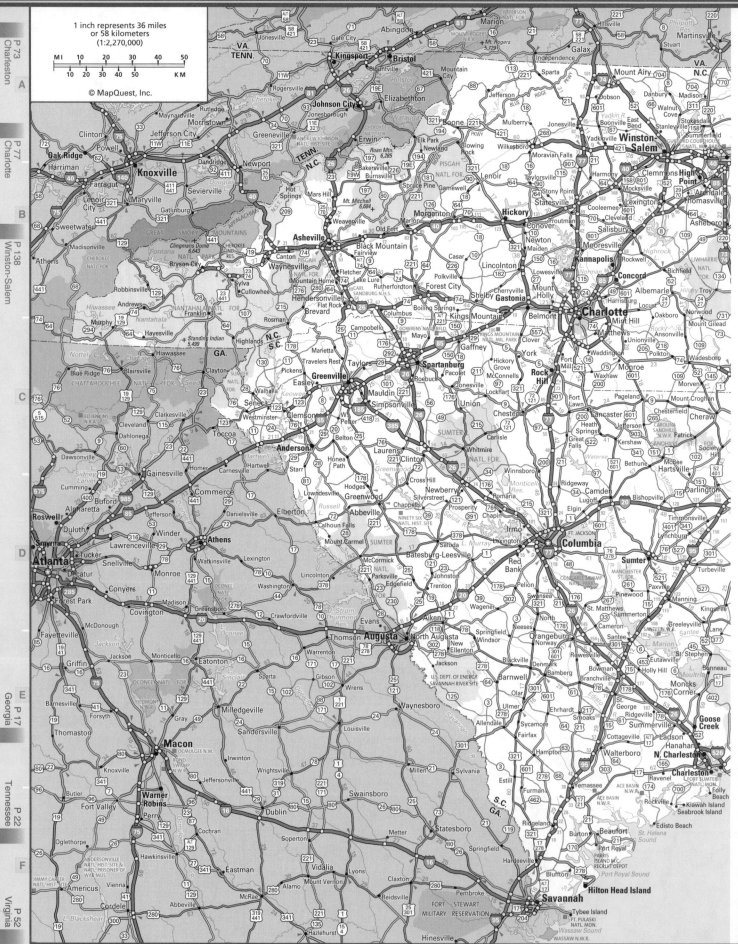

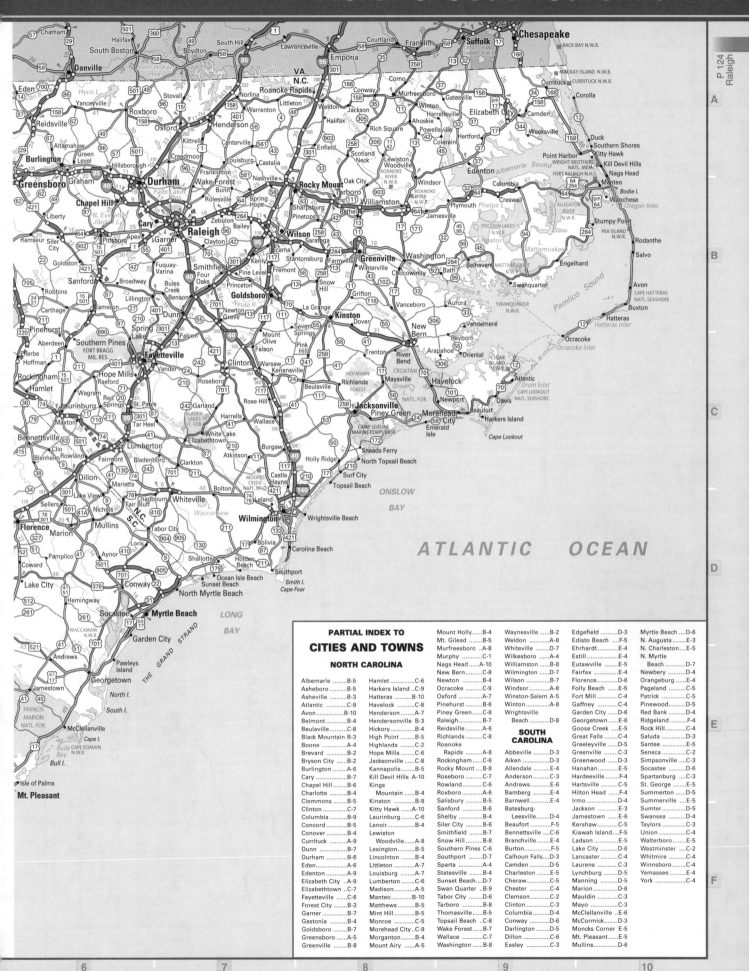

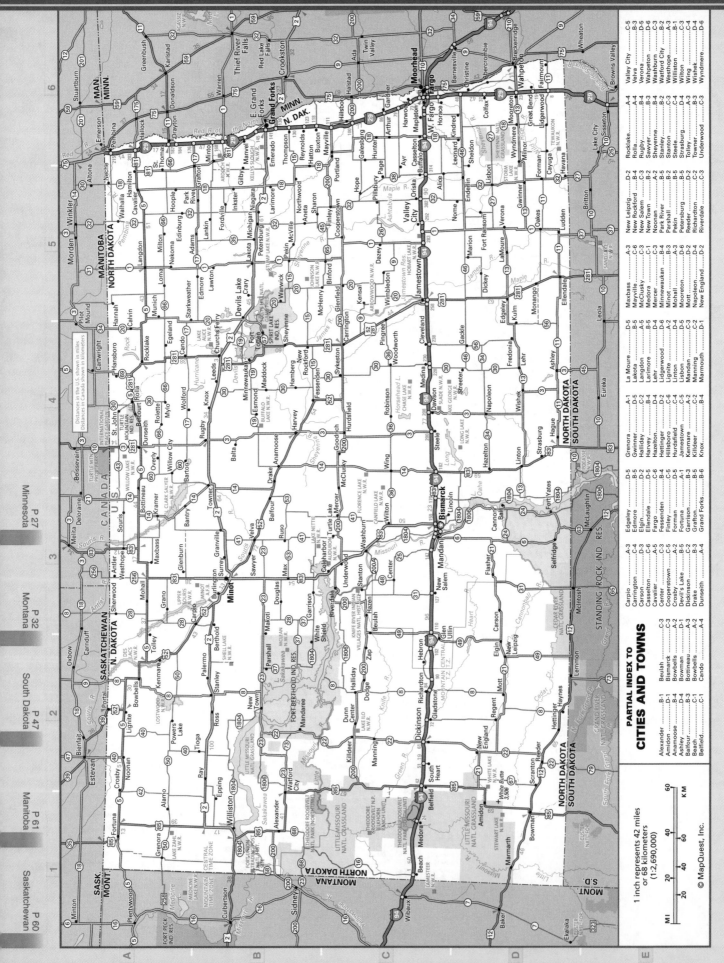

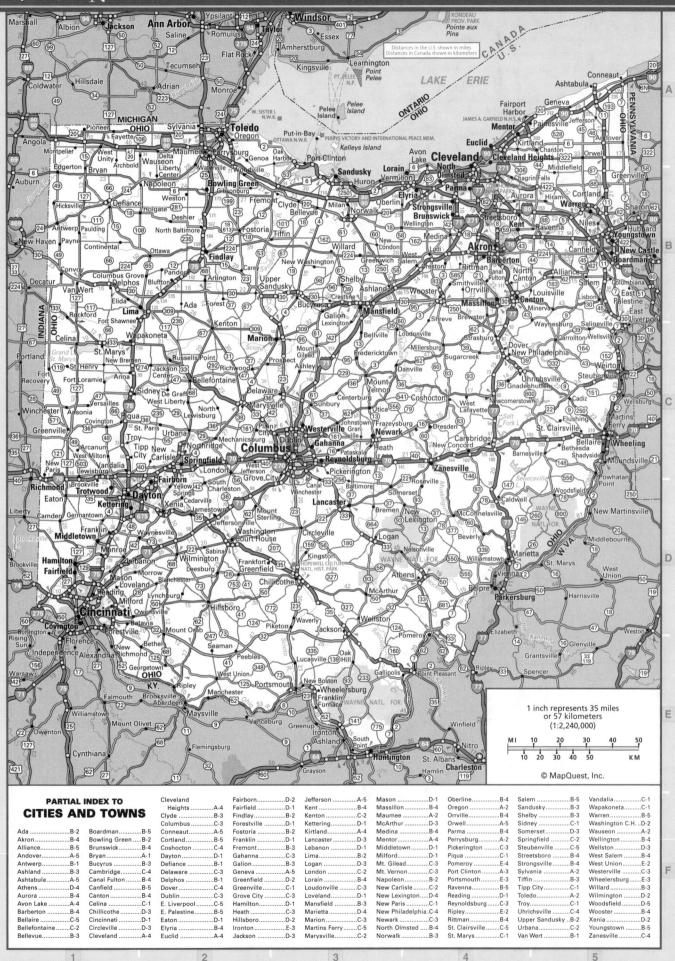

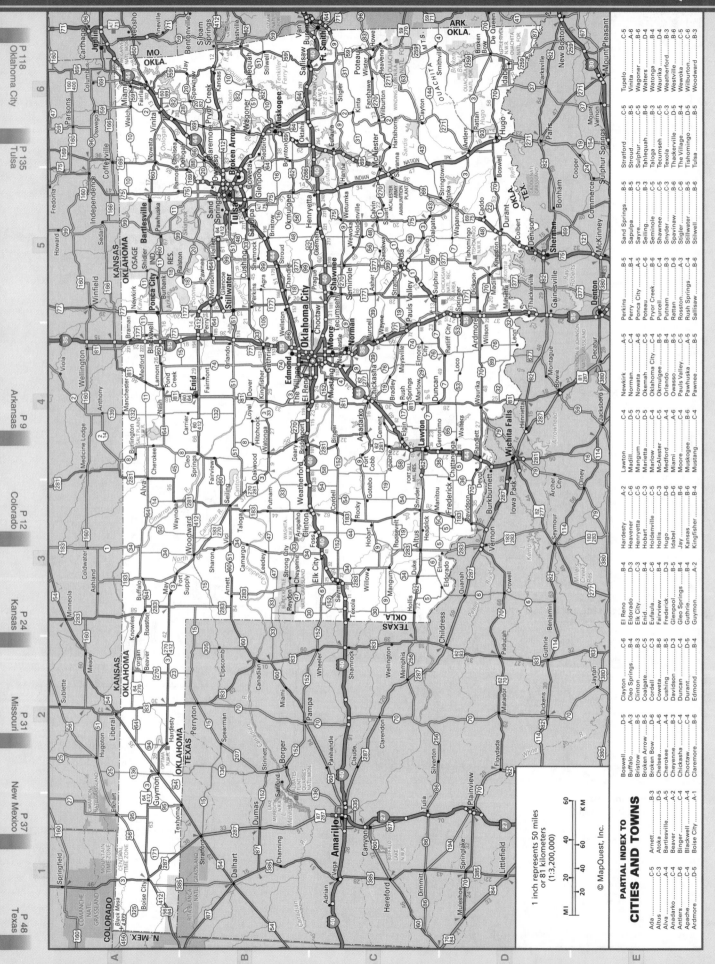

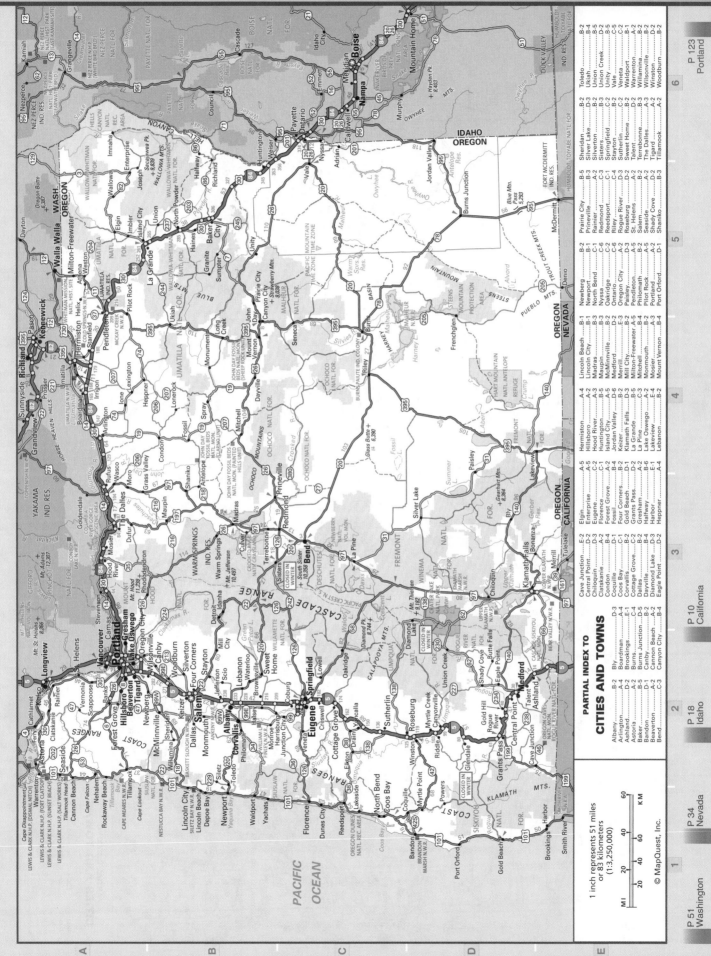

1 inch represents 51 miles
or 83 kilometers
(1:3,250,000)

MI 20   40   60
KM 20   40   60

PARTIAL INDEX TO
CITIES AND TOWNS

P 123 Portland

P 10 California

P 18 Idaho

P 34 Nevada

P 51 Washington

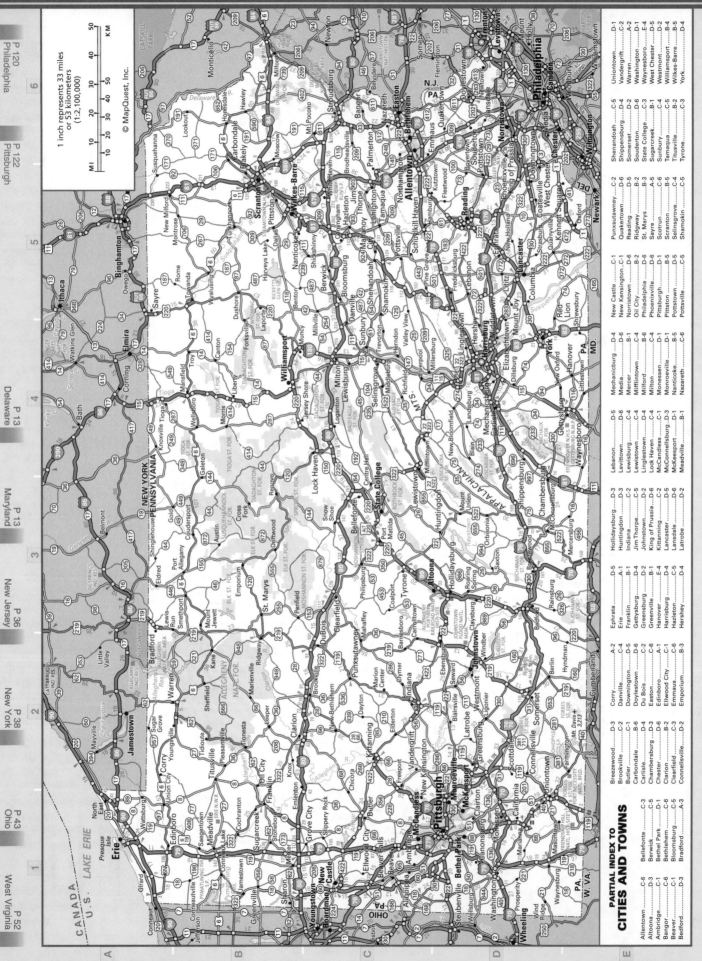

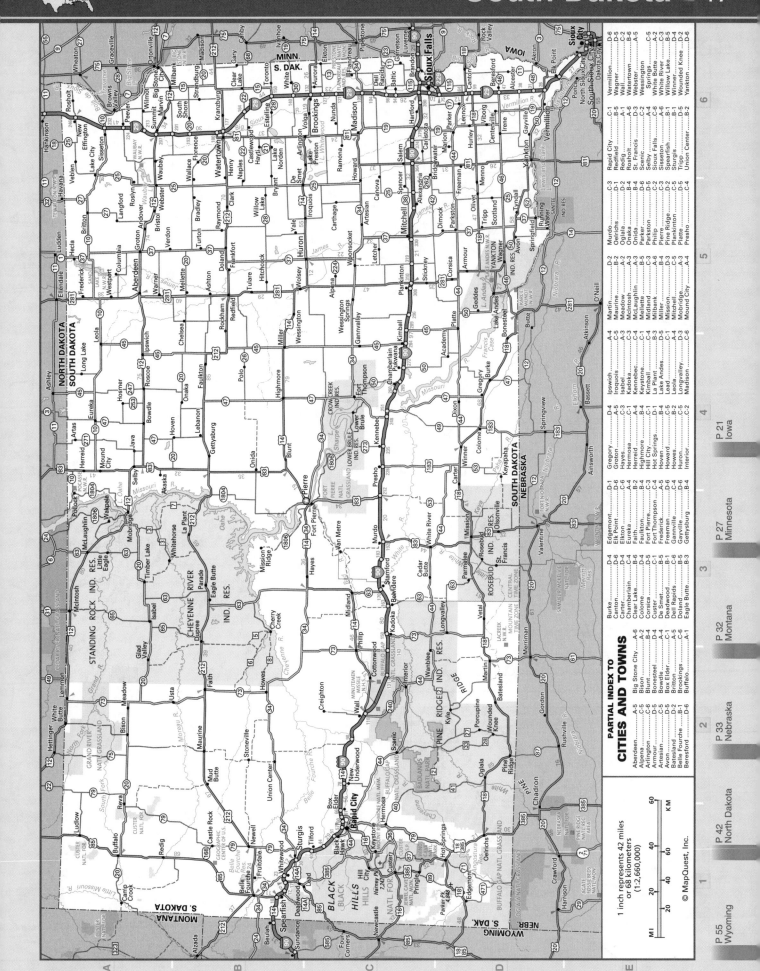

1 inch represents 42 miles
or 68 kilometers
(1:2,660,000)

© MapQuest, Inc.

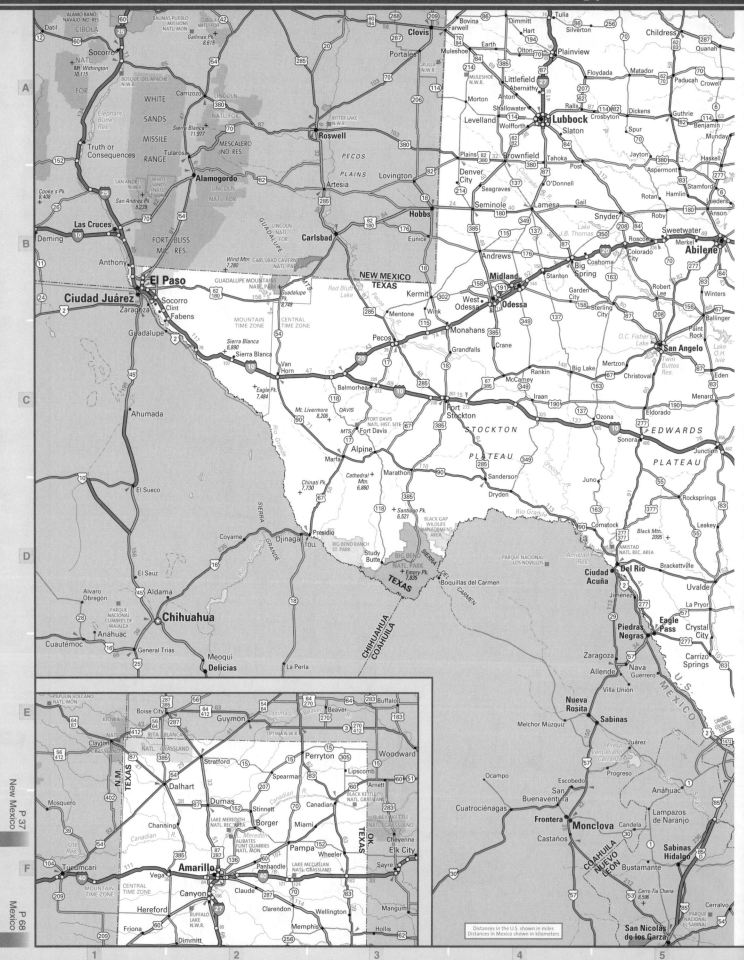

Distances in the U.S. shown in miles
Distances in Mexico shown in kilometers

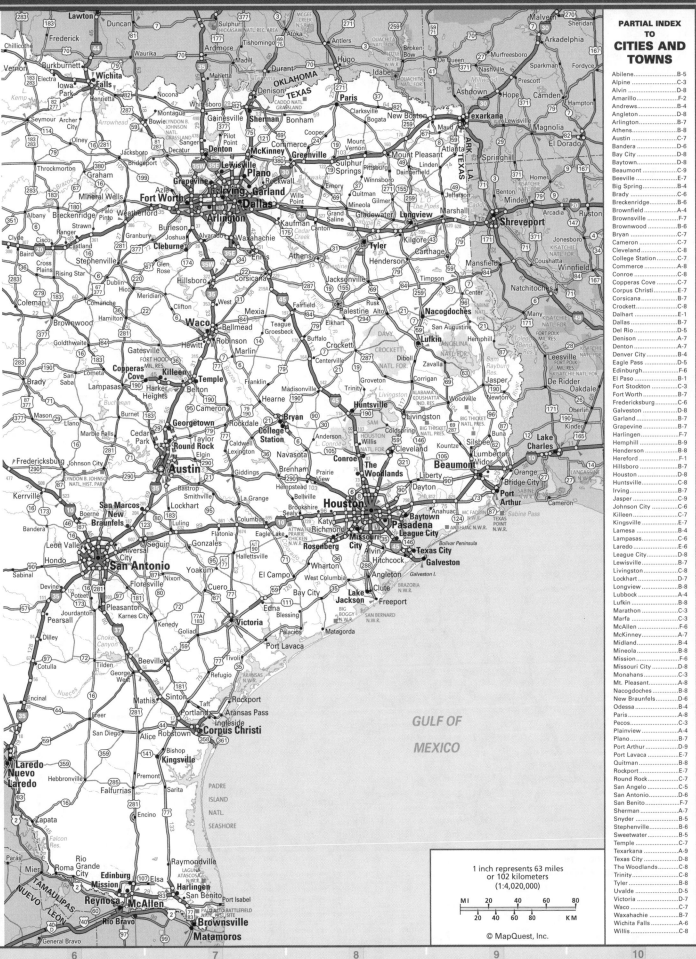

P 70 Austin

P 88 Dallas

P 93 Houston

P 129 San Antonio

P 9 Arkansas

P 25 Louisiana

P 44 Oklahoma

1 inch represents 63 miles
or 102 kilometers
(1:4,020,000)

MI   20   40   60   80
20   40   60   80   KM

© MapQuest, Inc.

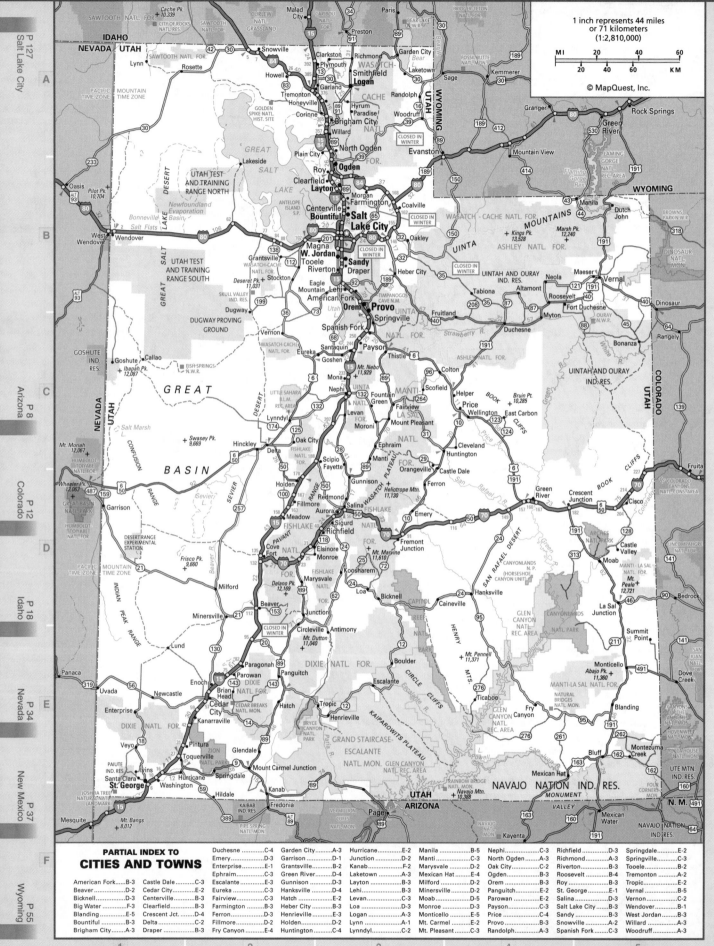

1 inch represents 44 miles
or 71 kilometers
(1:2,810,000)

© MapQuest, Inc.

P 127 Salt Lake City
P 8 Arizona
P 12 Colorado
P 18 Idaho
P 34 Nevada
P 37 New Mexico
P 55 Wyoming

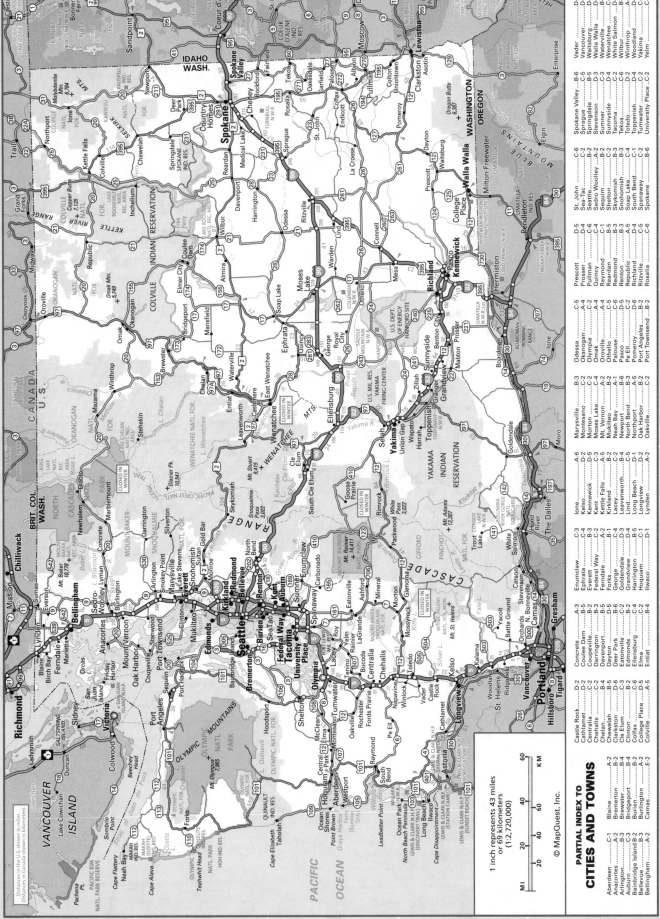

P 127 Spokane

P 132 Seattle

P 18 Idaho

P 45 Oregon

P 58 British Columbia

1 inch represents 43 miles or 69 kilometers (1:2,720,000)

© MapQuest, Inc.

PARTIAL INDEX TO CITIES AND TOWNS

Aberdeen	C-1	Concrete	D-2	Enumclaw	C-3	Marysville	A-6	Odessa	B-3	Prescott	D-5	St. John	C-5	Vader	D-2
Anacortes	A-2	Coulee Dam	D-2	Ephrata	C-4	Montesano	D-2	Okanogan	C-2	Prosser	D-4	Sea-Tac	A-4	Vancouver	C-5
Arlington	B-3	Coupeville	C-2	Everett	B-3	Morton	C-4	Olympia	C-2	Pullman	C-2	Seattle	B-2	Wahsburg	D-5
Auburn	C-3	Chelan	B-4	Federal Way	B-3	Moses Lake	B-5	Oroville	A-2	Quincy	B-4	Sedro Woolley	A-2	Walla Walla	D-5
Bainbridge Island	B-2	Chewelah	A-4	Ferndale	D-5	Mt. Vernon	A-2	Othello	C-4	Raymond	A-4	Sequim	C-1	Waterville	B-4
Bellevue	B-2	Cle Elum	C-2	Forks	D-5	Mukilteo	B-5	Pe Ell	C-4	Redmond	A-4	Shelton	B-5	Wenatchee	C-4
Bellingham	A-2	Clinton	B-2	George	C-4	Neah Bay	A-1	Pomeroy	D-6	Renton	B-3	Skykomish	B-3	White Salmon	D-3
Blaine	A-2	Colfax	C-2	Goldendale	C-2	Newport	B-6	Port Angeles	B-2	Republic	A-3	Snohomish	B-3	Wilbur	C-6
Bremerton	A-2	Colville	B-2	Grandview	C-4	North Bend	D-1	Port Townsend	B-6	Richland	D-4	Soap Lake	C-4	Winthrop	A-4
Brewster	B-4			Harrington	C-4	Northport	A-5			Ritzville	B-2	South Bend	C-1	Woodland	D-2
Bridgeport	B-2	Castle Rock	D-2	Hoquiam	C-1	Oak Harbor	B-2			Rosalia	C-2	Spanaway	B-2	Yakima	C-2
Burien	B-2	Cathlamet	D-2	Ilwaco	B-4	Oakville	A-2					Spokane	C-6	Yelm	C-2
Burlington	A-2	Centralia	C-2									Spokane Valley	B-6	University Place	C-2
Camas	B-2	Chehalis	C-2									Sprague	C-2	Turnwater	B-6
		Chelan	B-4									Stevenson	D-3	Toppenish	B-4
		Chewelah	B-4									Sumner	C-2	Toledo	C-6
		Cle Elum	C-2									Sunnyside	C-2	Tacoma	D-3
		Clinton	B-2												
		Colfax	C-6												
		Colville	B-5												

Distances in the U.S. shown in miles
Distances in Canada shown in kilometers

MI 0 20 40 60
KM 0 20 40 60

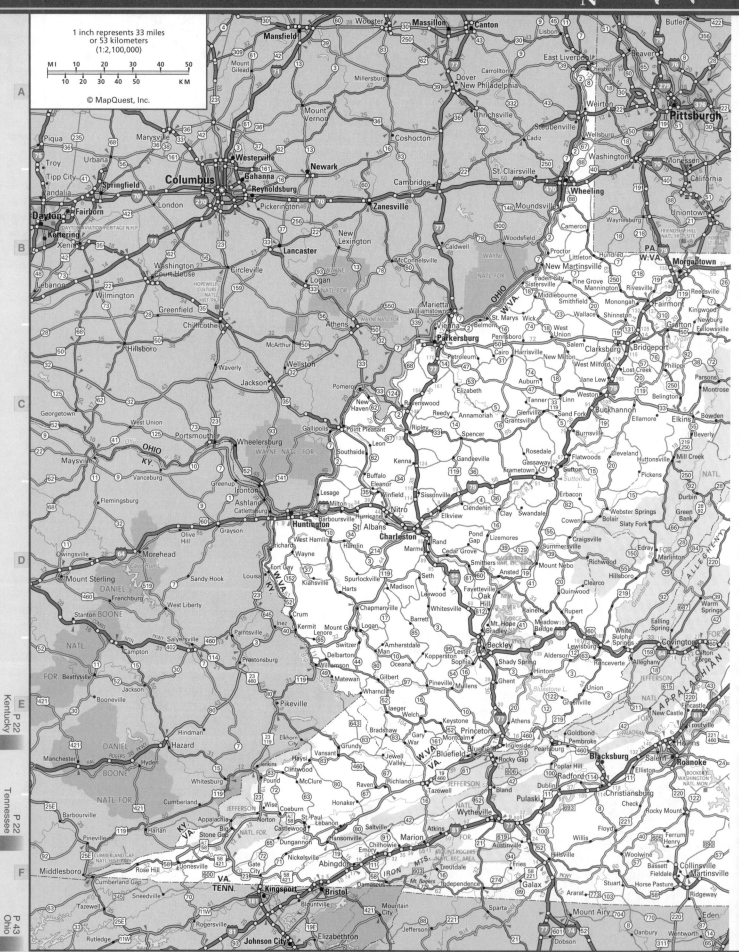

1 inch represents 33 miles
or 53 kilometers
(1:2,100,000)

© MapQuest, Inc.

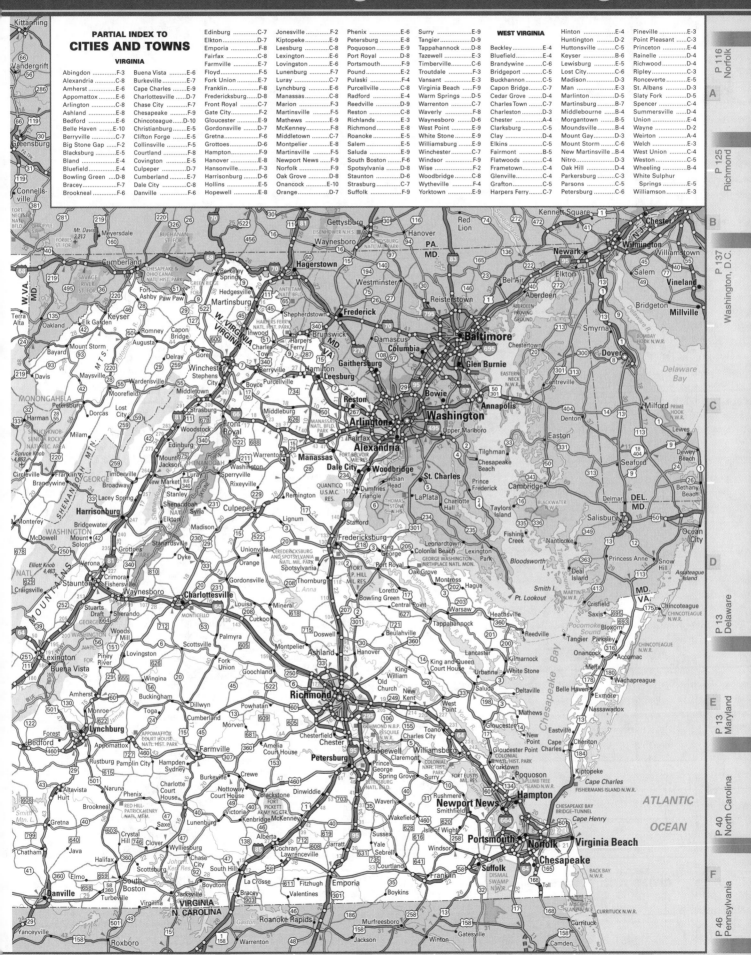

P 116 Norfolk

P 125 Richmond

P 137 Washington, D.C.

P 13 Delaware

P 13 Maryland

P 40 North Carolina

P 46 Pennsylvania

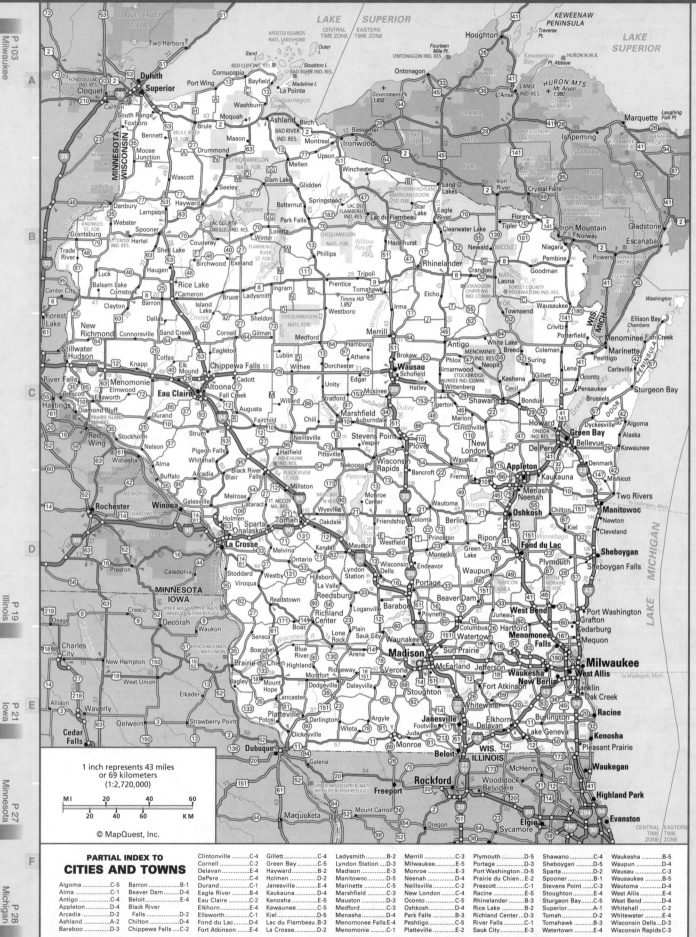

1 inch represents 43 miles
or 69 kilometers
(1:2,720,000)

MI   20   40   60
20   40   60
KM

© MapQuest, Inc.

PARTIAL INDEX TO
CITIES AND TOWNS

1   2   3   4   5

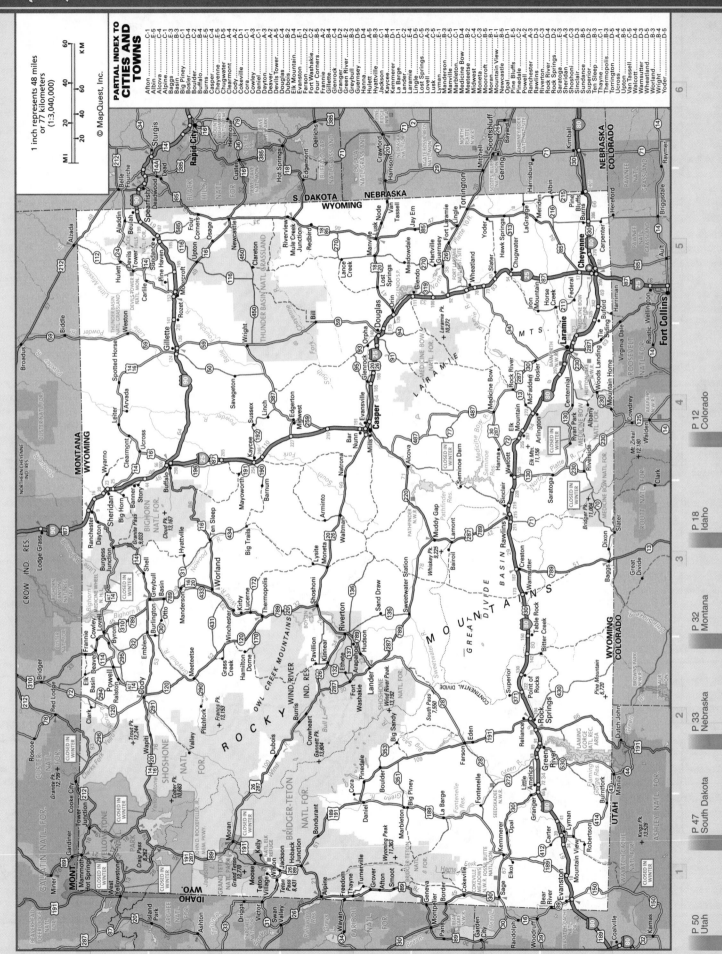

P 12 Colorado

P 18 Idaho

P 32 Montana

P 33 Nebraska

P 47 South Dakota

P 50 Utah

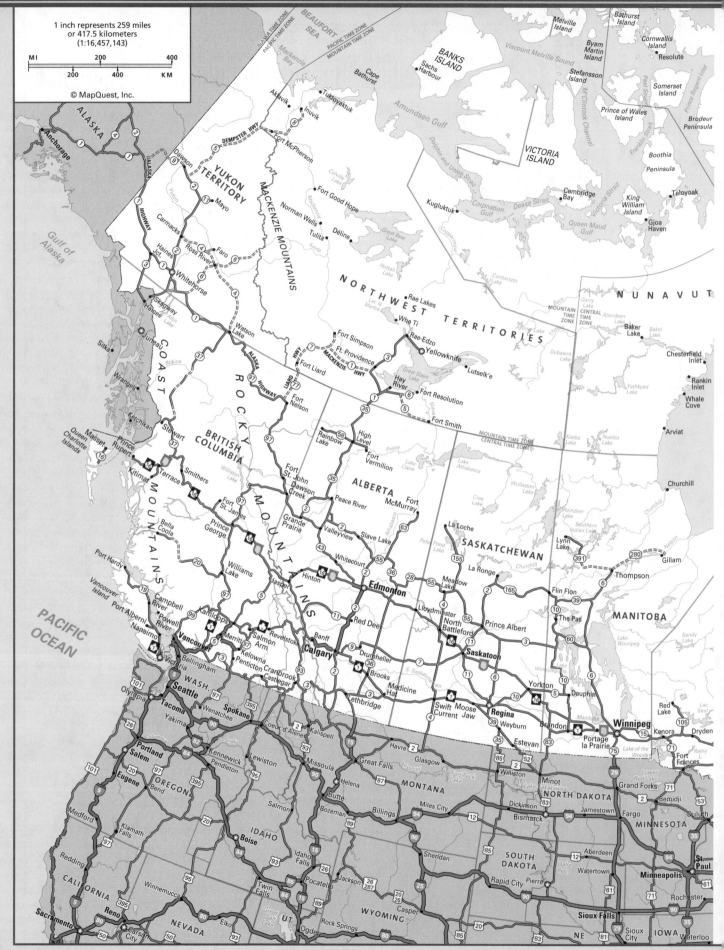

1 inch represents 259 miles
or 417.5 kilometers
(1:16,457,143)

© MapQuest, Inc.

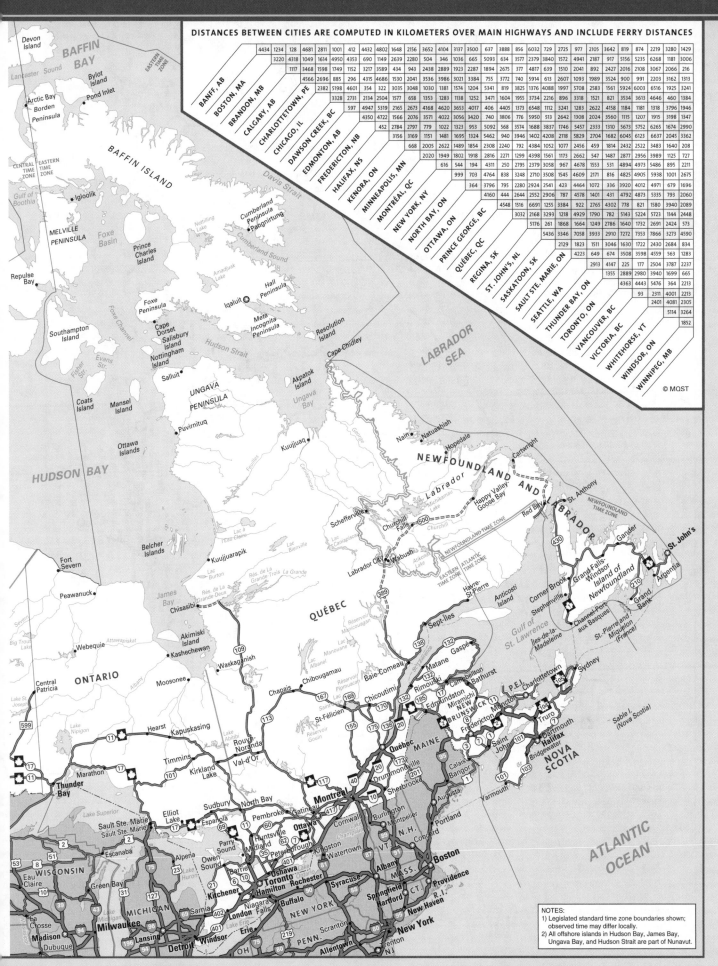

DISTANCES BETWEEN CITIES ARE COMPUTED IN KILOMETERS OVER MAIN HIGHWAYS AND INCLUDE FERRY DISTANCES

Distance chart (triangular matrix). City labels along the diagonal, in order:

BANFF, AB · BOSTON, MA · BRANDON, MB · CALGARY, AB · CHARLOTTETOWN, PE · CHICAGO, IL · DAWSON CREEK, BC · EDMONTON, AB · FREDERICTON, NB · HALIFAX, NS · KENORA, ON · MINNEAPOLIS, MN · MONTRÉAL, QC · NEW YORK, NY · NORTH BAY, ON · OTTAWA, ON · PRINCE GEORGE, BC · QUÉBEC, QC · REGINA, SK · ST. JOHN'S, NL · SASKATOON, SK · SAULT STE. MARIE, ON · SEATTLE, WA · THUNDER BAY, ON · TORONTO, ON · VANCOUVER, BC · VICTORIA, BC · WHITEHORSE, YT · WINDSOR, ON · WINNIPEG, MB

Distances read from each origin city across to the remaining cities:

- **BANFF, AB:** 4434 1234 128 4681 2811 1001 412 4432 4802 1648 2156 3652 4104 3137 3500 637 3888 856 6032 729 2725 977 2105 3642 819 874 2219 3280 1429
- **BOSTON, MA:** 3220 4318 1049 4950 4353 690 346 1036 665 5093 634 3577 2379 3840 1572 2187 917 5156 5235 6268 1181 3006
- **BRANDON, MB:** 1117 3468 1598 1749 1152 3217 3589 434 943 2438 1252 3471
- **CALGARY, AB:** 4566 2696 885 296 4315 4686 1530 2041 3536 3986 3384 755 3772 740 5914 613 2607 1093 1989 3524 900 991 2203 3162 1313
- **CHARLOTTETOWN, PE:** 2382 5198 4601 354 322 3035 3048 1030 1381 1574 1204 5341 819 3825 1376 4088 1997 5708 2583 1561 5924 6003 6516 1925 3241
- **CHICAGO, IL:** 3328 2731 2134 2504 1577 658 1353 1283 1138 1252 3471 896 3318 1521 821 3534 3613 4646 460 1384
- **DAWSON CREEK, BC:** 597 4947 5319 2165 2673 4168 4620 3653 4017 406 4405 1373 6548 1112 3241 1283 2622 4158 1184 1181 1318 3796 1946
- **EDMONTON, AB:** 4350 4722 1566 2076 3571 4022 3056 3420 740 3806 776 5950 513 2642 1308 2024 3560 1115 1207 1915 3198 1347
- **FREDERICTON, NB:** 452 2784 2797 779 1022 1323 953 5092 568 3574 1688 3837 1016 2333 1310 5673 5752 6265 1674 2990
- **HALIFAX, NS:** 3156 3169 1151 1481 1695 1324 5462 940 3946 1402 4208 2118 5829 2704 1682 6045 6123 6637 2045 3362
- **KENORA, ON:** 668 2005 2622 1489 1854 2308 2240 792 4384 1052 1077 2456 459 1814 2432 2522 3483 1640 208
- **MINNEAPOLIS, MN:** 2020 1949 1802 1918 2271 1299 4398 1561 1173 2662 547 1487 2877 2956 3989 1125 727
- **MONTRÉAL, QC:** 616 544 194 4311 250 2795 2379 3058 967 4678 1553 531 4894 4905 5938 1001 2675
- **NEW YORK, NY:** 999 703 4764 838 3248 2710 3508 1545 4609 2171 816 4825 4905 5938 1001 1696
- **NORTH BAY, ON:** 364 3796 795 2280 2924 2541 423 4464 1072 336 3920 4012 4971 679 1696
- **OTTAWA, ON:** 4160 444 2644 2552 2690 787 4578 1401 431 4792 4873 5335 793 2060
- **PRINCE GEORGE, BC:** 4548 1516 6691 1255 3384 922 2765 4302 778 821 1580 3940 2089
- **QUÉBEC, QC:** 3032 2168 3293 1218 4929 1790 782 5143 5224 5723 1144 2448
- **REGINA, SK:** 5176 261 1868 1664 1249 2786 1640 1732 2691 2424 573
- **ST. JOHN'S, NL:** 5436 3346 7058 3933 2910 7272 7353 7866 3273 4590
- **SASKATOON, SK:** 2129 1823 1511 3046 1630 1722 2430 2684 834
- **SAULT STE. MARIE, ON:** 4223 649 674 3508 3598 4659 563 1283
- **SEATTLE, WA:** 2913 4147 225 177 2504 3787 2237
- **THUNDER BAY, ON:** 1355 2889 2980 3940 1699 665
- **TORONTO, ON:** 4363 4443 5476 364 2213
- **VANCOUVER, BC:** 93 2311 4001 2213
- **VICTORIA, BC:** 2401 4081 2305
- **WHITEHORSE, YT:** 5114 3264
- **WINDSOR, ON:** 1852

© MQST

NOTES:
1) Legislated standard time zone boundaries shown; observed time may differ locally.
2) All offshore islands in Hudson Bay, James Bay, Ungava Bay, and Hudson Strait are part of Nunavut.

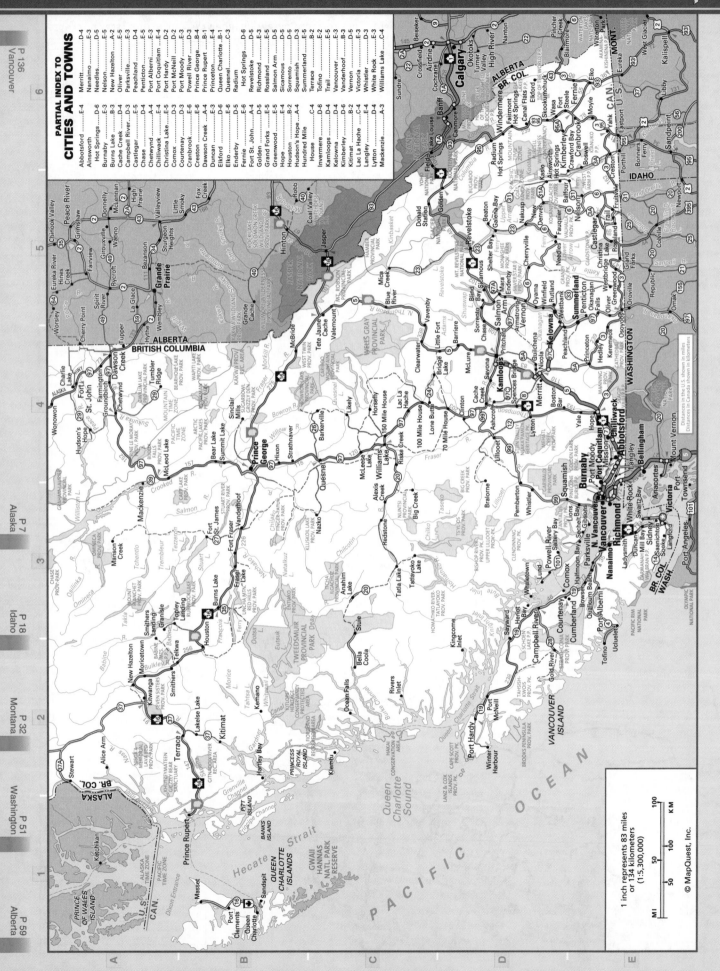

PARTIAL INDEX TO CITIES AND TOWNS

Abbotsford	E-4	Merritt	D-4
Ainsworth	E-3	Nanaimo	D-5
Burnaby	E-5	Needles	E-3
Burns Lake	B-3	Nelson	E-3
Cache Creek	D-4	New Hazelton	A-2
Campbell River	E-5	Oliver	E-4
Castlegar	E-3	Parksville	D-4
Chase	D-4	Peachland	E-5
Chetwynd	A-3	Penticton	E-4
Chilliwack	E-5	Port Alberni	E-3
Comox	D-2	Port Coquitlam	D-4
Courtenay	E-3	Port Hardy	D-2
Cranbrook	E-4	Port McNeill	D-3
Creston	E-4	Port Moody	E-5
Dawson Creek	A-4	Powell River	E-6
Duncan	E-3	Prince George	B-4
Elkford	D-2	Prince Rupert	B-1
Elko	E-6	Princeton	E-4
Enderby	D-5	Quesnel	C-3
Fernie	E-6	Radium Hot Springs	D-6
Fort St. John	A-4	Revelstoke	D-5
Golden	D-6	Richmond	E-5
Grand Forks	E-3	Rossland	E-5
Greenwood	E-3	Salmon Arm	D-5
Hope	D-4	Sicamous	D-3
Houston	B-2	Sorrento	D-3
Hudson's Hope	A-4	Squamish	E-5
Hundred Mile House	C-4	Summerland	E-5
Invermere	E-2	Terrace	B-2
Kamloops	D-4	Tofino	E-5
Kelowna	D-5	Trail	E-3
Kimberley	E-3	Vancouver	D-6
Kitimat	B-2	Vanderhoof	B-3
Lac La Hache	C-4	Vernon	D-5
Langley	E-4	Victoria	D-3
Lytton	D-4	Whistler	E-3
Mackenzie	A-3	White Rock	E-4
		Williams Lake	C-4

P 136 Vancouver
P 7 Alaska
P 18 Idaho
P 32 Montana
P 51 Washington
P 59 Alberta

1 inch represents 83 miles or 134 kilometers (1:5,300,000)

© MapQuest, Inc.

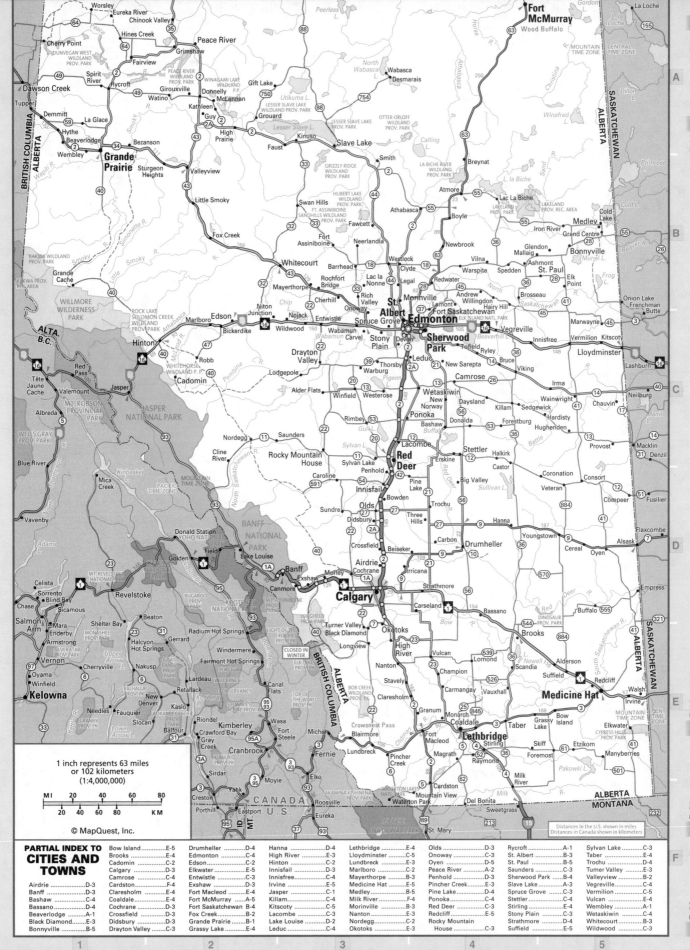

1 inch represents 63 miles
or 102 kilometers
(1:4,000,000)

MI   20   40   60   80

KM   20   40   60   80

© MapQuest, Inc.

PARTIAL INDEX TO CITIES AND TOWNS

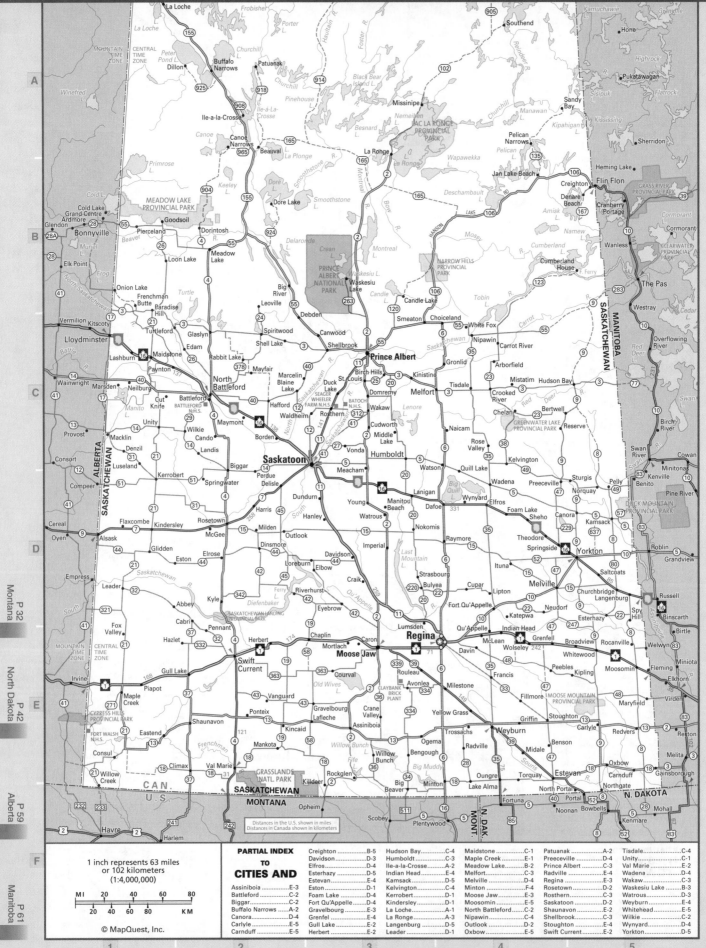

P 32 Montana

P 42 North Dakota

P 59 Alberta

P 61 Manitoba

Distances in the U.S. shown in miles
Distances in Canada shown in kilometers

1 inch represents 63 miles
or 102 kilometers
(1:4,000,000)

MI   20   40   60   80

20   40   60   80   KM

© MapQuest, Inc.

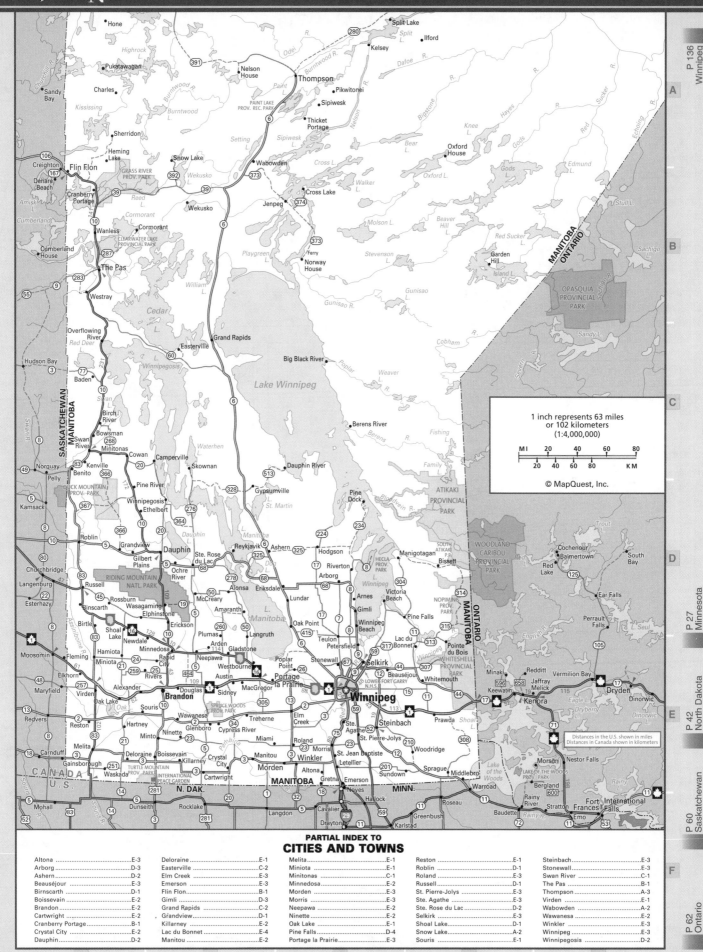

P 136 Winnipeg

1 inch represents 63 miles
or 102 kilometers
(1:4,000,000)

MI   20   40   60   80

20   40   60   80
KM

© MapQuest, Inc.

P 27 Minnesota

P 42 North Dakota

P 60 Saskatchewan

Distances in the U.S. shown in miles
Distances in Canada shown in kilometers

PARTIAL INDEX TO
CITIES AND TOWNS

P 62 Ontario

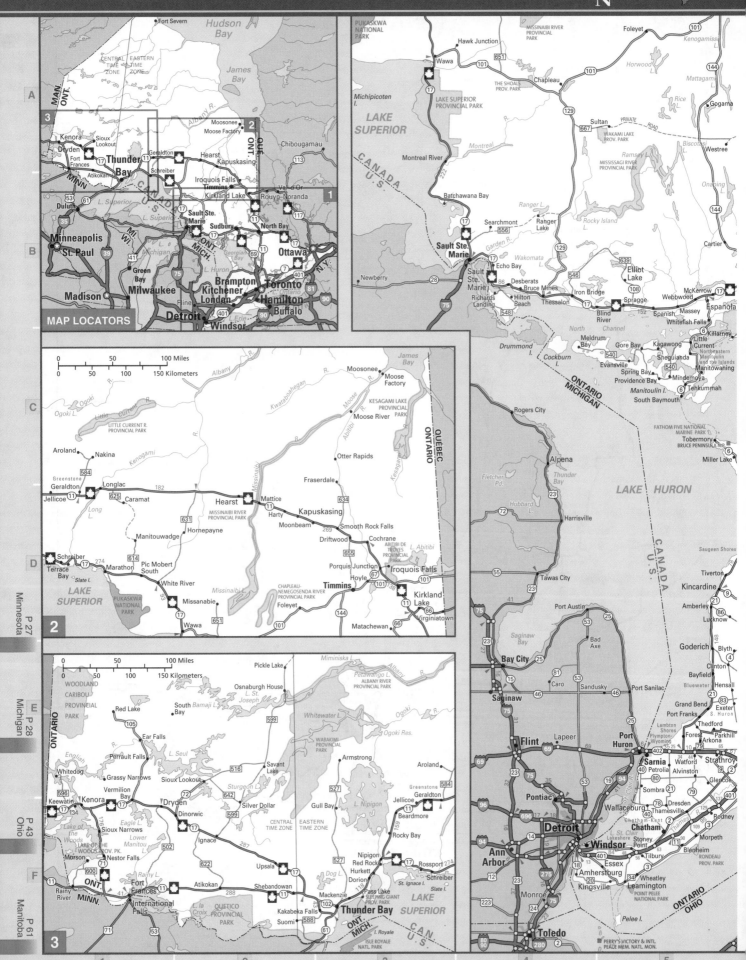

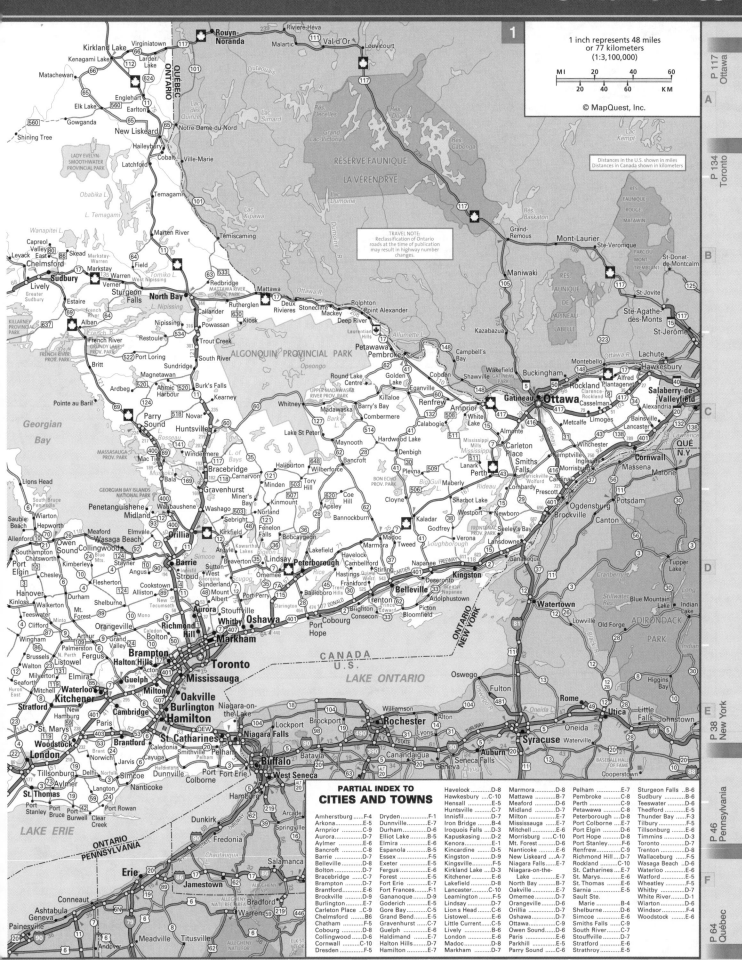

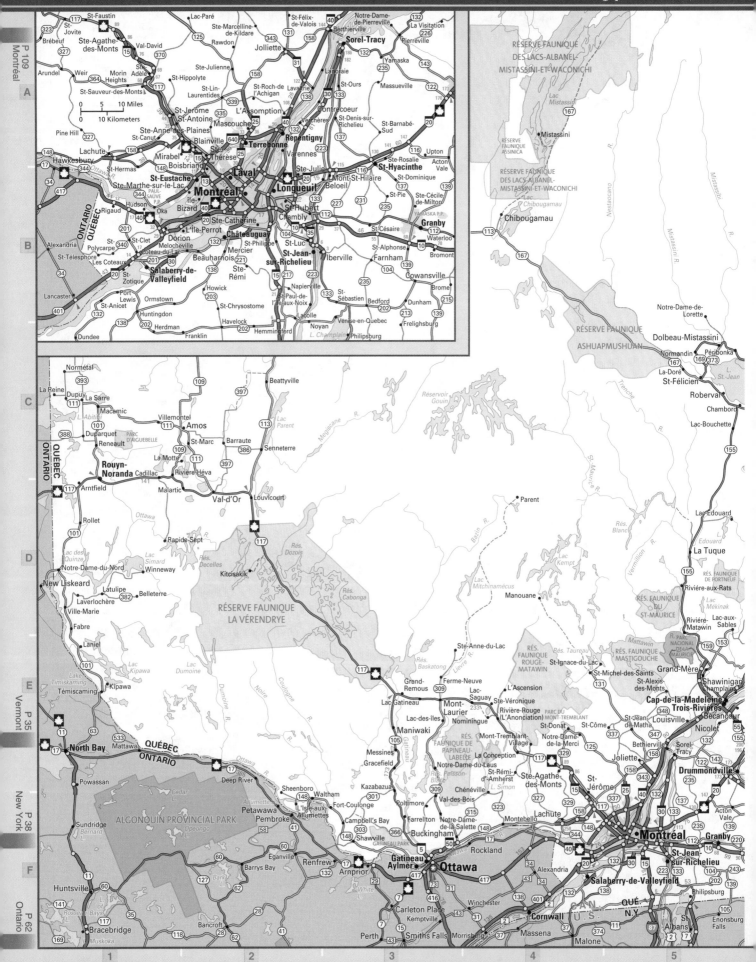

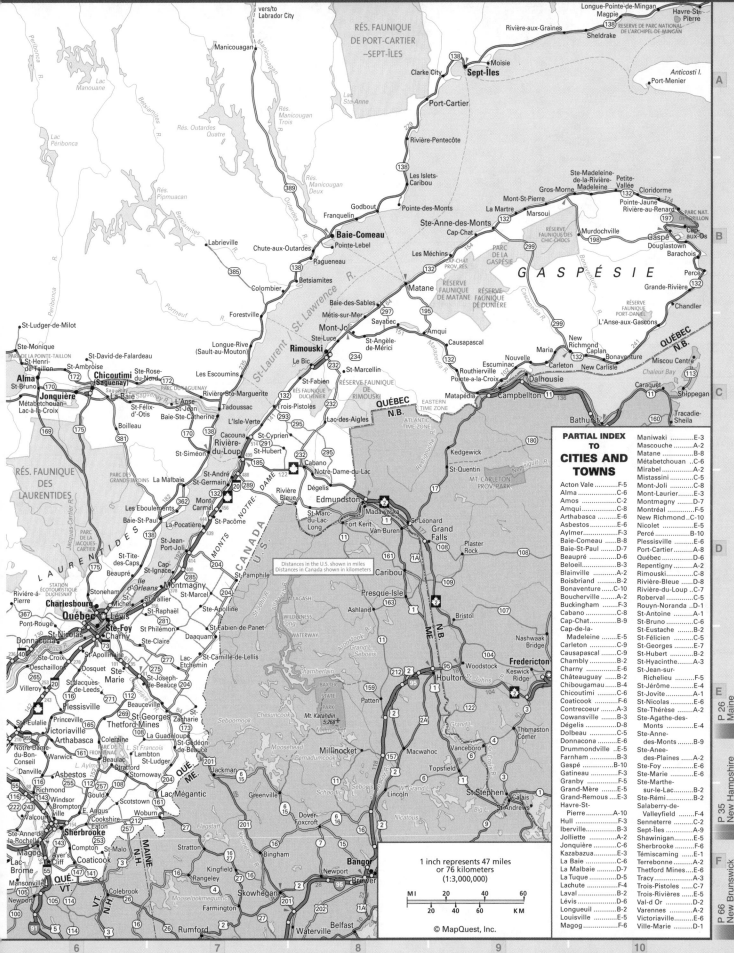

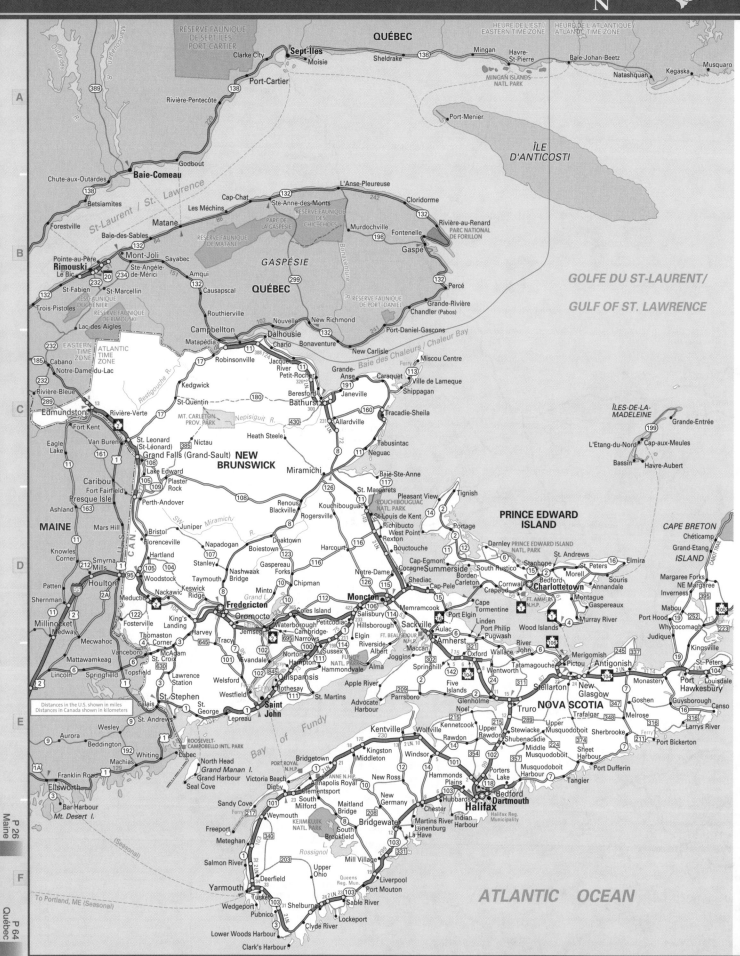

RÉSERVE FAUNIQUE
DE SEPT-ILES -
PORT-CARTIER

Clarke City
Sept-Îles
Moisie

Mingan
Havre-
St-Pierre
Baie-Johan-Beetz

Musquaro

Port-Cartier

Sheldrake
138

Natashquan
Kegaska

Rivière-Pentecôte

MINGAN ISLANDS
NATL. PARK

Port-Menier

ÎLE
D'ANTICOSTI

Godbout

Chute-aux-Outardes

Baie-Comeau

138

Betsiamites

L'Anse-Pleureuse

Cap-Chat

Cloridorme

132

Forestville

Matane

Ste-Anne-des-Monts
RÉSERVE FAUNIQUE
DES
CHIC-CHOCS

242

Murdochville

Fontenelle

132

Rivière-au-Renard
PARC NATIONAL
DE FORILLON

Baie-des-Sables
132

PARC DE
LA GASPÉSIE

198

Gaspé

Pointe-au-Père
Rimouski
Le Bic
Mont-Joli
Sayabec
20
234
Ste-Angèle-
de-Mérici

St-Fabien
232
St-Marcellin

132
Trois-Pistoles

Amqui

RÉSERVE FAUNIQUE
DE MATANE

GASPÉSIE

QUÉBEC

Causapscal

GOLFE DU ST-LAURENT /

GULF OF ST. LAWRENCE

185
Cabano
Notre-Dame-du-Lac
232

Rivière-Bleue
289

Edmundston

Lac-des-Aigles

RÉSERVE FAUNIQUE
DUCHENIER

RÉSERVE FAUNIQUE
DE RIMOUSKI

Routhierville

RÉSERVE FAUNIQUE
DE PORT-DANIEL

Campbellton

Matapédia
Dalhousie
Charlo

Nouvelle
New Richmond
Bonaventure

241
Port-Daniel-Gascons

132

Grande-Rivière

Chandler (Pabos)

Percé

232
EASTERN
TIME
ZONE
ATLANTIC
TIME
ZONE

17

Robinsonville

188 224

132

New Carlisle

Baie des Chaleurs / Chaleur Bay

Miscou Centre

Rivière-Verte

Fort Kent

Eagle
Lake
161

Van Buren
St. Leonard
(St-Léonard)
Grand Falls (Grand-Sault)
385
Nictau
Lake Edward

105
109
Plaster
Rock
Perth-Andover

Kedgwick

St-Quentin
180

MT. CARLETON
PROV. PARK
430

Heath Steele

Nepisiguit R.

Jacquet
River
Petit-Rocher

Beresford
Bathurst
300

231

Grande-
Anse
191
Janeville

160

8

11

Allardville

72

Tabusintac

Neguac

Ville de Lameque
Shippagan

113
Caraquet

Tracadie-Sheila

ÎLES-DE-LA-
MADELEINE

199
Grande-Entrée

L'Etang-du-Nord
Cap-aux-Meules

Bassin
Havre-Aubert

MAINE

Caribou
Fort Fairfield
Presque Isle
163
Ashland

11

Mars Hill

NEW
BRUNSWICK

Miramichi

126

Baie-Ste-Anne

117
St. Margarets

KOUCHIBOUGUAC
NATL. PARK
St-Louis de Kent
Richibucto
West Point
Rexton

Pleasant View

Tignish

14
2

PRINCE EDWARD
ISLAND

CAPE BRETON

Chéticamp

Grand-Etang
ISLAND

CABOT TRAIL

Knowles
Corner

212

Smyrna
Mills

Bristol
Florenceville
Hartland

Napadogan
107
Stanley

Juniper

Renous
Blackville

Rogersville

116

Bouctouche

11

Darnley
PRINCE EDWARD ISLAND
NATL. PARK

South Rustico
Stanhope

St. Andrews
16
St. Peters
Elmira

Margaree Forks
NE Margaree

Patten
Houlton
95
2A

Woodstock
105
104

Taymouth
Nashwaak
Bridge

Boiestown
123

Deaktown

116

Harcourt

126

Notre-Dame
Shediac
Cap-Pele

Summerside
Borden-
Carleton

15
Crapaud
Cornwall
58

Bedford
Morell

Souris

Montague
Gaspereaux

Inverness

395

Mabou

Shernman
11
2

Caribou
Medway

122
Fosterville

Keswick
Ridge
Fredericton
Oromocto

Minto
Grand L.
Chipman
10

112

Salisbury

Moncton

106
114
Memramcook

115
FT. AMHERST
N.H.P.
Charlottetown

4
Murray River

Port Hood
19
Judique

Whycocomagh

Millinocket

Mecwahoc

Thomaston
Corner
McAdam
St. Croix
630

King's
Landing
Harvey

Tracy
645

Jemseg
102
695
Waterborough
Cambridge-
Narrows

Coles Island
423
106

233
114

Hillsborough

Elgin
Riverside-
Albert

Cape
Tormentine

Linden
Port Elgin

Port Philip
Pugwash

Wood Islands

River
John
106

Merigomish
245
337

Antigonish

Kingsville
St-Peters
104

Vanceboro
6
Lincoln
Springfield
Topsfield
3

101

Evandale
Norton
111
Hampton
845

Sussex
Welsford

209

FUNDY
NATL. PARK
Alma

Springhill
142

104

Wentworth
24
15

Oxford
Wallace

311

Tatamagouche

New
Glasgow
347

Port
Hawkesbury

104
Louisdale

Millinocket
Mattawamkeag

St. Stephen
Calais
9

St. George
Lepreau

Welsford
Westfield
Rothesay
Quispamsis
111
Saint
John

St. Martins

Advocate
Harbour

Parrsboro

Five
Islands

Glenholme
Truro

Stellarton

NOVA SCOTIA

Trafalgar
348

Melrose

Monastery
19
7

Guysborough
16
Canso

Aurora
9
Beddington

Wesley

St. Andrews

1A
Whiting
Lubec

North Head
Grand Manan I.
Grand Harbour
Seal Cove

ROOSEVELT-
CAMPOBELLO INTL. PARK

PORT ROYAL
N.H.P.

Bridgetown
21
Middleton
12

Kentville
230

17E
Kingston

Wolfville
14
Windsor
354

Upper
Rawdon
101

Rawdon

Stewiacke

215
289

Upper
Musquodoboit

Goshen

347
Sherbrooke

211

Larrys River
316

Port Bickerton

Machias

Franklin Road

Ellsworth

Bar Harbour
Mt. Desert I.

1A

Victoria Beach
Annapolis Royal
ANNE N.H.P.
Clementsport
South
Milford

Digby

Weymouth

New Ross

New
Germany

103

Hammonds
Plains

Middle
Musquodoboit

Musquodoboit
Harbour

224

Sheet
Harbour

374

Porters
Lake

7

Port Dufferin

Tangier

Sandy Cove
217
Freeport

Meteghan

340

KEJIMKUJIK
NATL. PARK
South
Brookfield

Mill Village

Bridgewater
331

Martins River
Indian
Harbour

Lunenburg
La Have

Chester

Hubbards

Bedford
Dartmouth
Halifax

Halifax Reg.
Municipality

Salmon River
Deerfield

203
Upper
Ohio

Queens
Reg. Mun.
Rossignol

209

Liverpool
Port Mouton

ATLANTIC OCEAN

Yarmouth

Tusket
Wedgeport
Pubnico

103
Shelburne

Sable River

Lockeport

Lower Woods Harbour

Clyde River

Clark's Harbour

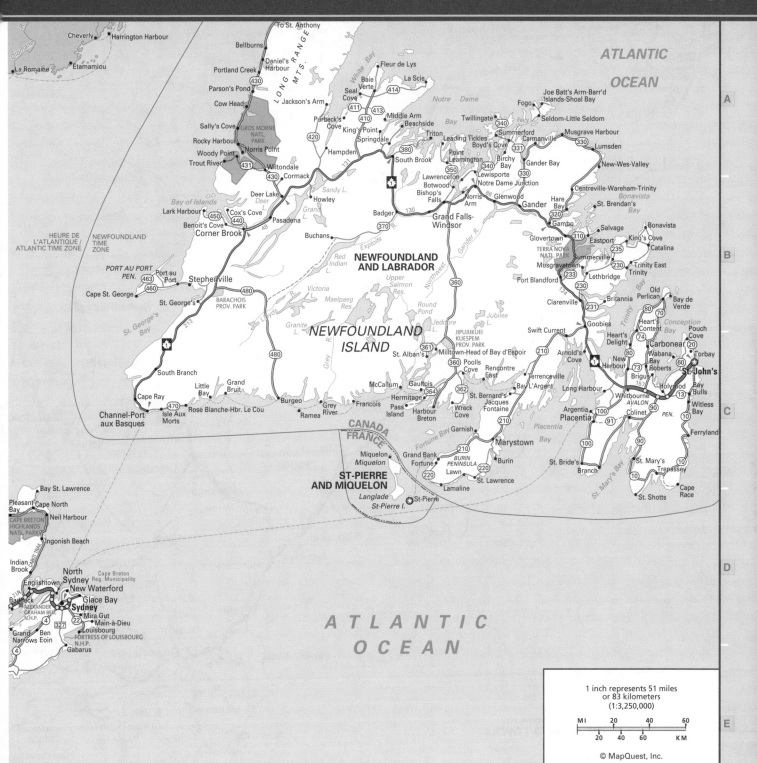

ATLANTIC OCEAN

To St. Anthony

Cheverly · Harrington Harbour

La Romaine · Etamamiou

Bellburns

Portland Creek

Daniel's Harbour

Parson's Pond

Cow Head

Sally's Cove

Rocky Harbour

Woody Point

Trout River

GROS MORNE NATL. PARK

Norris Point

Wiltondale

Cormack

Deer Lake

Howley

Lark Harbour

Cox's Cove

Benoit's Cove

Corner Brook

Pasadena

Buchans

Bay of Islands

NEWFOUNDLAND TIME ZONE

HEURE DE L'ATLANTIQUE / ATLANTIC TIME ZONE

PORT AU PORT PEN.

Cape St. George

Port au Port

St. George's

Stephenville

BARACHOIS PROV. PARK

South Branch

Cape Ray

Little Bay

Grand Bruit

Channel-Port aux Basques

Isle Aux Morts

Rose Blanche-Hbr. Le Cou

Burgeo

Ramea

Grey River

Francois

Hermitage

Gaultois

McCallum

Pass Island

Harbour Breton

Wreck Cove

Garnish

CANADA FRANCE

Miquelon

Grand Bank

Fortune

Lamaline

St. Lawrence

Lawn

BURIN PENINSULA

Burin

ST-PIERRE AND MIQUELON

Langlade

St-Pierre I.

St-Pierre

Jackson's Arm

Purbeck's Cove

King's Point

Hampden

South Brook

Badger

Springdale

Baie Verte

Seal Cove

Middle Arm

Beachside

Triton

Leading Tickles

Point Leamington

Lawrenceton

Botwood

Bishop's Falls

Grand Falls-Windsor

Fleur de Lys

La Scie

Notre Dame Bay

Twillingate

Summerford

Carmanville

Boyd's Cove

Birchy Bay

Gander Bay

Lewisporte

Notre Dame Junction

Glenwood

Norris Arm

Fogo

Joe Batt's Arm-Barr'd Islands-Shoal Bay

Seldom-Little Seldom

Musgrave Harbour

Lumsden

New-Wes-Valley

Centreville-Wareham-Trinity

Gander

Hare Bay

Gambo

St. Brendan's

Salvage

Eastport

Glovertown

TERRA NOVA NATL. PARK

Summerville

Musgravetown

Port Blandford

Clarenville

Goobies

Swift Current

Milltown-Head of Bay d'Espoir

JIPUJIJKUEI KUESPEM PROV. PARK

St. Alban's

Pools Cove

Rencontre East

Terrenceville

Bay L'Argent

St. Bernard's-Jacques Fontaine

Long Harbour

Arnold's Cove

New Harbour

Brigus

Whitbourne

Argentia

Placentia

Marystown

Bonavista

King's Cove

Catalina

Trinity East

Trinity

Lethbridge

Britannia

Old Perlican

Heart's Content

Heart's Delight

Wabana

Bay Roberts

Holyrood

AVALON PEN.

Colinet

Long Harbour

St. Bride's

Branch

Bay de Verde

Pouch Cove

Carbonear

Torbay

St. John's

Bay Bulls

Witless Bay

Ferryland

St. Mary's

Trepassey

Cape Race

St. Shotts

St. Mary's Bay

Conception Bay

Trinity Bay

NEWFOUNDLAND AND LABRADOR

NEWFOUNDLAND ISLAND

Red Indian L.

Upper Salmon Res.

Maelpaeg Res.

Victoria L.

Grey R.

Granite L.

Round Pond

Jeddore L.

Jubilee L.

Placentia Bay

Fortune Bay

Marystown

Sydney

North Sydney

New Waterford

Glace Bay

Baddeck

Bay St. Lawrence

Cape North

Pleasant Bay

Neil Harbour

Ingonish Beach

Indian Brook

Englishtown

CAPE BRETON HIGHLANDS NATL. PARK

Cape Breton Reg. Municipality

ALEXANDER GRAHAM BELL N.H.P.

Mira Gut

Main-à-Dieu

Louisbourg

FORTRESS OF LOUISBOURG N.H.P.

Grand Narrows

Ben Eoin

Gabarus

ATLANTIC OCEAN

1 inch represents 51 miles or 83 kilometers (1:3,250,000)

MI   20   40   60

20   40   60   KM

© MapQuest, Inc.

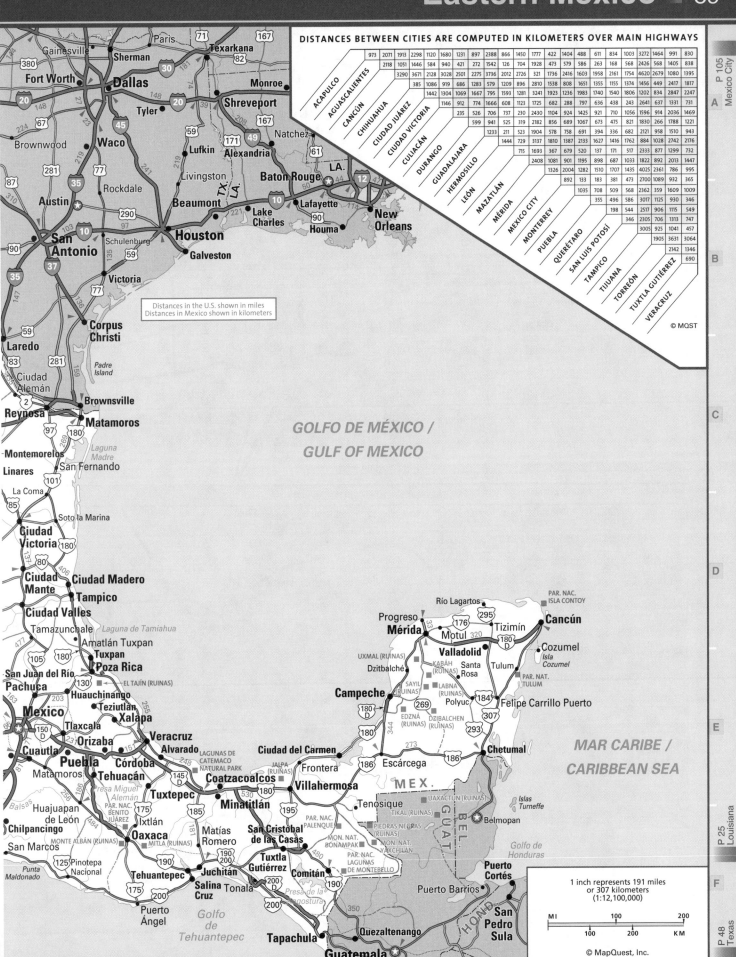

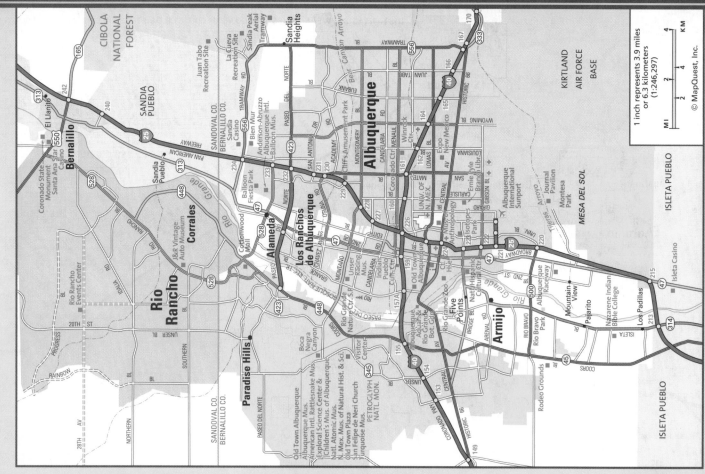

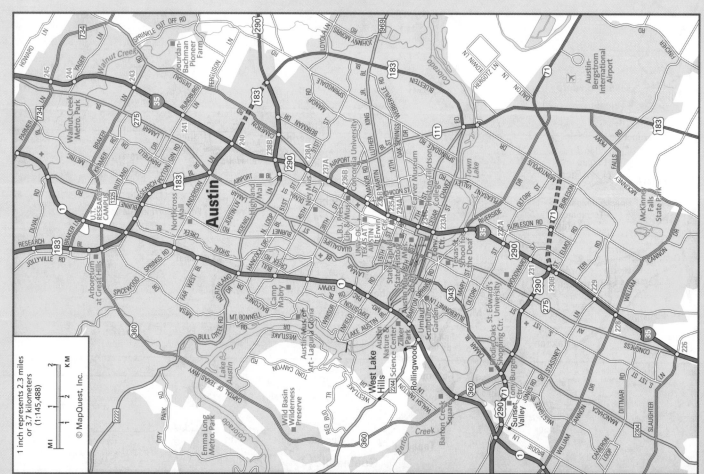

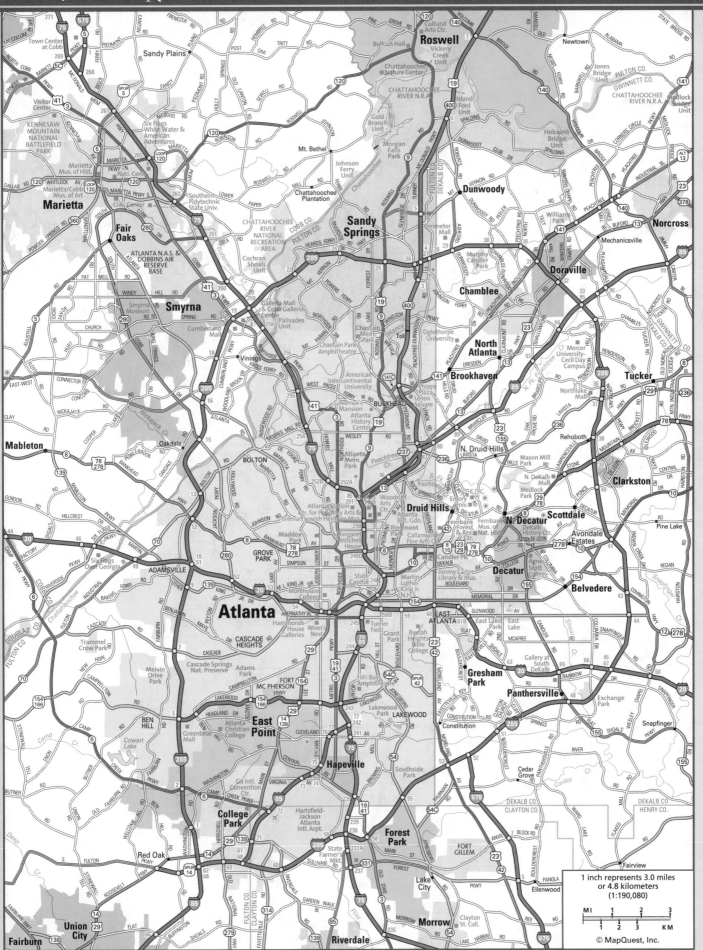

1 inch represents 3.0 miles
or 4.8 kilometers
(1:190,080)

© MapQuest, Inc.

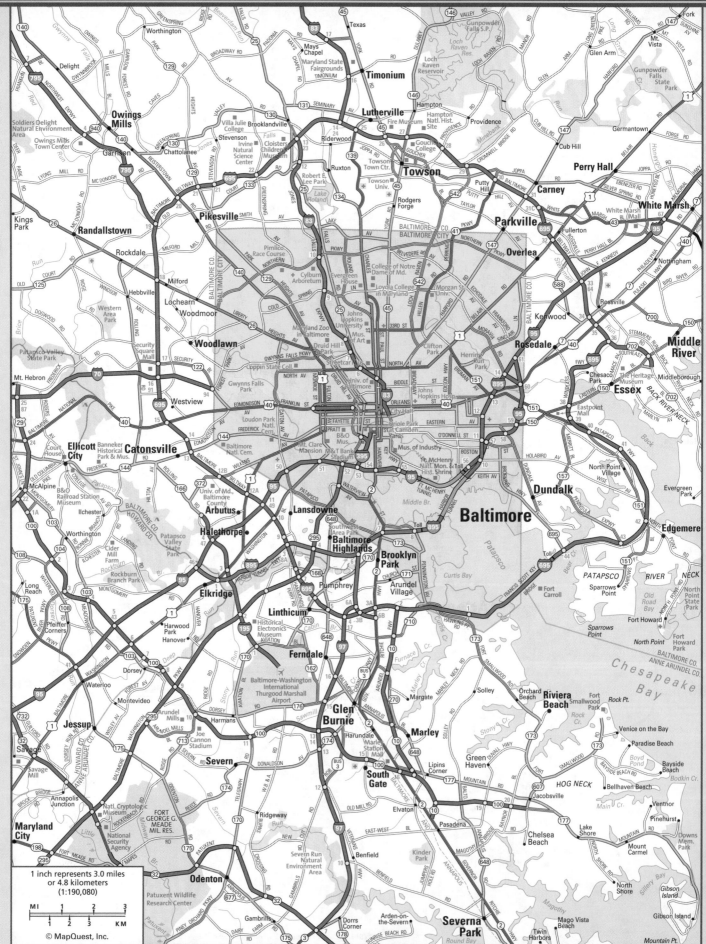

N

1 inch represents 3.0 miles
or 4.8 kilometers
(1:190,080)

© MapQuest, Inc.

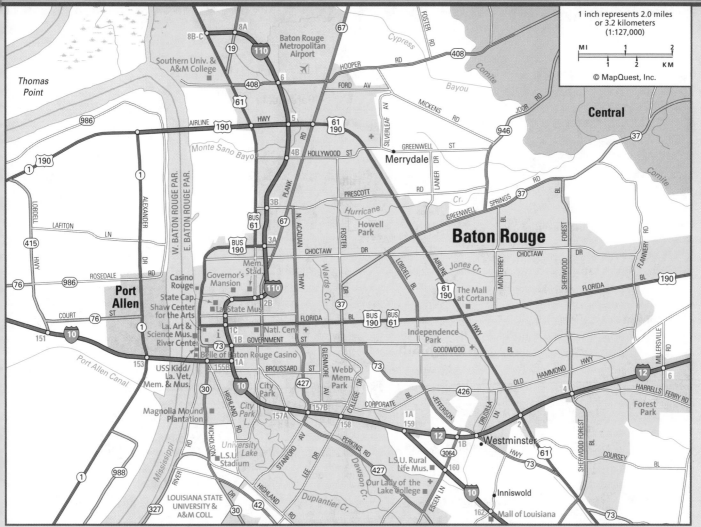

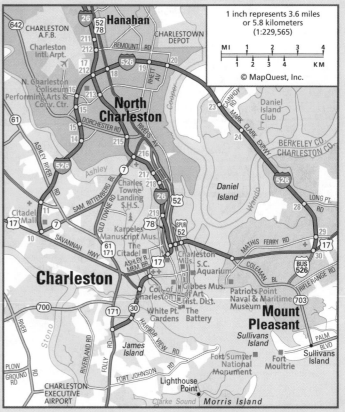

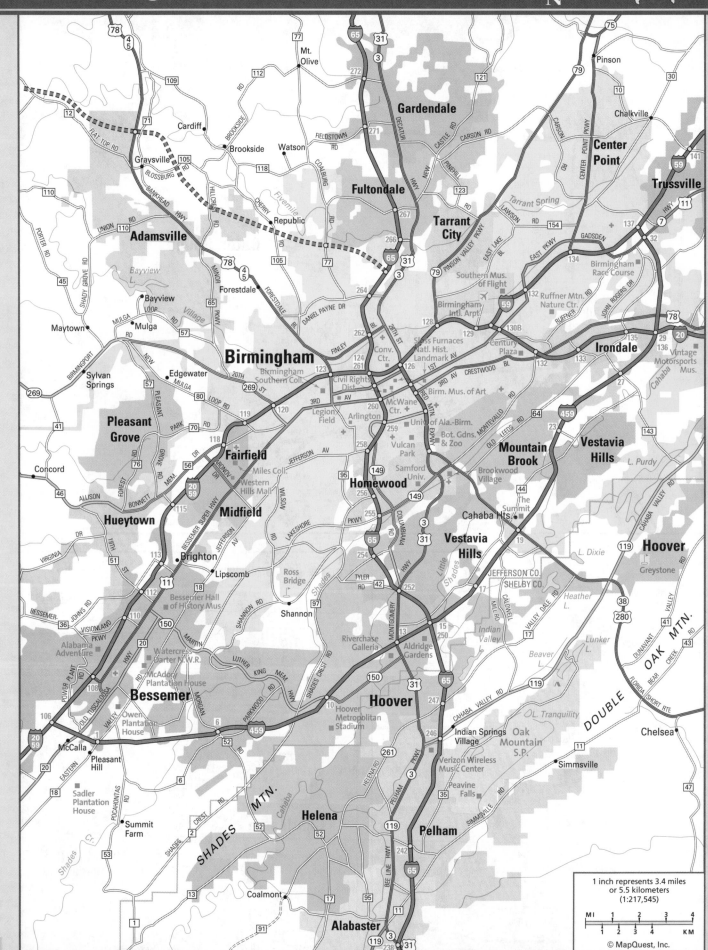

74 ■ **Birmingham**

N

78
45

Mt. Olive

78
71
Cardiff
Brookside
Graysville
105
Brookside
Watson

109
112
FIELDSTOWN RD
272
77
65
31
3

FLAT TOP RD
BLOSSBURG RD
BANKHEAD HWY
Republic
Fivemile
COALBURG RD

DECATUR HWY

Gardendale

121

75

79
Pinson

10
Chalkville

30

141
59

Center Point

Trussville

110
UNION RD
110
Adamsville
HILLCREST RD
CHERRY RD
118
105

78
45
5
Forestdale
266
267
271

Fultondale

NEW PINEHILL RD
CASTLE RD
CARSON RD

123

Tarrant Spring
LAWSON RD
154

137
7

11
HWY

32

SHADY GROVE RD
PORTER RD
45
Bayview L.
65
MINOR PKWY
MULGA LOOP RD
57
264
Bayview

Tarrant City

79
PINSON VALLEY PKWY
Southern Mus. of Flight
Birmingham Intl. Arpt.

EAST LAKE BL
EAST PKWY
134

CARSON RD
CENTER POINT PKWY

GADSDEN

Birmingham Race Course

135
29
20
136
Vintage Motorsports Mus.

Maytown
MULGA RD
Mulga
BIRMINGPORT RD
57
NEW PLEASANT GROVE RD
80 LOOP RD
MULGA RD
269
Edgewater
262
BL
Sylvan Springs
269
57
Birmingham Southern Coll.
123

26TH ST
1ST

128
130B
Ruffner Mtn. Nature Ctr.
132
RUFFNER RD
132
133
23
64
459

JOHN ROGERS DR
78
20

DANIEL PAYNE DR
FINLEY
Birmingham
Civil Rights Dist.
124
261
Conv. Ctr.
126
Sloss Furnaces Natl. Hist. Landmark AV
129
3RD AV
CRESTWOOD BL
Century Plaza

Irondale

143

Pleasant Grove
FOREST GROVE RD
76
MEM
56
Fairfield
119
120
3RD AV
Legion Field
260
McWane Ctr.
Arlington
Birm. Mus. of Art
259
Univ. of Ala.-Birm.
RED MTN EXPWY
Bot. Gdns. & Zoo

MONTEVALLO RD
OLD LEEDS RD

Vestavia Hills

L. Purdy

Concord
46
41
ALLISON RD
BONNETT RD
118
JERONV DR
Miles Coll.
Western Hills Mall
JEFFERSON AV
258
Vulcan Park
Samford Univ.
149
256
149
Brookwood Village
Mountain Brook
The Summit
44

119
Hoover
Greystone

115
Midfield
WILSON RD
95
Homewood
255
3
Cahaba Hts.
JEFFERSON CO.
SHELBY CO.
19
L. Dixie
38
280

Hueytown
HIGH SCHOOL RD
51
113
Brighton
LAKESHORE PKWY
PKWY
254
252
17
Vestavia Hills
CALDWELL MILL RD
Heather L.
VALLEY DALE RD
17

VIRGINIA DR
BESSEMER SUPER HWY
JEFFERSON AV
18
Lipscomb
Ross Bridge
Shades
TYLER RD
42
HWY
Little Shades
Indian Valley

DOUBLE OAK MTN.
41
Lunker L.
Beaver L.
DUNAVANT VALLEY RD
FLORIDA SHORT RTE

BESSEMER RD
36
JOHNS RD
110
Bessemer Hall of History Mus.
SHANNON RD
97
Shannon
MONTGOMERY HWY
15
250
13
Riverchase Galleria
Aldridge Gardens

112
11
112
VISIONLAND PKWY
20
150
MARTIN
WATERCRESS DARTER N.W.R.
LUTHER KING MEM HWY
SHADES CREST RD
150
247
65
119

Alabama Adventure
McAdory Plantation House
PARKWOOD RD
10
Hoover
Hoover Metropolitan Stadium

CAHABA VALLEY RD
L. Tranquility
Chelsea
11

106
108
POWER PLANT RD
Owen Plantation House
6
459
246
Indian Springs Village
Oak Mountain S.P.

20
59
McCalla
Pleasant Hill
OLD TUSCALOOSA RD
1 VALLEY RD
52
261
Verizon Wireless Music Center
Simmsville

18
EASTERN VALLEY RD
Sadler Plantation House
POCAHONTAS RD
6
HELENA RD
3
35
Peavine Falls
SIMMSVILLE RD
47

SHADES CREST RD
Summit Farm
53
2
SHADES MTN.
Cahaba
52
52
Helena
119
Pelham
242

13
Coalmont
17
95
BEE LINE HWY
11
65
3

1
91
Alabaster
119
3
31
238

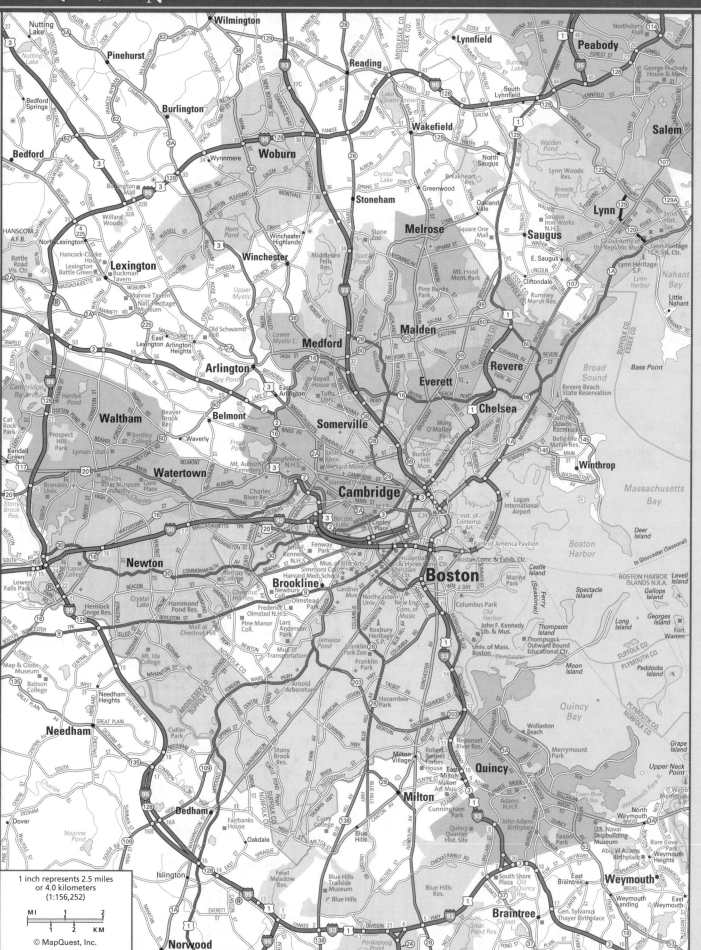

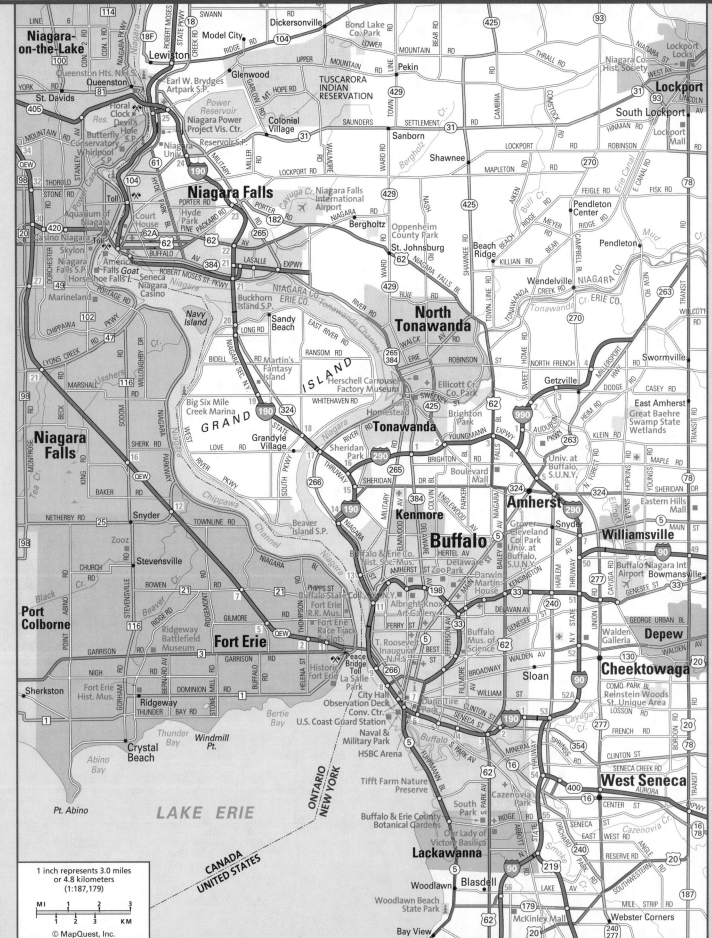

1 inch represents 3.0 miles
or 4.8 kilometers
(1:187,179)

MI   1   2   3

1   2   3   KM

© MapQuest, Inc.

Chicago

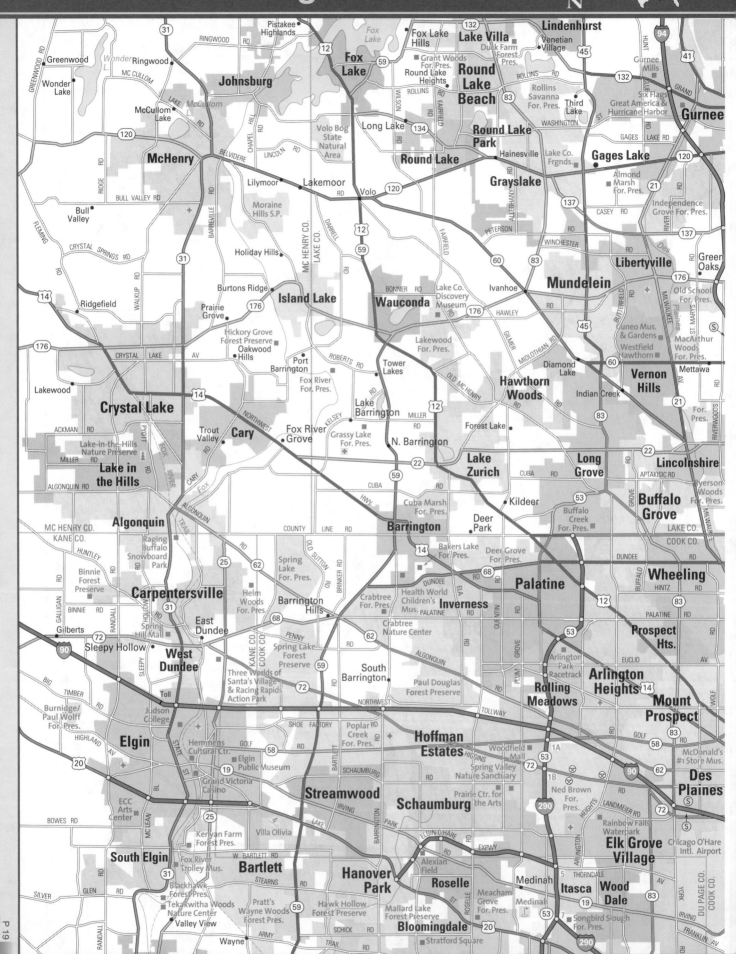

LAKE MICHIGAN

Beach Park
131 137
SUNSET AV
Waukegan
AV
137
GREEN BAY
Park
City
LEWIS AV
Illinois Beach State Park
NORTH SHORE BIKE PATH
SHERIDAN RD
Shimer College
Genesee Theatre
43
131
Greenbelt For. Pres.
14TH ST
North Chicago
GREAT LAKES NAVAL TRAINING CENTER
SKOKIE
S
Knollwood
Rondout
Middle Fork Savanna F.P.
Lake Bluff
Lake Forest College
Lake Forest
SHERIDAN RD
43
EVERETT RD
HALF DAY RD
TRI-STATE TOLLWAY
94
Prairie Wolf Slough Forest Preserve
Bannockburn
Trinity Intl. Univ.
41
WAUKEGAN RD
Highwood
Highland Park
Riverwoods
DEERFIELD RD
GREEN BAY RD
Ravinia Festival Music Center
Deerfield
LAKE COOK RD
94
Northbrook Court
Chicago Botanic Garden
For. Pres.
68
Glencoe
Northbrook
29
EDENS EXPWY
30
PFINGSTEN RD
WILLOW RD
43
31
TOWER RD
Northbrook Hist. Soc. Museum
294
Glenview
Northfield
33
SHERIDAN RD
Winnetka
River Trail Nature Ctr.
For. Pres.
The Glen Club
The Grove
41
34A
Kenilworth
Mitchell Mus. of the Am. Indian
Chicago Sports Hall of Fame
GLENVIEW RD
34B-C
LAKE AV
Wilmette
Baha'i House of Worship
Westfield Old Orchard
GREEN BAY RD
Grosse Point Lighthouse & Lakefront
35
North Shore Ctr. for Performing Arts
21
GOLF RD
58
Golf
Forest Preserve
Northwestern University
Golf Mill Shopping Ctr.
37
Skokie
Charles Gates Dawes House
14
DEMPSTER ST
Morton Grove
Skokie Heritage Mus.
N SHORE Channel
Evanston
12 45
OAKTON ST
Niles
CRAWFORD AV
WESTERN AV
Allstate Arena
Park Ridge
TOUHY AV
43
DEVON AV
14
39
41
Lincolnwood Town Center
DEVON AV
Loyola University Chicago
190
294
Rosemont Theatre
KENNEDY EXPWY
81A
LAWRENCE
DES PLAINES RIVER RD
79
41
83 AV
94
Lincolnwood
14
Chicago
RIDGE
Swedish American Museum Center
Schiller Park
Toll
Norridge
171
19
Harwood Hts.
Northeastern Ill. Univ.
41C
FOSTER AV
42
Aragon Entertainment Center
ELSTON AV
LINCOLN AV
ASHLAND AV
41
Lincoln Park
Harlem Irving Plaza
HARLEM AV
For. Pres.
50
44
IRVING PARK RD
43B
19
Wrigley Field

LAKE

MICHIGAN

INDIANA DUNES NATIONAL LAKESHORE
Gary Chicago Intl. Airport
West Beach Visitor Center
Ogden Dunes
Dune Acres
Indiana Dunes State Park
Bailly-Chellberg Visitor Center
Burns Harbor
Porter
90 13
15
20
FIFTH
261
Grand
Calumet
17
12
249
19
22
149
12
94
Chesterton
Gary
GRANT ST
BURR ST
53
U.S. Steel Yard
21
Ditch
S 20
Portage
80 90
6
9
10
80 94
Calumet
12 259
Burns
16
Lake Station
S
23
BROADWAY
Lit.
Indiana Univ. N.W.
258
Calumet Prairie St. Nature Preserve
New Chicago
51
GRAND ARMY OF THE REPUBLIC HWY
6
RIDGE RD
Ross
55
MAIN ST
Hobart
L. George
Deep
149
WILLOW CREEK RD
130
Wheeler
LAKE CO.
PORTER CO.
Oak Ridge Prairie Co. Park
53
255
61ST ST
51
Deep River County Park
0 1 2 mi
0 1 2km
Merrillville
73RD AV
Star Plaza Theatre
30
253
Westfield Southlake
Deep River Waterpark
LINCOLN
30
HIGHWAY
Valparaiso
130

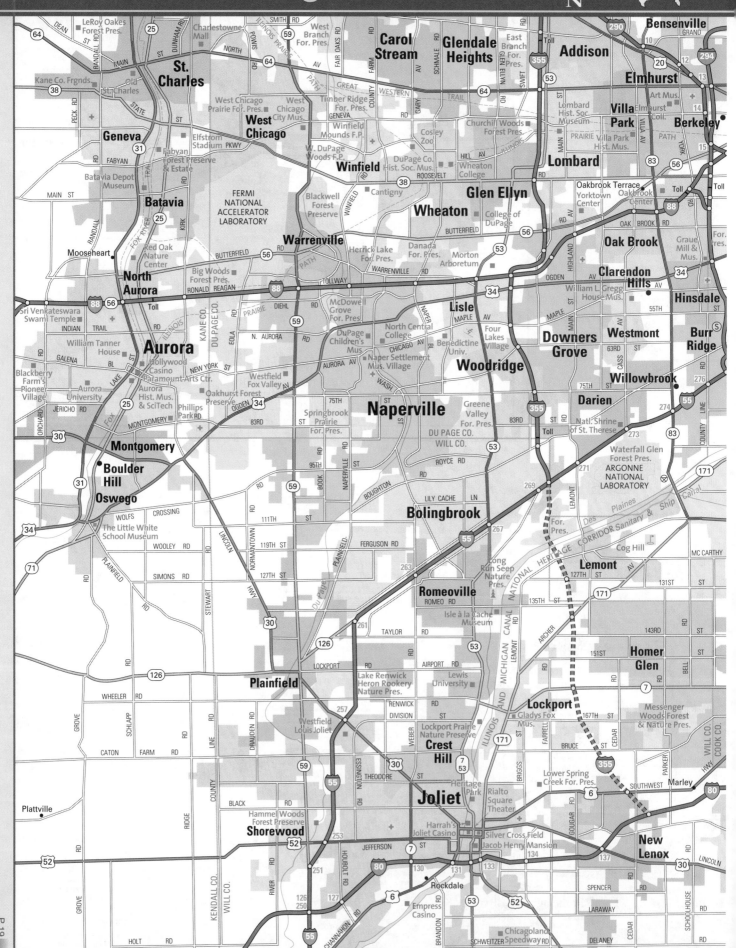

1 inch represents 3.3 miles
or 5.3 kilometers
(1:209,801)

© MapQuest, Inc.

LAKE

MICHIGAN

Franklin Park
River Grove
Elmwood Park
BELMONT
AV
MILWAUKEE
Chicago
FULLERTON
AV
De Paul Univ.
Peggy Notebaert Nature Center
Lincoln Park Zoo
Steppenwolf Theatre
International Mus. of Surgical Science
Chicago History Museum

Northlake
Stone Park
Maywood Park Race Track
Concordia Univ.
CHICAGO
Polish Mus. of America
Ukrainian Natl. Mus.
Mus. of Holography

Melrose Park
Oak Park
GRAND
AV
NORTH
AV
Garfield Park
Sears Tower

Bellwood
River Forest
Frank Lloyd Wright Home
WASHINGTON
United Center
Chicago

Hillside
Maywood
Forest Park
EISENHOWER
EXPWY
Mexican Fine Arts Ctr. Mus.

Broadview
Berwyn
ROOSEVELT RD
OGDEN AV
CERMAK RD

Westchester
CERMAK RD
North Riverside
Park Mall

La Grange Park
Brookfield Zoo
Cicero
U.S. Cellular Field
Illinois Institute of Technology

Brookfield
Riverside
Lyons
PERSHING RD
Douglas Tomb State Historic Site

Western Sprs.
La Grange
McCook
Stickney
Forest View
Hawthorne Race Course
47TH ST
DuSable Museum of African-American History

Countryside
Summit
Chicago Portage N.H.S.
55TH ST
63RD
University of Chicago
Museum of Science & Industry
Jackson Park

Indian Head Park
Hodgkins
Bedford Park
Balzekas Museum of Lithuanian Culture
Bridgeview Stadium
MARQUETTE
71ST ST
Marquette Park
Washington Park

Justice
Ford City Shopping Center
79TH ST
87TH

Willow Sprs.
Burbank
Dan Ryan Expwy
Chicago State Univ.

Hickory Hills
Bridgeview
Westfield Chicagoland Ridge
Evergreen Park
95TH

Palos Hills
Oak Lawn
Chicago Ridge
103RD ST
The Plaza
103RD ST

107TH ST
St. Xavier University
Beverly Hills/Morgan Park Historic Dist.
Beverly Arts Ctr.
Pullman Hist. District

Palos Park
Worth
Merrionette Park
115TH ST

Palos Forest Pres.
Alsip
Blue Island
Calumet Park
130TH ST

Palos Heights
Crestwood
Robbins
Posen
Riverdale
Dolton
Calumet City

Orland Square
Midlothian
Dixmoor
SIBLEY
Burnham

Orland Park
Oak Forest
Markham
Harvey
Phoenix
S. Holland
Whiting
East Chicago

Orland Hills
Hazel Crest
Thornton
E. Hazel Crest
Lansing
Hammond

Tinley Park
Country Club Hills
Homewood
Flossmoor
Glenwood
Lynwood
Munster
Highland
Griffith

Mokena
Arbury Hills
Odyssey Fun World
Olympia Fields
Chicago Heights
Ford Heights
Dyer
Schererville

Frankfort
Matteson
Park Forest
S. Chicago Heights
Sauk Village
Crete
Richton Park
Steger

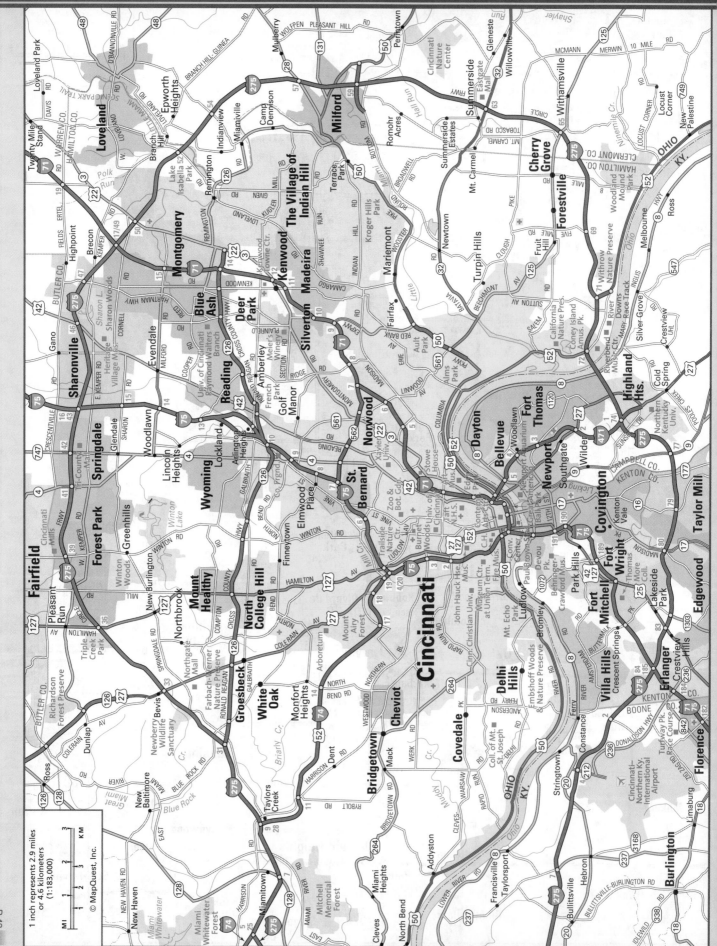

1 inch represents 2.9 miles
or 4.6 kilometers
(1:183,000)

© MapQuest, Inc.

N

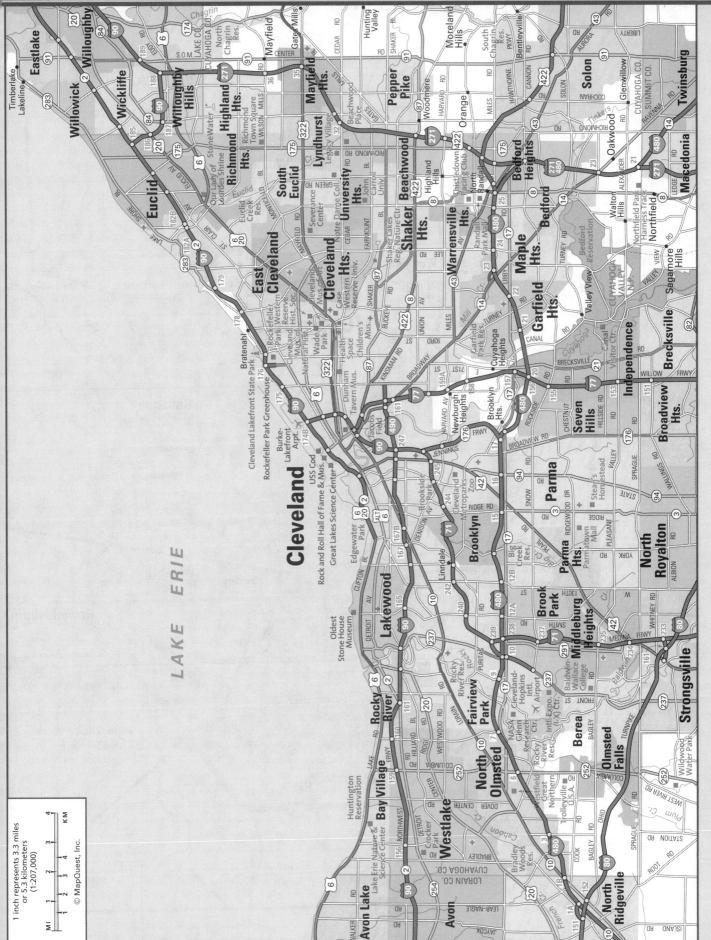

1 inch represents 3.3 miles
or 5.3 kilometers
(1:207,000)

© MapQuest, Inc.

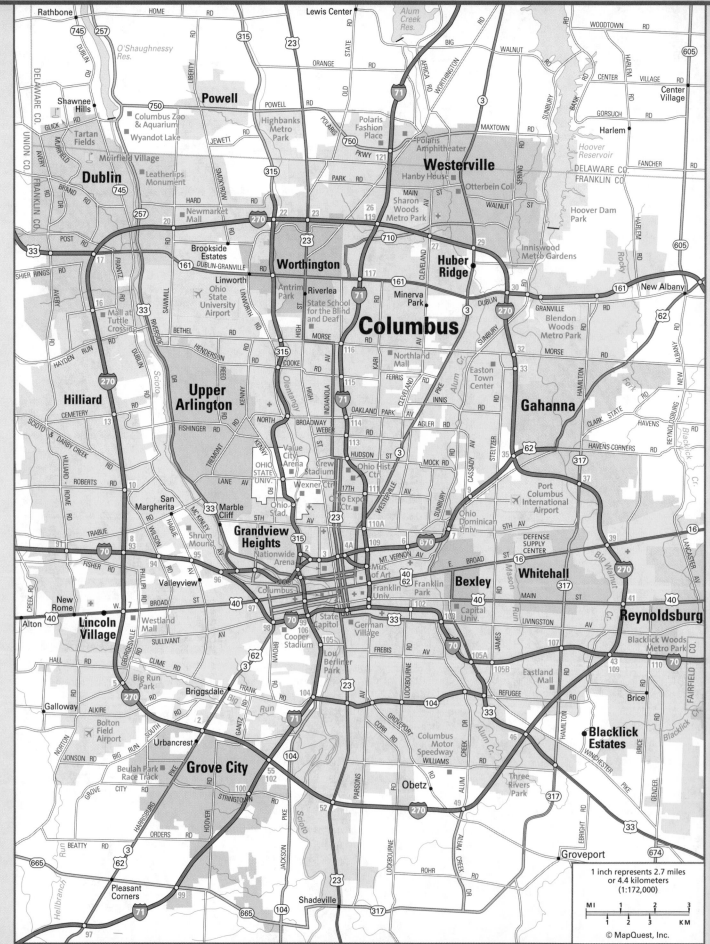

N

Rathbone
HOME
RD
Lewis Center
Alum Creek Res.
WOODTOWN
745 257
O'Shaughnessy Res.
315
23
STATE
3
HARLEM
RD
CENTER
VILLAGE
RD
Center Village
605

DUBLIN RD
DELAWARE CO.
UNION CO.
GLICK
MURFIELD
LIBERTY
ORANGE
RD
AFRICA RD
WORTHINGTON
BANK
SUNBURY
GORSUCH
RD
Harlem

Shawnee Hills
Columbus Zoo & Aquarium
750
Highbanks Metro Park
POWELL
RD
Polaris Fashion Place
Polaris Amphitheater
MAXTOWN
Hoover Reservoir

Tartan Fields
Wyandot Lake
JEWETT
POLARIS
PKWY 121
Westerville
Hanby House
Otterbein Coll.
WALNUT
Hoover Dam Park
FANCHER

Muirfield Village
Leatherlips Monument
315
PARK
RD
MAIN ST
Sharon Woods Metro Park
WALNUT ST
DELAWARE CO.
FRANKLIN CO.

Dublin
745
257
Newmarket Mall
HARD RD
SMOKYRUN
270
22
23
26 119
Inniswood Metro Gardens
605

33
POST RD
Brookside Estates
161
DUBLIN-GRANVILLE
Worthington
710
27
29
30
161
New Albany
62

17
SAWMILL
FRANTZ
RD
Linworth
Antrim Park
Riverlea
117
71
CLEVELAND
Minerva Park
DUBLIN
270
GRANVILLE
Blendon Woods Metro Park

16
RIVERSIDE DR
BETHEL
Ohio State University Airport
State School for the Blind and Deaf
161
Columbus
3
SUNBURY
32
MORSE

Mall at Tuttle Crossing
33
315
COOKE RD
116
KARL
Northland Mall
33

HAYDEN RUN RD
DUBLIN RD
HENDERSON
REED
315
HIGH
INDIANOLA
115
FERRIS
CLEVELAND
INNIS
Easton Town Center

Hilliard
270
KENNY
NORTH
OLENTANGY
114
OAKLAND PARK
AV
AGLER RD
Port Columbus International Airport
37

CEMETERY
13
Upper Arlington
FISHINGER RD
BROADWAY
WEBER
113
HUDSON ST
3
MOCK RD
STELTZER RD
CASSADY
62
317
16

SCIOTO & DARBY CREEK
TREMONT
LANE AV
Value City Arena
Crew Stadium
Ohio Hist. Ctr.
Ohio Dominican Univ.
35
9

HILLIARD-ROBERTS RD
10
San Margherita
33
Marble Cliff
OHIO STATE UNIV.
Ohio Stad.
Wexner Ctr.
17TH
Ohio Expo Ctr.
WESTERVILLE
110A
670
7
DEFENSE SUPPLY CENTER
39
270
16

TRABUE
91
8 93
WILSON
McKINLEY
5TH
Grandview Heights
315
23
109
MT. VERNON AV
5TH AV
Whitehall

70
FISHER
94
95
Shrum Mound
Nationwide Arena
2
3
4A
Mus. of Art
E. BROAD
16
MAIN ST
317
41
40

New Rome
PHILLIPI RD
Valleyview
96
COR Columbus
40
62
Franklin Park
Bexley
40
Capital Univ.
LIVINGSTON
AV
Reynoldsburg

Alton
40
Lincoln Village
W. 7
BROAD ST
97
State Capitol
33
German Village
102
40
JAMES RD
107
110 70

HALL RD
Westland Mall
SULLIVANT
AV
70
99
Cooper Stadium
Lou Berliner Park
FREBIS AV
105
105A
Blacklick Woods Metro Park

Galloway
GEORGESVILLE RD
CLIME RD
62
3
104
LOCKBOURNE
Eastland Mall
105B
43 109
110 70

ALKIRE
Big Run Park
Briggsdale
FRANK RD
Big Run
23
AV
104
REFUGEE
HAMILTON
Brice
FAIRFIELD CO.

Bolton Field Airport
270
2
GANTZ RD
71
GROVEPORT RD
104
33
Blacklick Estates

Urbancrest
SOUTH
BIG RUN RD
Columbus Motor Speedway
WILLIAMS
ALUM CR
46
BRICE RD
Blacklick Cr.
317

Beulah Park Race Track
Grove City
GROVE CITY RD
PIKE
55 102
100
STRINGTOWN RD
104
PARSONS AV
Obetz
49
270
WINCHESTER PIKE
674
33

665
62
3
HARRISBURG
ORDERS RD
HOOVER RD
52
SCIOTO
JACKSON RD
Three Rivers Park
EBRIGHT RD
GENDER RD
Groveport
674

BEATTY RD
Hellbranch
71
97
Pleasant Corners
99
665
104
23
Shadeville
317
ROHR RD

1 inch represents 2.7 miles or 4.4 kilometers (1:172,000)

MI
0   1   2   3
KM
0   1   2   3   4   5

© MapQuest, Inc.

N

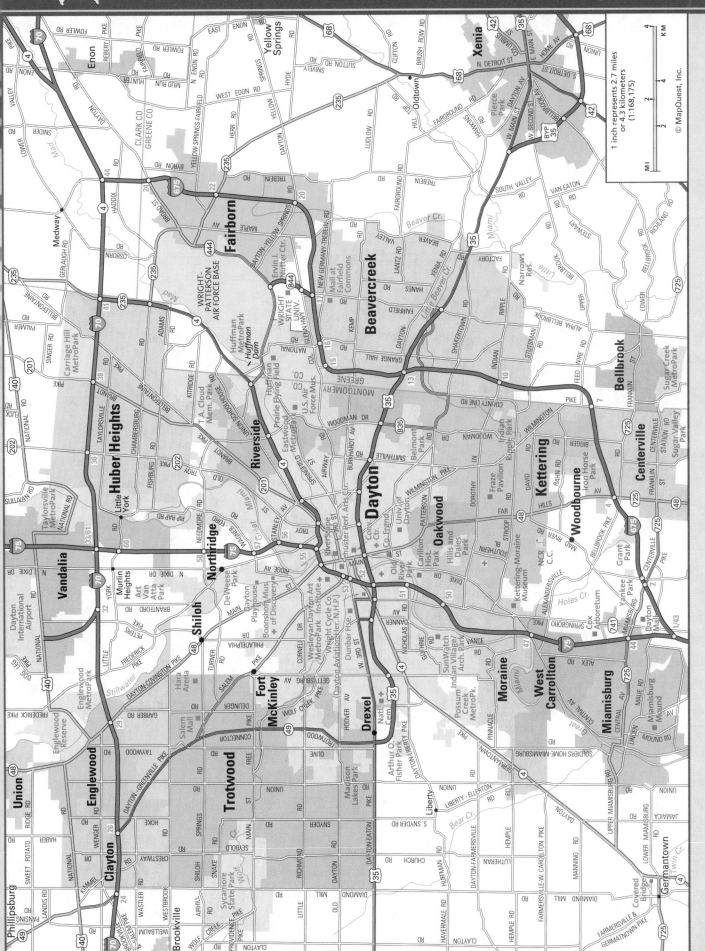

1 inch represents 2.7 miles
or 4.3 kilometers
(1:168,175)

© MapQuest, Inc.

Enon

Yellow
Springs

Xenia

Oldtown

Fairborn

WRIGHT-
PATTERSON
AIR FORCE BASE

Beavercreek

Medway

Huber Heights

Bellbrook

Riverside

MONTGOMERY CO.
GREENE CO.

Dayton

Kettering

Centerville

Vandalia

Little York

Murlin
Heights

Woodbourne

Northridge

Oakwood

Shiloh

Dayton
International
Airport

Fort
McKinley

Drexel

Moraine

West
Carrollton

Miamisburg

Union

Englewood

Clayton

Trotwood

Phillipsburg

Brookville

Germantown

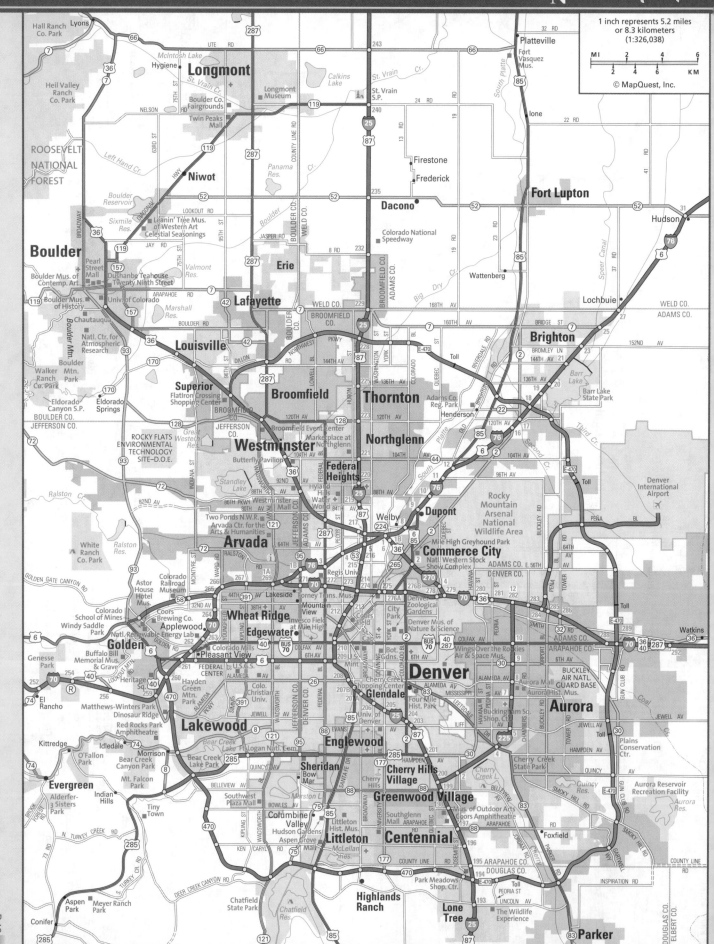

N

1 inch represents 5.2 miles
or 8.3 kilometers
(1:326,038)

© MapQuest, Inc.

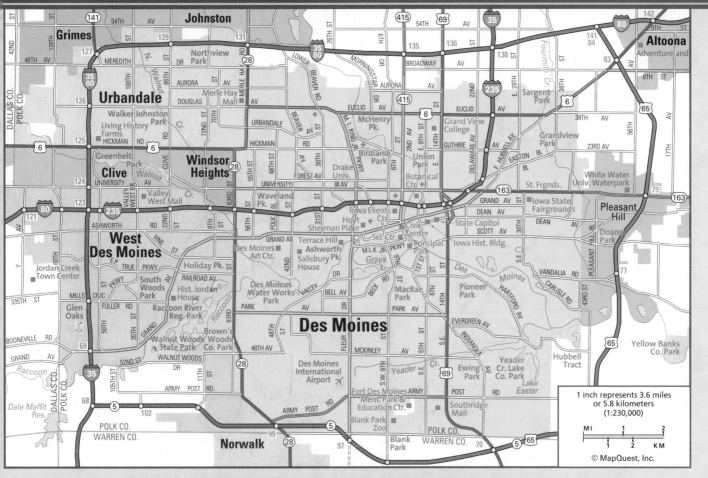

Edmonton

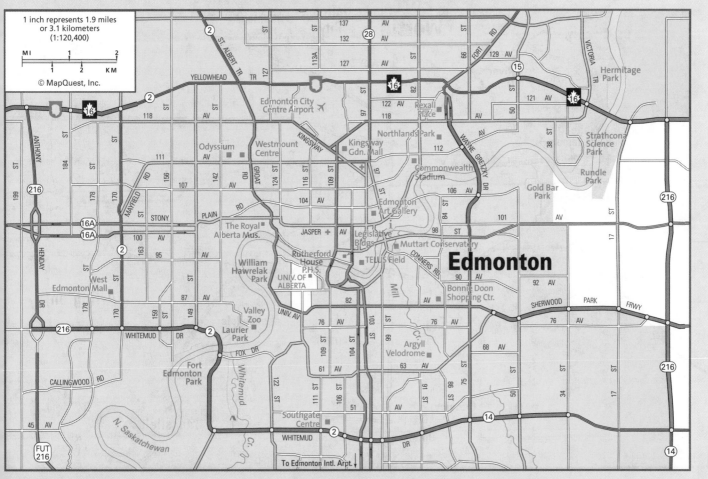

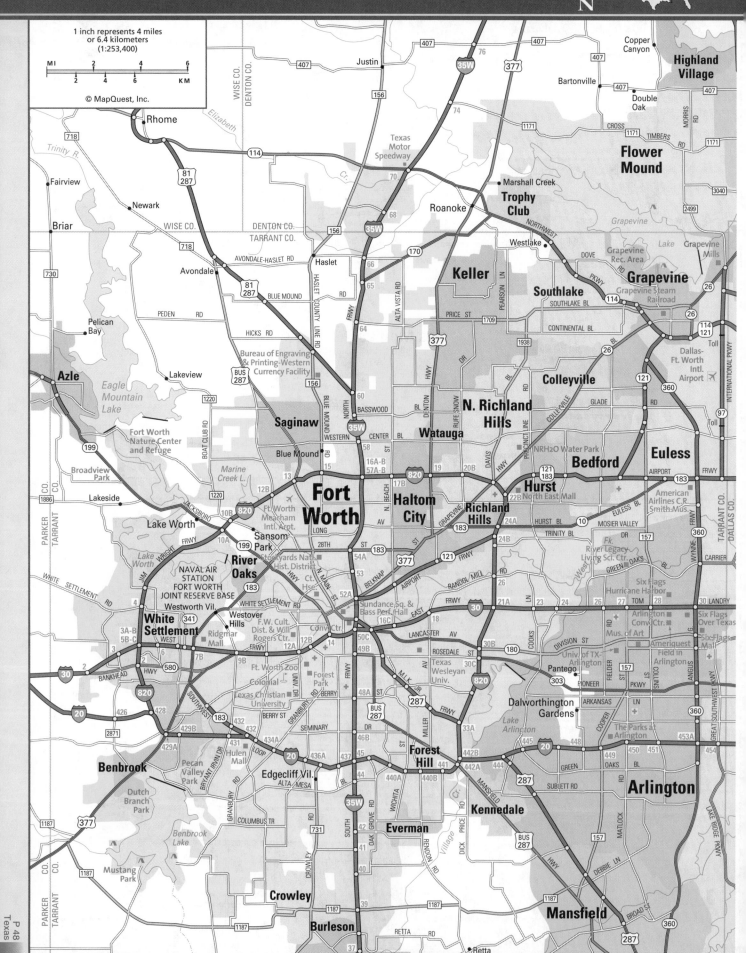

1 inch represents 4 miles
or 6.4 kilometers
(1:253,400)

MI 2 4 6

KM 2 4 6

© MapQuest, Inc.

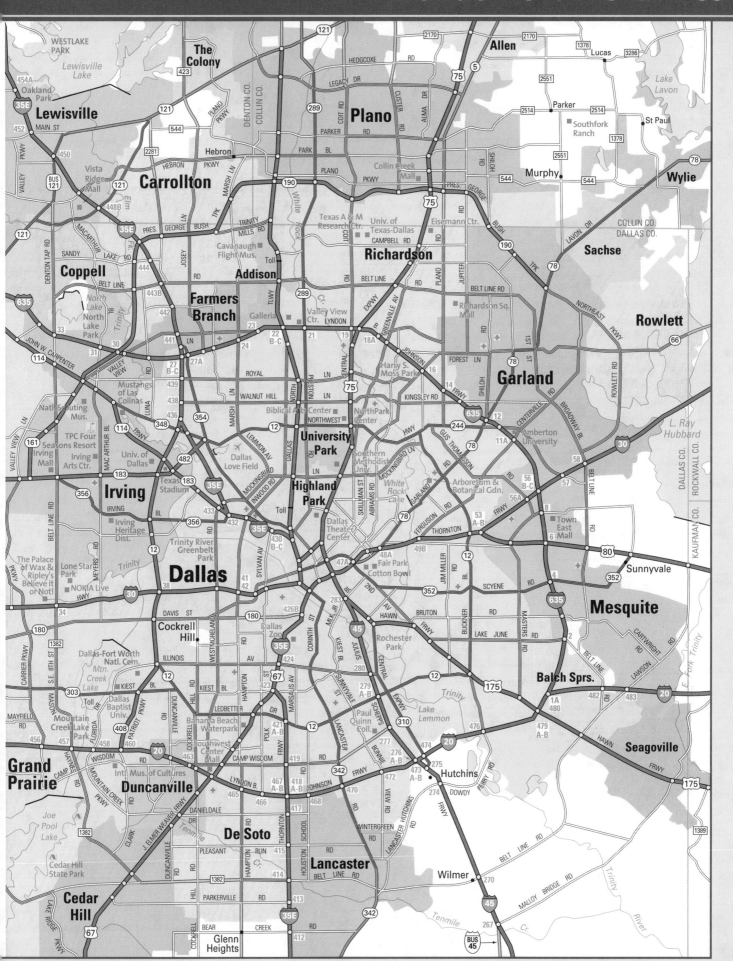

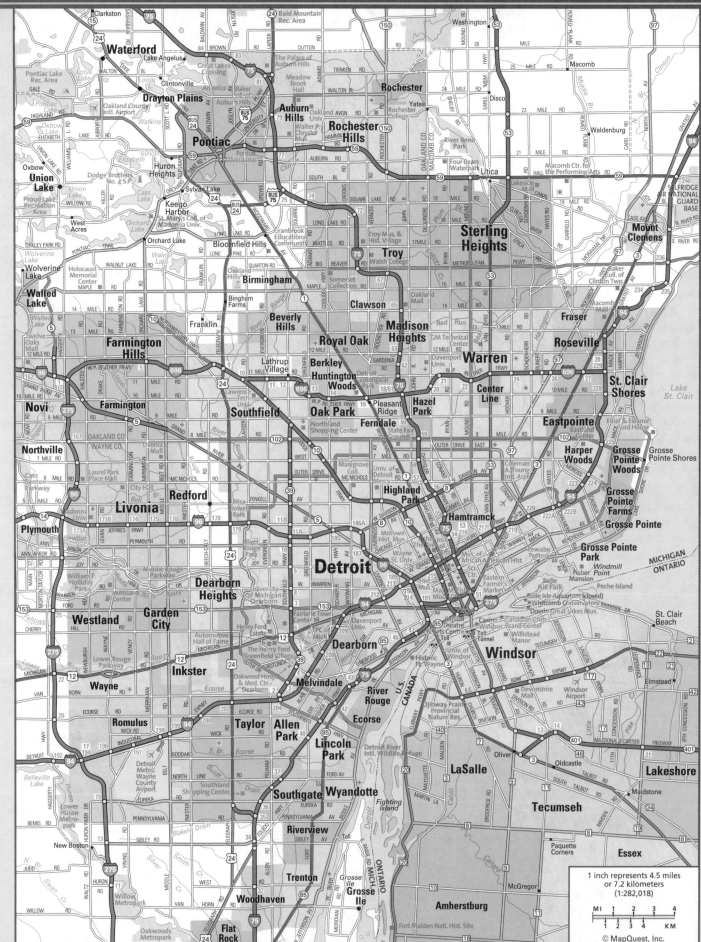

N

1 inch represents 4.5 miles
or 7.2 kilometers
(1:282,018)

© MapQuest, Inc.

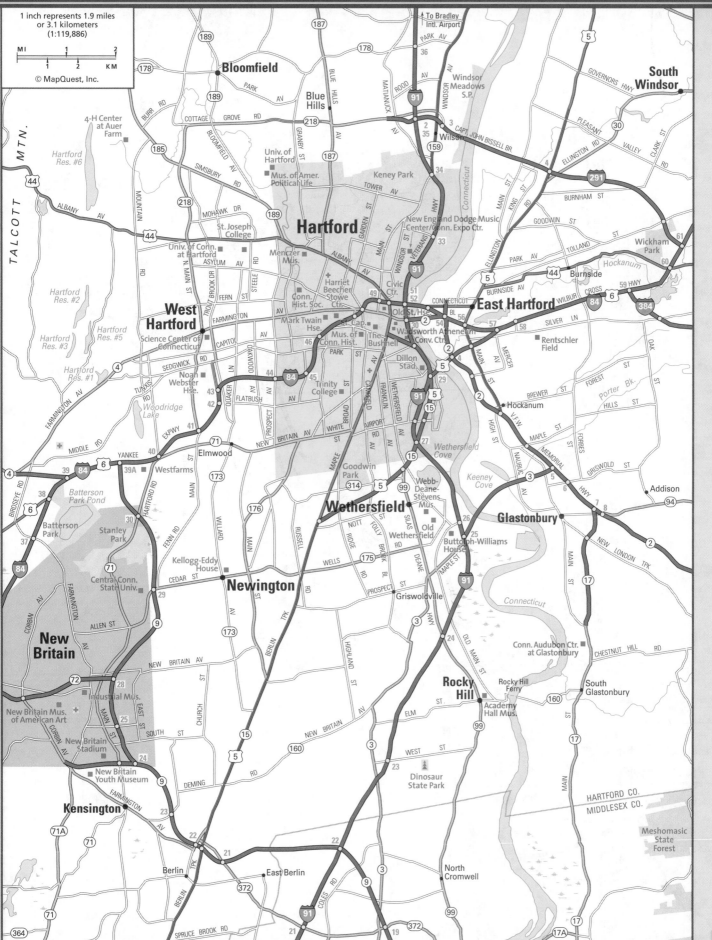

1 inch represents 1.9 miles
or 3.1 kilometers
(1:119,886)

MI · 1 · 2

KM 1 · 2

© MapQuest, Inc.

Hartford

TALCOTT MTN.

Hartford Res. #6

Hartford Res. #2

Hartford Res. #5

Hartford Res. #3

Hartford Res. #1

4-H Center at Auer Farm

Woodridge Lake

Batterson Park Pond

Batterson Park

Stanley Park

Central Conn. State Univ.

New Britain

Industrial Mus.

New Britain Mus. of American Art

New Britain Stadium

New Britain Youth Museum

Kensington

Berlin

East Berlin

Bloomfield

Blue Hills

Univ. of Hartford

Mus. of Amer. Political Life

Keney Park

Hartford

St. Joseph College

Univ. of Conn. at Hartford

Menczer Mus.

West Hartford

Conn. Hist. Soc.

Harriet Beecher Stowe Ctr.

Science Center of Connecticut

Mark Twain Hse.

St. Cap.

Mus. of Conn. Hist.

The Bushnell

Noah Webster Hse.

Trinity College

Elmwood

Westfarms

Kellogg-Eddy House

Newington

Goodwin Park

Wethersfield

Webb-Deane-Stevens Mus.

Old Wethersfield

Buttolph-Williams House

Griswoldville

Rocky Hill

Dinosaur State Park

North Cromwell

Windsor Meadows S.P.

Wilson

To Bradley Intl. Airport

South Windsor

New England Dodge Music Center/Conn. Expo Ctr.

Civic Ctr.

Old St. Hse.

Wadsworth Atheneum Conv. Ctr.

Dillon Stad.

Wethersfield Cove

East Hartford

Burnside

Rentschler Field

Hockanum

Wickham Park

Keeney Cove

Glastonbury

Addison

Conn. Audubon Ctr. at Glastonbury

Rocky Hill Ferry

South Glastonbury

Academy Hall Mus.

HARTFORD CO.
MIDDLESEX CO.

Meshomasic State Forest

Connecticut

N

Honolulu

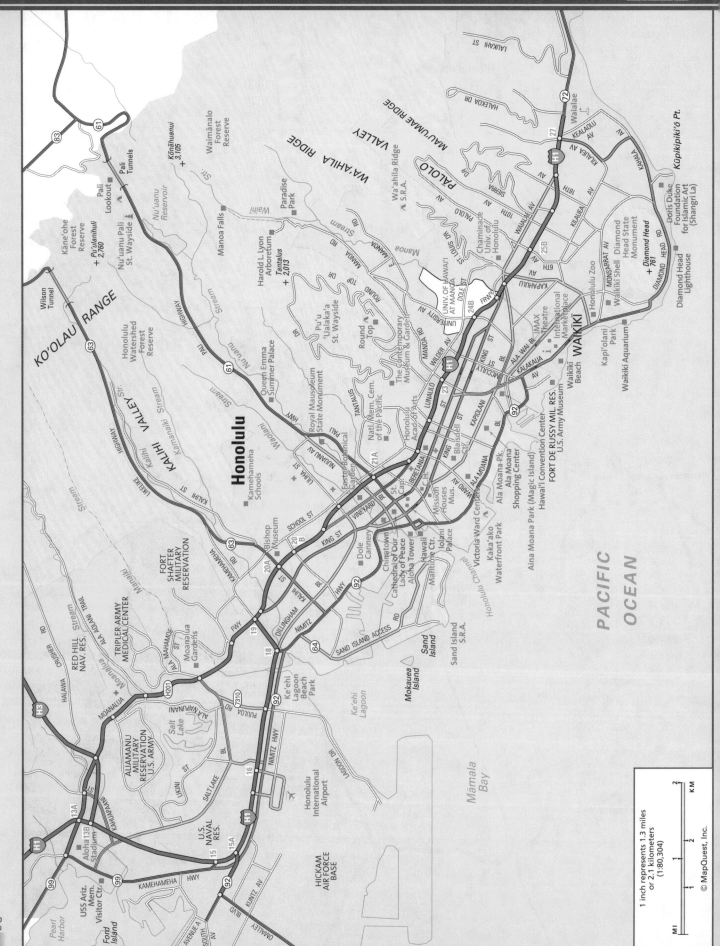

LAUKAHI ST

83

61

Pali Tunnels

Pali Lookout

72

HALEKOA DR

WA'AHILA RIDGE

MAU'UMAE RIDGE

27

Waialae

KEALAOLU

Waialae

KILAUEA AV

Kūpikipiki'ō Pt.

H1

KEALAHOU

Kāne'ohe Forest Reserve

Pu'ulanihuli + 2,760

Nu'uanu Pali St. Wayside

Kōnāhuanui + 3,105

Waimānalo Forest Reserve

PALOLO

VALLEY

Wa'ahila Ridge S.R.A.

Chaminade Univ. of Honolulu

25B

Doris Duke Foundation for Islamic Art (Shangri La)

Nu'uanu Reservoir

Manoa Falls

Waihī

Paradise Park

SIERRA

KAPAHULU

Diamond Head State Monument

Diamond Head Lighthouse

61

Wilson Tunnel

KO'OLAU RANGE

63

Honolulu Watershed Forest Reserve

Harold L Lyon Arboretum

Tantalus + 2013

Pu'u 'Ualaka'a St. Wayside

Round Top

The Contemporary Museum & Garden

UNIV. OF HAWAI'I AT MANOA

24B

MONSARRAT AV

+ Diamond Head 761

DIAMOND HEAD RD

6TH

Honolulu Zoo

Waikīkī Shell

Queen Emma Summer Palace

Royal Mausoleum State Monument

TANTALUS

Natl. Mem. Cem. of the Pacific

Honolulu Acad. of Arts

KING ST

H1

WAIALAE AV

IMAX Theatre

International Marketplace

WAIKIKI

Kapi'olani Park

Waikīkī Aquarium

Honolulu

Kamehameha Schools

63

FORT SHAFTER MILITARY RESERVATION

Bishop Museum

21A

St. Capt.

LUNALILO

Mission Houses Mus.

Blaisdell Ctr.

KAPIOLANI

Ala Moana Pk.

Ala Moana Shopping Center

Hawai'i Convention Center

FORT DE RUSSY MIL RES.

U.S. Army Museum

Waikīkī Beach

KALAKAUA AV

92

Dole Cannery

20B

SCHOOL ST

KING ST

Chinatown Cathedral of Our Lady of Peace

Aloha Tower

Hawaii Maritime Ctr.

'Iolani Palace

Victoria Ward Center

Kaka'ako Waterfront Park

Aina Moana Park (Magic Island)

20A

19

DILLINGHAM

NIMITZ

92

64

SAND ISLAND ACCESS RD

Honolulu Channel

Sand Island S.R.A.

PACIFIC

OCEAN

18

Mokauea Island

Sand Island

H3

H201

H1

ALA MAHAMOE ST

Moanalua Gardens

MOANALUA

Salt Lake

7310

92

Ke'ehi Lagoon Beach Park

Ke'ehi Lagoon

Māmala Bay

TRIPLER ARMY MEDICAL CENTER

RED HILL NAV. RES.

CRUSHER RD

HALAWA

Ala 'Aolani Trail

ALIAMANU MILITARY RESERVATION U.S. ARMY

SALT LAKE BL

16

LAGOON DR

Honolulu International Airport

13A

Aloha 13B Stadium

U.S. NAVAL RES.

15

15A

HICKAM AIR FORCE BASE

99

USS Ariz. Mem. Visitor Ctr.

Ford Island

99

KAMEHAMEHA HWY

92

KUNTZ AV

AVENUE A

SOUTH AV

QMALLEY BLVD

Pearl Harbor

1 inch represents 1.3 miles or 2.1 kilometers (1:80,304)

MI

KM

© MapQuest, Inc.

1 inch represents 4.2 miles
or 6.8 kilometers
(1:268,000)

© MapQuest, Inc.

MI 0 1 2 3 4

KM 0 1 2 3 4

Eagle Village

Zionsville

334

Patrick Henry
Sullivan Mus.

129
Royalton

865
BOONE CO.
MARION CO.

421

Carmel

Fishers

116TH ST   ST   RD   116TH ST   RD   5

WESTFIELD RD
Home
Place
31

96TH ST
31

431

465
31
421

HAMILTON CO.
MARION CO.

69

106TH ST

33
Fashion Mall
Keystone
at the Crossing

Castleton
Square Mall

ELLER
ALLISONVILLE RD

HAGUE
37

3

CUMBERLAND

52
65

HENDRICKS CO.
MARION CO.

LAFAYETTE RD

465

COOPER RD

86TH ST
23
27

MICHIGAN RD

CROOKED Cr.

86TH ST

MERIDIAN ST

COLLEGE AV

82ND ST

35

1

82ND ST

Mud Cr.

FALL CREEK RD

Indian Lake

79TH ST
124

EAGLE CREEK RD

GEORGETOWN RD

ZIONSVILLE RD

79TH ST

ST

ST

DR

73RD ST

Williams
Creek

79TH ST

Marott
Park

71ST ST

Broad
Ripple Park

ALLISONVILLE RD

BINFORD BL

Woollen's
Garden

63RD ST

Ft. Harrison
State Park

21
71ST ST
62ND ST

GRANDVIEW

Meridian
Hills
Holliday Park
North
Crows
Nest

KESSLER BL

BL

Glendale
Shopping
Center

56TH ST

40

**Eagle
Creek
Park**

20
123

Northwestway
Park

BL

Crows
Nest

White

KEYSTONE AV

56TH ST

56TH ST
19
*Eagle
Creek
Res.*
52

SCHOOL RD

121

65

KESSLER BL

M.L. KING JR. ST

Rocky
Ripple

52ND ST

Holcomb
Bot. Gdns.
46TH ST

State
Fairgrounds

52ND ST

Lawrence
36

RACEWAY RD

Spring
Hills
Indianapolis Mus.
of Art

Butler
Univ.

42
31

67

74
136
Clermont

HIGH ST

17

465

38TH ST

Lafayette
Square

GEORGETOWN RD
119

LAFAYETTE RD

Wynnedale

Crown Hill
Natl. Cem.
38TH ST

Indianapolis

Pepsi Coliseum

Martin Univ.
Washington
Park

38TH ST

SHADELAND AV

FRANKLIN RD

38TH ST

ST

30TH ST

Indianapolis
Raceway Park

16
73

30TH ST

Marian
College

TIBBS AV

Lt. Eagle Cr.

117
116

Riverside
Park

65

Fall Cr.

30TH ST

SHERMAN DR

The Children's
Museum

85

AV

87

89

30TH ST
465
91
70

25TH ST

Indianapolis Motor
Speedway & Hall
of Fame Mus.

115

16TH ST

M.L. KING JR. ST

MERIDIAN ST

President
Benjamin
Harrison
Home

70

Brookside
Park

16TH ST

EMERSON AV

RURAL ST

44
90

RD
36
421

Warren
Park

Washington
Square Mall

40

14
21ST ST

CLUB RD

10TH ST
Speedway

COUNTRY CLUB RD

SCHOOL RD

10TH ST

113

St.
Cap.

WASHINGTON ST

ENGLISH AV

Pleasant Run

48

47

PROSPECT ST

BROOKVILLE RD

POST RD

52

ROCKVILLE RD
36
13

Avon

GIRLS SCHOOL RD

HIGH SCHOOL RD

MORRIS ST

Eagle Cr.

Indiana Conv.
Ctr. & RCA Dome

70
77
78
79A

80
110

TIBBS AV

Pleasant Run

MADISON AV

SOUTHEASTERN AV

49
94

40

12

LYNHURST DR

HOLT RD

RAYMOND ST

Garfield
Park

109

74
465

Marion Co.
Fairgrounds

TROY AV

96

74

AIRPORT EXPWY
75
11

KENTUCKY AV

65
KEYSTONE AV

107

31
36

40
52

SOUTHEASTERN AV

DAVIS RD

**Indianapolis
International
Airport**

36
52

9
73

TROY AV

AV

**Beech
Grove**

Univ. of
Indianapolis

THOMPSON RD

421

40

8

74
465
7

HARDING ST

Lick Cr.

EAST ST

2

37

54
106

EMERSON AV

EDGEWOOD AV

SHELBYVILLE RD

SIX POINTS RD

70

Plainfield

HIGH SCHOOL RD

White R.

4

BLUFF RD

MADISON AV

AMERIPLEX BLVD

67

MANN RD

Buck Cr.

Little Buck

Homecroft
Southport

103

FRANKLIN RD

HICKORY RD

East Fork

Camby

CAMBY RD

SOUTHPORT RD

BANTA RD

SOUTHPORT RD

MERIDIAN ST

Perry
Park

SHELBY ST

MC FARLAND RD

65

ARLINGTON AV

FIVE POINTS RD

SOUTHPORT RD

MC GREGOR RD

MOORESVILLE RD
SOUTHPORT RD
West Newton
RALSTON RD

Friendswood

37

Southwestway
Park

STOP 11 RD

135

COUNTY LINE RD

31

Greenwood
Park Mall

SHERMAN DR

101

MARION CO.
JOHNSON CO.

525 EAST

600 EAST

MARION CO.
JOHNSON CO.

FAIRVIEW RD

Pleasant Run

Greenwood

MAIN ST

99

Rocklane

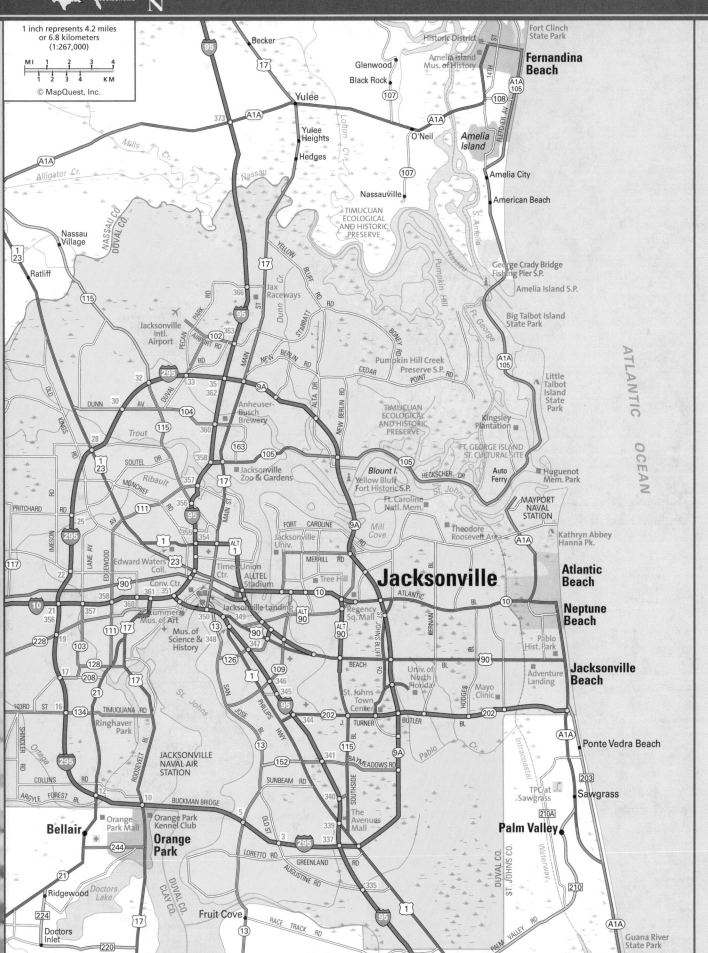

Becker

Glenwood

Black Rock

Yulee

Yulee
Heights

Hedges

Nassauville

O'Neil

Historic District

Fort Clinch
State Park

Amelia Island
Mus. of History

**Fernandina
Beach**

Amelia
Island

Amelia City

American Beach

George Crady Bridge
Fishing Pier S.P.

Amelia Island S.P.

Big Talbot Island
State Park

Little
Talbot
Island
State
Park

TIMUCUAN
ECOLOGICAL
AND HISTORIC
PRESERVE

Nassau
Village

Ratliff

Jax
Raceways

Jacksonville
Intl.
Airport

Anheuser-
Busch
Brewery

Pumpkin Hill Creek
Preserve S.P.

TIMUCUAN
ECOLOGICAL
AND HISTORIC
PRESERVE

FT. GEORGE ISLAND
ST. CULTURAL SITE

Kingsley
Plantation

Auto
Ferry

Huguenot
Mem. Park

**MAYPORT
NAVAL
STATION**

Kathryn Abbey
Hanna Pk.

Jacksonville
Zoo & Gardens

Blount I.

Yellow Bluff
Fort Historic S.P.

Ft. Caroline
Natl. Mem.

Theodore
Roosevelt Area

**Atlantic
Beach**

**Neptune
Beach**

Edward Waters
Coll.

FORT CAROLINE

Jacksonville
Univ.

MERRILL RD.

Tree Hill

Mill
Cove

Jacksonville

ATLANTIC

Conv. Ctr.

Times Union
Ctr.

ALLTEL
Stadium

Pablo
Hist. Park

Cummer
Mus. of Art

Jacksonville Landing

Mus. of
Science &
History

Regency
Sq. Mall

Univ. of
North
Florida

Mayo
Clinic

Adventure
Landing

**Jacksonville
Beach**

St. Johns
Town
Center

BEACH

J. TURNER
BUTLER

**ATLANTIC
OCEAN**

Bellair

Orange
Park Mall

Orange Park
Kennel Club

**Orange
Park**

JACKSONVILLE
NAVAL AIR
STATION

BUCKMAN BRIDGE

SUNBEAM

SOUTHSIDE

The
Avenues
Mall

TPC at
Sawgrass

Sawgrass

Ponte Vedra Beach

Palm Valley

Ridgewood

Doctors
Lake

Doctors
Inlet

LORETTO RD.

GREENLAND

AUGUSTINE RD.

Fruit Cove

RACE TRACK RD.

Guana River
State Park

Ringhaver
Park

BAYMEADOWS RD.

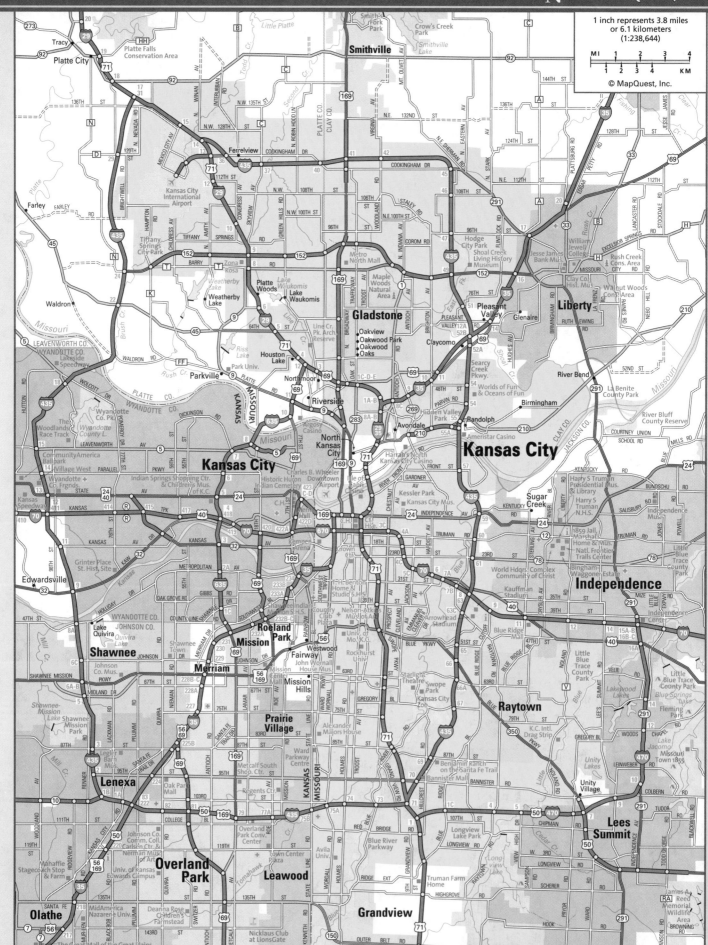

1 inch represents 3.8 miles
or 6.1 kilometers
(1:238,644)

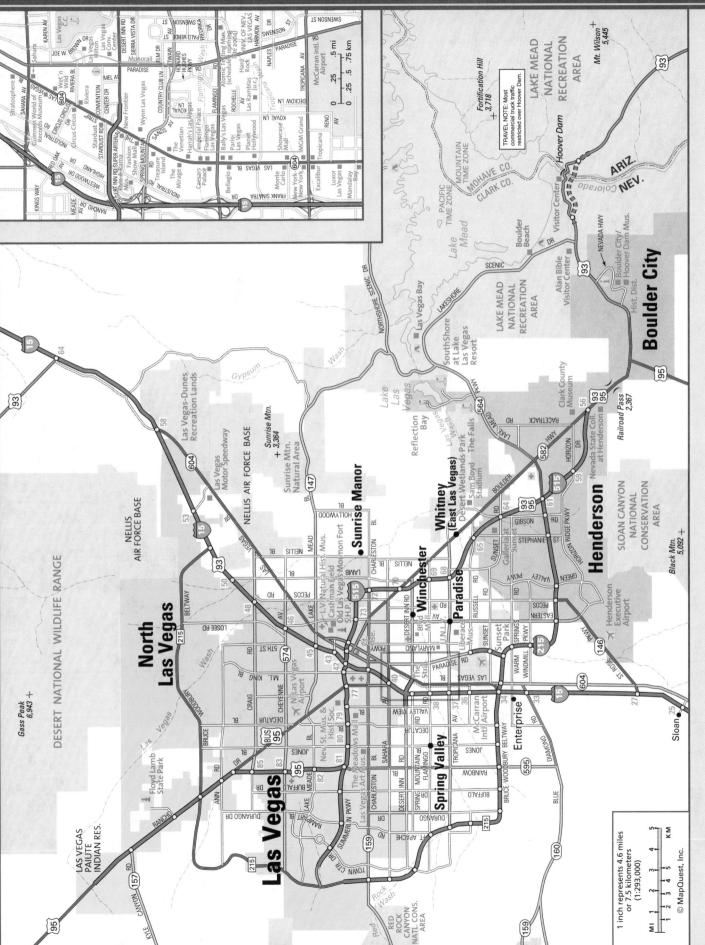

N

TRAVEL NOTE: Most commercial truck traffic restricted over Hoover Dam.

1 inch represents 4.6 miles or 7.5 kilometers (1:293,000)

© MapQuest, Inc.

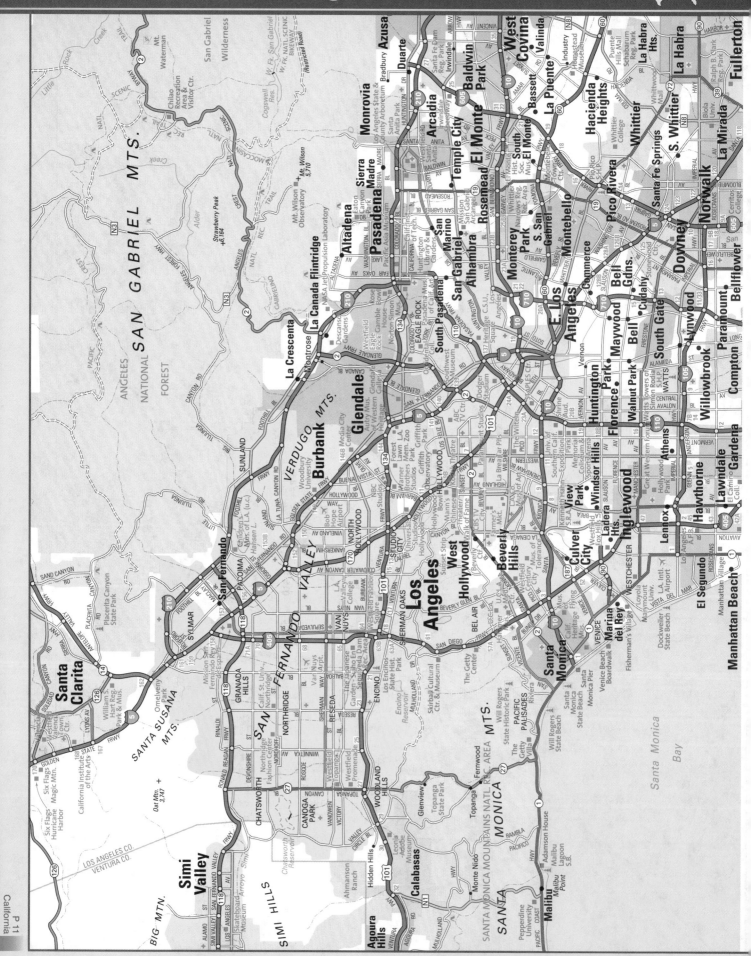

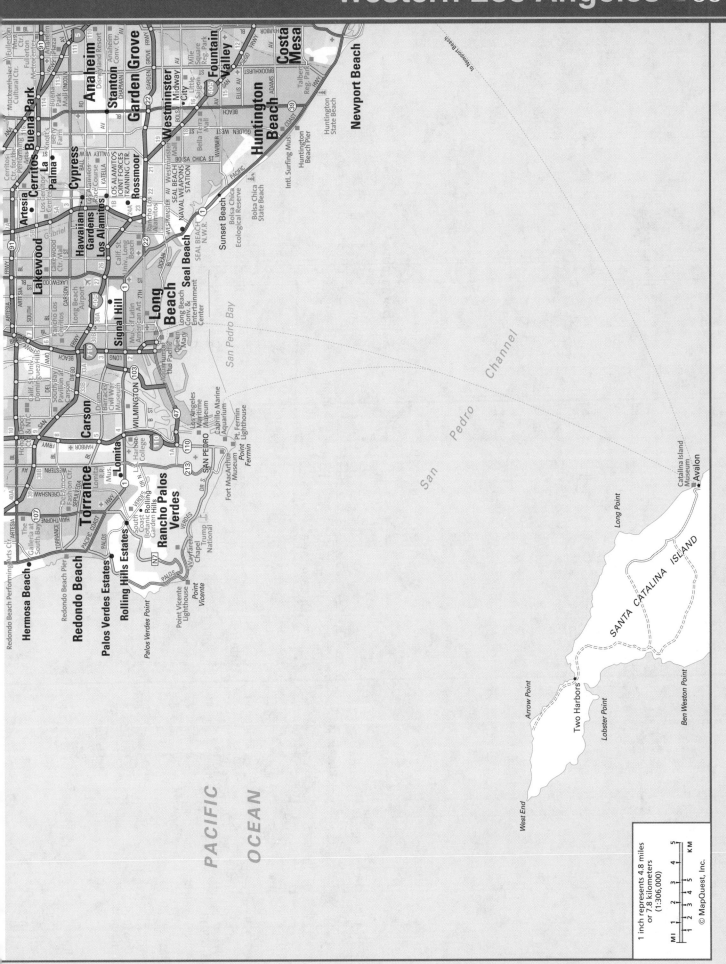

1 inch represents 4.8 miles
or 7.8 kilometers
(1:306,000)

PACIFIC

OCEAN

San Pedro Bay

San Pedro Channel

SANTA CATALINA ISLAND

Catalina Island Museum
Avalon

Long Point

West End

Arrow Point

Two Harbors

Lobster Point

Ben Weston Point

KM
MI

Newport Beach

Costa Mesa

Huntington Beach

Fountain Valley

Westminster

Garden Grove

Anaheim

Stanton

Cypress

La Palma

Buena Park

Cerritos

Artesia

Rossmoor

Los Alamitos

Hawaiian Gardens

Lakewood

Seal Beach

Long Beach

Signal Hill

Carson

WILMINGTON

Lomita

Torrance

Redondo Beach

Hermosa Beach

Palos Verdes Estates

Rolling Hills Estates

Rancho Palos Verdes

SAN PEDRO

Sunset Beach

to Newport Beach

PACIFIC OCEAN

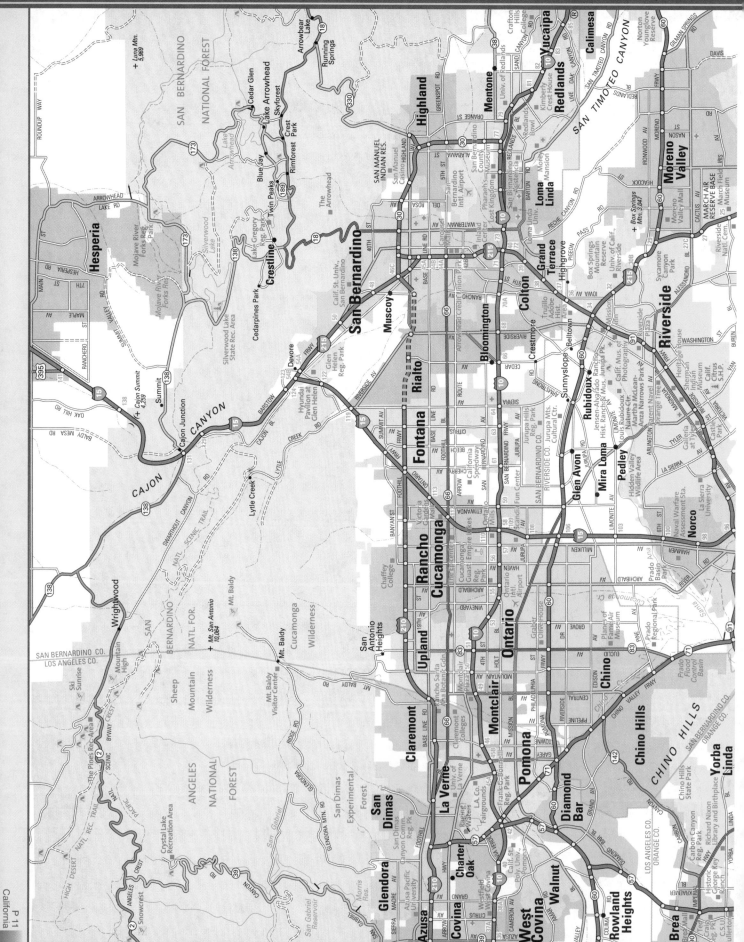

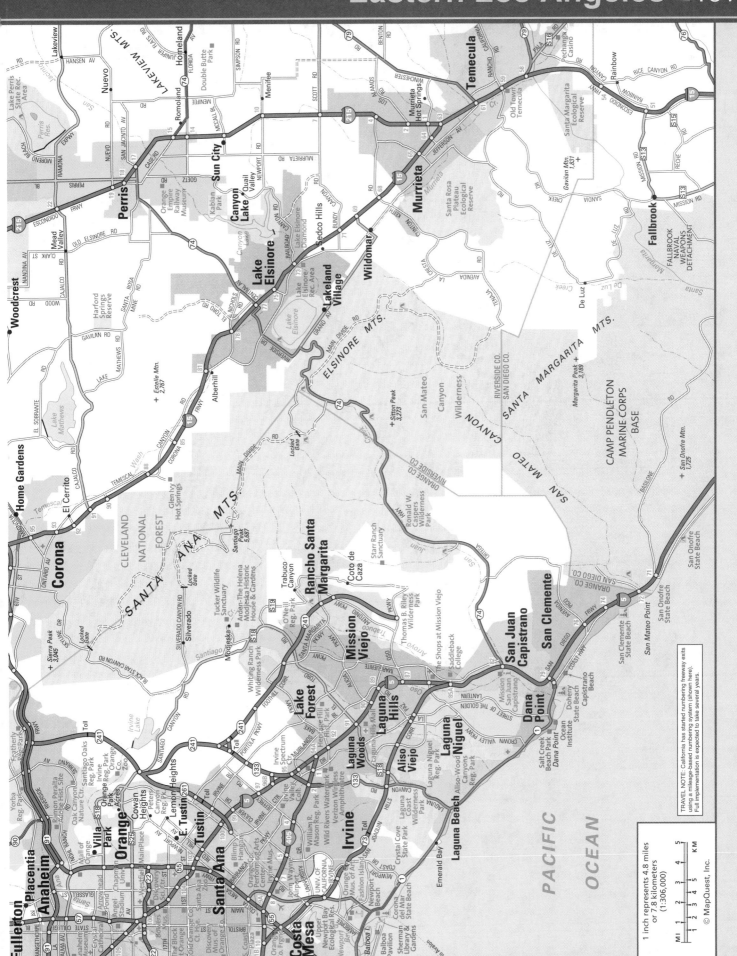

TRAVEL NOTE: California has started numbering freeway exits using a mileage-based numbering system (shown here). Full implementation is expected to take several years.

1 inch represents 4.8 miles
or 7.8 kilometers
(1:306,000)

© MapQuest, Inc.

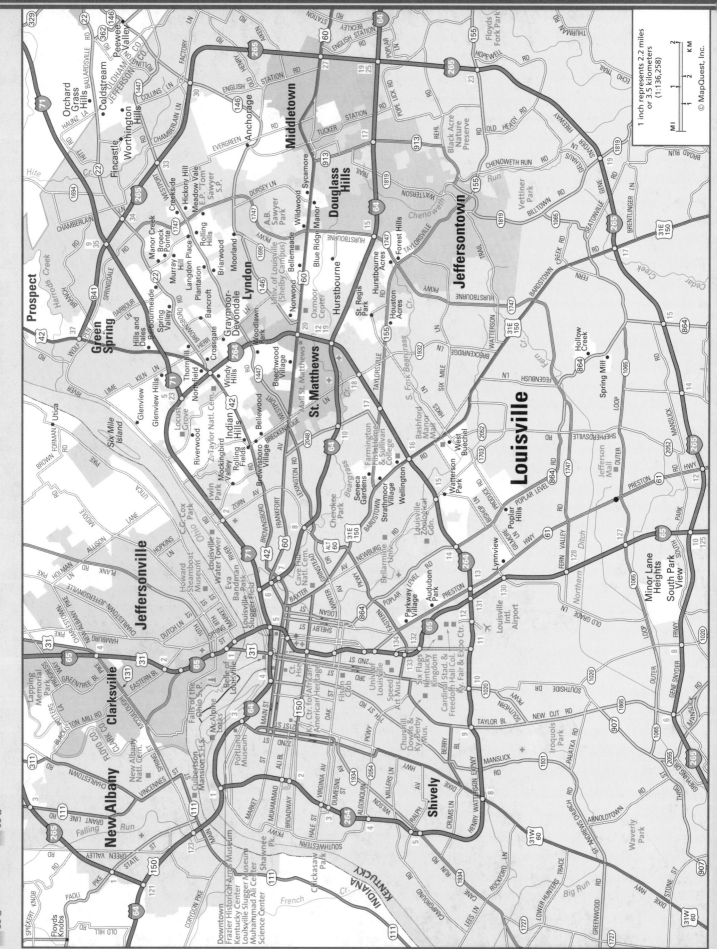

N

Louisville

1 inch represents 2.2 miles
or 3.5 kilometers (1:136,258)

© MapQuest, Inc.

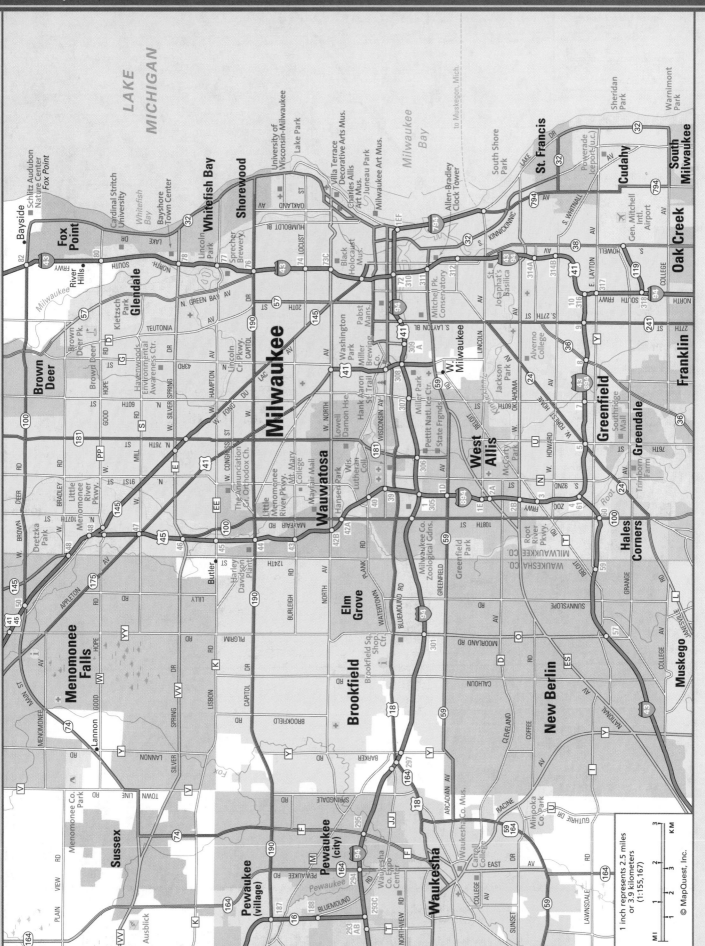

N

LAKE MICHIGAN

Bayside

Fox Point

Schlitz Audubon Nature Center
Fox Point

Cardinal Stritch University

Whitefish Bay

Bayshore Town Center

Whitefish Bay

Shorewood

University of Wisconsin-Milwaukee

Lake Park

Villa Terrace Decorative Arts Mus.

Charles Allis Art Mus.

Juneau Park

Milwaukee Art Mus.

Milwaukee Bay

to Muskegon, Mich.

Sheridan Park

Warnimont Park

South Shore Park

St. Francis

Allen-Bradley Clock Tower

Powerade Iceport (u.c.)

Cudahy

South Milwaukee

Gen. Mitchell Airport

Oak Creek

Brown Deer

Glendale

Lincoln Park

Sprecher Brewery

Black Holocaust Mus.

Pabst Mans.

Miller Brewing Co.

Mitchell Pk. Conservatory

St. Josaphat's Basilica

Alverno College

Franklin

Menomonee Falls

Milwaukee

Wauwatosa

The Annunciation Gr. Orthodox Ch.

Mayfair Mall

Mt. Mary College

Lowell Damon Hse.

Hank Aaron St Trail

Pettit Natl. Ice Ctr.

State Frgnds.

Wis. Lutheran Coll.

West Allis

McCarty Park

Jackson Park

Greenfield

Southridge Mall

Greendale

Trimborn Farm

Hales Corners

Harley Davidson Plant

Butler

Dretzka Park

Little Menomonee River Pkwy.

Elm Grove

Milwaukee Co. Zoological Gdns.

Greenfield Park

Root River Pkwy.

WAUKESHA CO.

MILWAUKEE CO.

Sussex

Menomonee Co. Park

Lannon

Brookfield

Brookfield Sq. Shop. Ctr.

New Berlin

Muskego

Minooka Co. Park

Pewaukee (village)

Pewaukee (city)

Pewaukee

Waukesha Co. Expo Center

Waukesha

Carroll College

Ausblick

1 inch represents 2.5 miles or 3.9 kilometers
(1:155,167)

KM

TENN.
ARK.

Meeman-
Shelby
Forest
S.P.

Mississippi

Redman
Point
Bar

Loosahatchie

Loosahatchie Bar

SHELBY CO.
CRITTENDEN CO.

West
Memphis

Memphis Motorsports Park

FITE RD

Canal
Drainage
Loosahatchie

Bartlett

Raleigh Springs Mall

Presidents Island

Treasure Island

Chucalissa Museum

T.O. Fuller S.P.

Lake McKellar

Harbor Channel

Nonconnah

Cr.

Slave Haven Underground Railroad Mus.
Univ. of Tenn. Health Sci.
The Pyramid
Convention Center
Mud Island
Victorian Village
AutoZone Park
Ctr. for Southern Folklore
Beale St. Hist. Dist.
FedExForum/Rock 'n Soul Mus.
Natl. Civil Rights Mus.
Natl. Ornamental Metal Mus.

Sun Studio

Stax

Rhodes Coll.

Zoo Overton Park
Brooks Mus. of Art

Memphis College of Art

Christian Bros. Univ.
Liberty Bowl
Memphis Frgnds. Pink Palace Mus.

Univ. of Memphis

Memphis

Memphis Natl. Cem.

Shelby Farms

Oak Court Mall

Memphis Bot. Gdn.

The Dixon Gallery & Gdns.

Memphis Mem. Park

Lichterman Nature Ctr.

Germantown

Barron Av

Rhodes Av

Graceland

Memphis Intl. Airport

Hickory Ridge Mall

Southland Mall

Capleville

TENNESSEE
MISSISSIPPI

SHELBY CO.
DESOTO CO.

North Horn Lake

Cora L.
Robco L.

Horn L.

Southaven

Southaven Towne Center

Horn Lake

Olive Branch

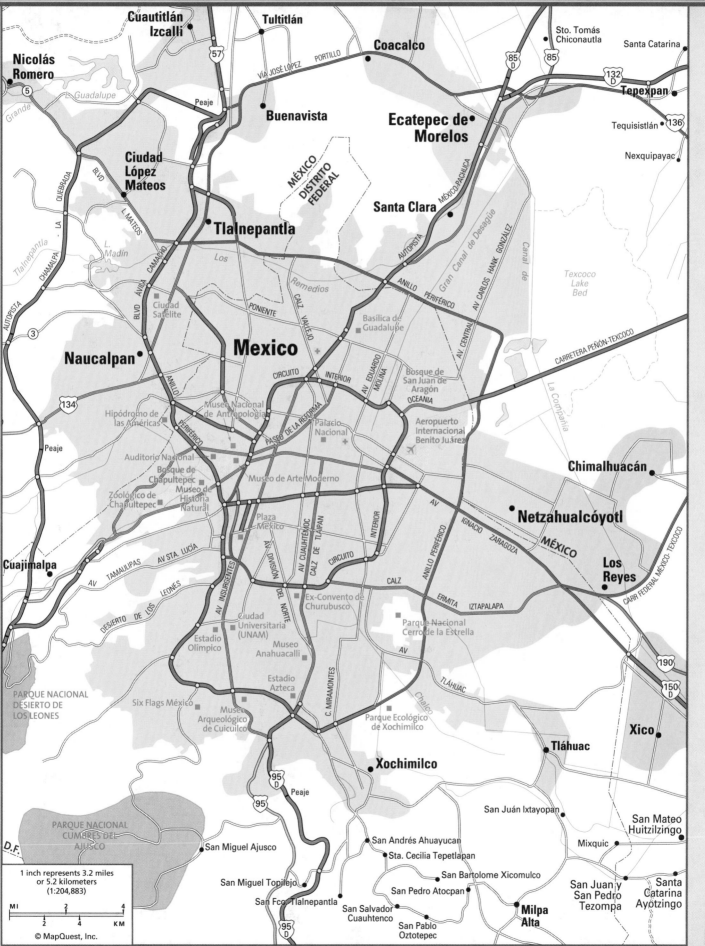

Cuautitlán Izcalli

Tultitlán

Coacalco

Nicolás Romero

Sto. Tomás Chiconautla

Santa Catarina

Tepexpan

Buenavista

Ecatepec de Morelos

Tequisistlán

Nexquipayac

Ciudad López Mateos

MÉXICO DISTRITO FEDERAL

Santa Clara

Tlalnepantla

Los Remedios

Texcoco Lake Bed

Basílica de Guadalupe

Mexico

Bosque de San Juan de Aragón

CARRETERA PEÑÓN-TEXCOCO

Naucalpan

Museo Nacional de Antropología

Palacio Nacional

Aeropuerto Internacional Benito Juárez

Hipódromo de las Américas

Auditorio Nacional

Chimalhuacán

Bosque de Chapultepec

Museo de Arte Moderno

Zoológico de Chapultepec

Museo de Historia Natural

Netzahualcóyotl

MÉXICO

Plaza México

Cuajimalpa

Los Reyes

Ex-Convento de Churubusco

Ciudad Universitaria (UNAM)

Parque Nacional Cerro de la Estrella

Estadio Olímpico

Museo Anahuacalli

Estadio Azteca

PARQUE NACIONAL DESIERTO DE LOS LEONES

Six Flags México

Museo Arqueológico de Cuicuilco

Parque Ecológico de Xochimilco

Xico

Tláhuac

Xochimilco

San Juán Ixtayopan

San Mateo Huitzilzingo

PARQUE NACIONAL CUMBRES DEL AJUSCO

San Andrés Ahuayucan

Mixquic

D.F.

San Miguel Ajusco

Sta. Cecilia Tepetlapan

San Bartolome Xicomulco

San Juan y San Pedro Tezompa

Santa Catarina Ayotzingo

San Miguel Topilejo

San Pedro Atocpan

San Fco. Tlalnepantla

San Salvador Cuauhtenco

San Pablo Oztotepec

Milpa Alta

1 inch represents 3.2 miles or 5.2 kilometers (1:204,883)

MI

KM

© MapQuest, Inc.

Minneapolis-St. Paul

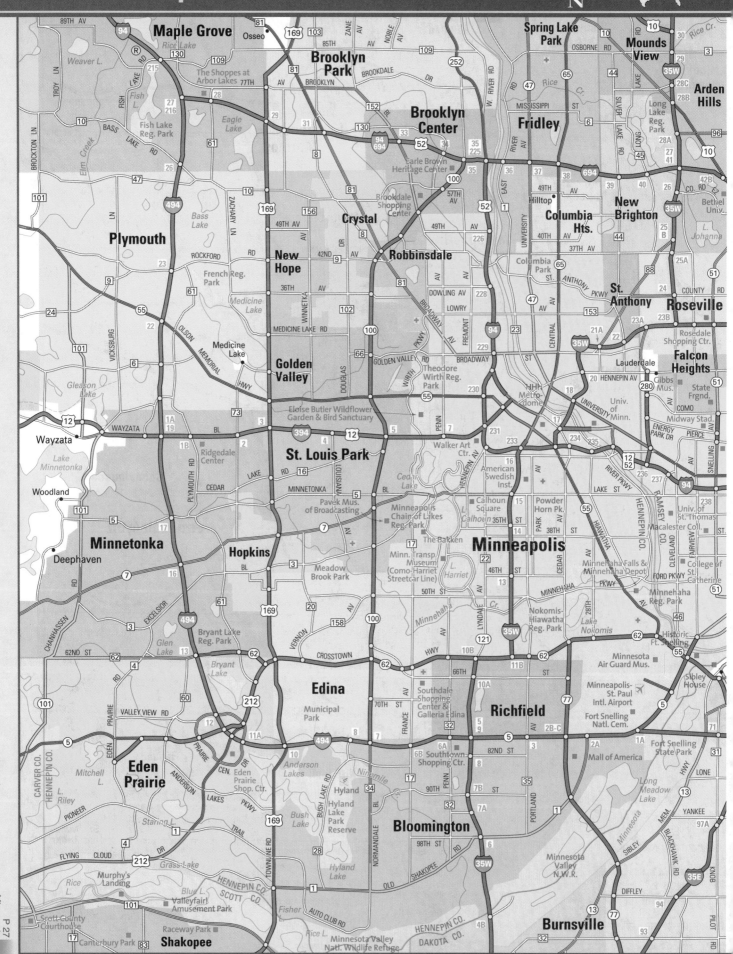

Maple Grove

Osseo

Weaver L.

Rice Lake

The Shoppes at Arbor Lakes

Fish Lake Reg. Park

Eagle Lake

Bass Lake

Brooklyn Park

Brooklyn Center

Earle Brown Heritage Center

Brookdale Shopping Center

Spring Lake Park

Mounds View

Arden Hills

Long Lake Reg. Park

Bethel Univ.

Fridley

Plymouth

French Reg. Park

Medicine Lake

New Hope

Crystal

Robbinsdale

Columbia Hts.

Hilltop

New Brighton

L. Johanna

Columbia Park

St. Anthony

Roseville

Rosedale Shopping Ctr.

Dowling Av

Lowry

Golden Valley

Theodore Wirth Reg. Park

Falcon Heights

Gibbs Mus.

State Frgnd.

Como

Midway Stad.

Gleason Lake

Eloise Butler Wildflower Garden & Bird Sanctuary

Wayzata

HHH Metro-dome

Univ. of Minn.

Energy Park Dr

Pierce

Lake Minnetonka

Ridgedale Center

St. Louis Park

Walker Art Ctr.

American Swedish Inst.

Woodland

Pavek Mus. of Broadcasting

Cedar Lake

Minneapolis Chain of Lakes Reg. Park

Calhoun Square

L. Calhoun

Powder Horn Pk.

Univ. of St. Thomas

Macalester Coll.

Minnetonka

Hopkins

The Bakken

Minneapolis

College of St. Catherine

Deephaven

Meadow Brook Park

Minn. Transp. Museum (Como-Harriet Streetcar Line)

L. Harriet

Minnehaha Falls & Minnehaha Depot

Minnehaha Reg. Park

Bryant Lake Reg. Park

Glen Lake

Bryant Lake

Nokomis-Hiawatha Reg. Park

Lake Nokomis

Historic Ft. Snelling

Minnesota Air Guard Mus.

Sibley House

Edina

Municipal Park

Southdale Shopping Center & Galleria Edina

Richfield

Minneapolis-St. Paul Intl. Airport

Fort Snelling Natl. Cem.

Fort Snelling State Park

Eden Prairie

Eden Prairie Shop. Ctr.

Anderson Lakes

Southtown Shopping Ctr.

Mall of America

Mitchell L.

L. Riley

Hyland

Bloomington

Hyland Lake Park Reserve

Bush Lake

Staring L.

Long Meadow Lake

Murphy's Landing

Rice L.

Valleyfair! Amusement Park

Raceway Park

Hyland Lake

Minnesota Valley N.W.R.

Burnsville

Scott County Courthouse

Shakopee

Canterbury Park

Fisher

Minnesota Valley Natl. Wildlife Refuge

HENNEPIN CO.
DAKOTA CO.

HENNEPIN CO.
SCOTT CO.

CARVER CO.
HENNEPIN CO.

P 27
Minnesota

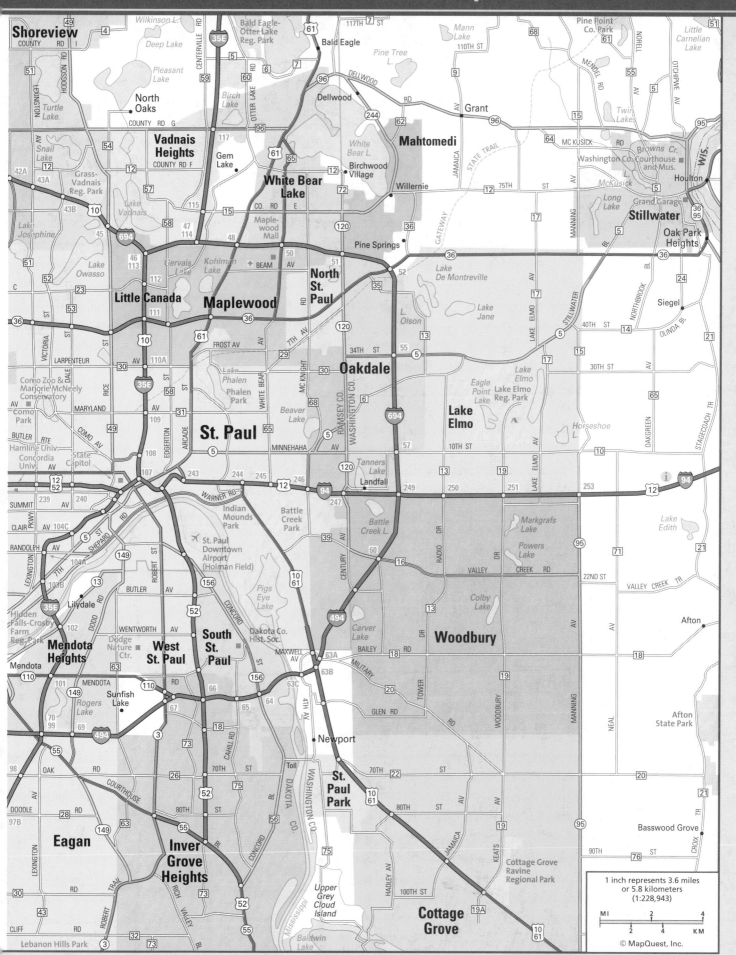

1 inch represents 3.6 miles
or 5.8 kilometers
(1:228,943)

© MapQuest, Inc.

N

Miami

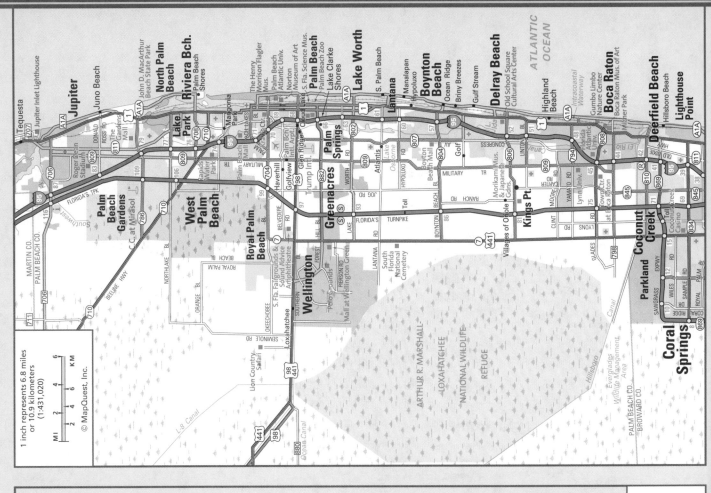

1 inch represents 6.8 miles
or 10.9 kilometers
(1:431,020)

© MapQuest, Inc.

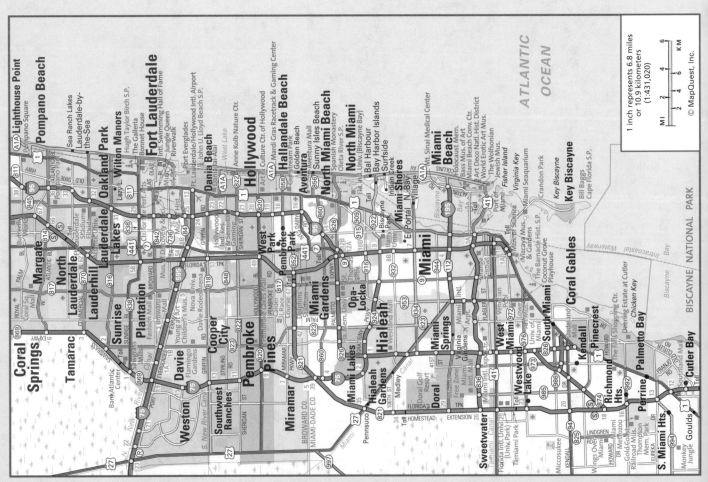

1 inch represents 6.8 miles
or 10.9 kilometers
(1:431,020)

© MapQuest, Inc.

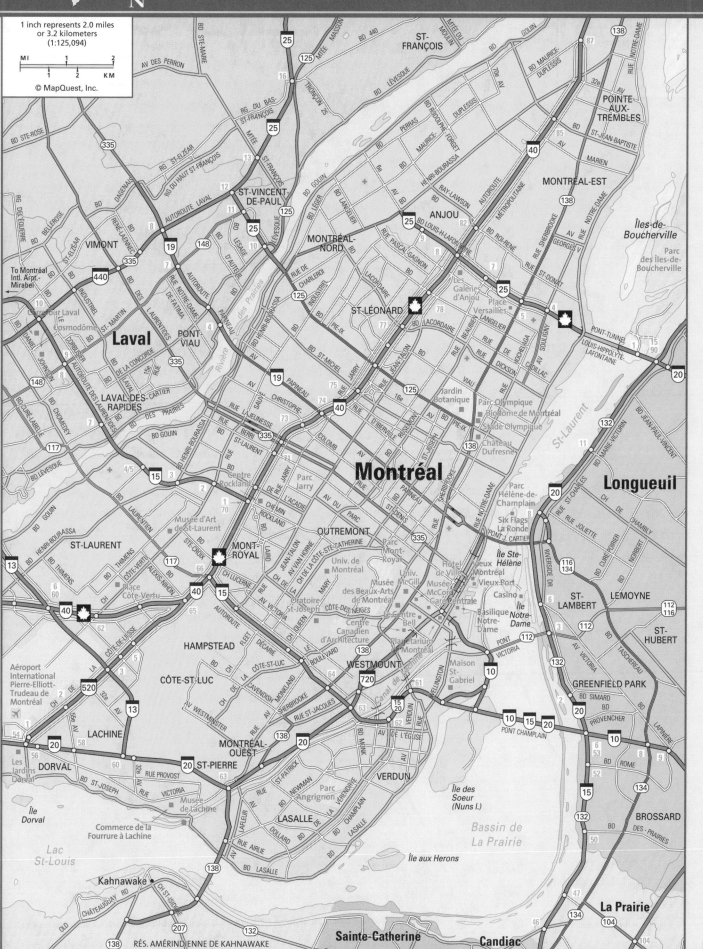

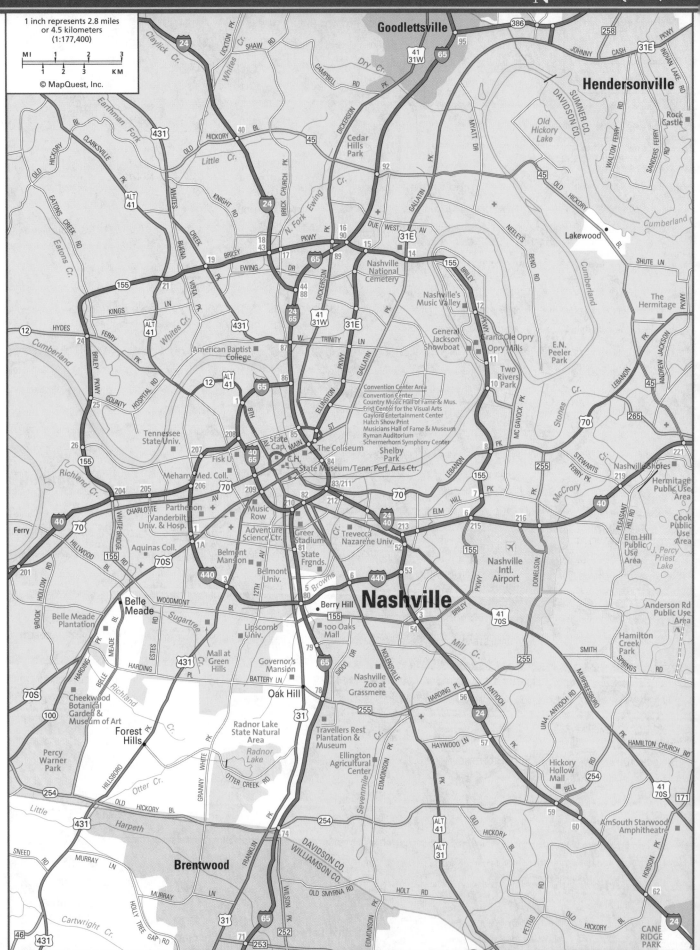

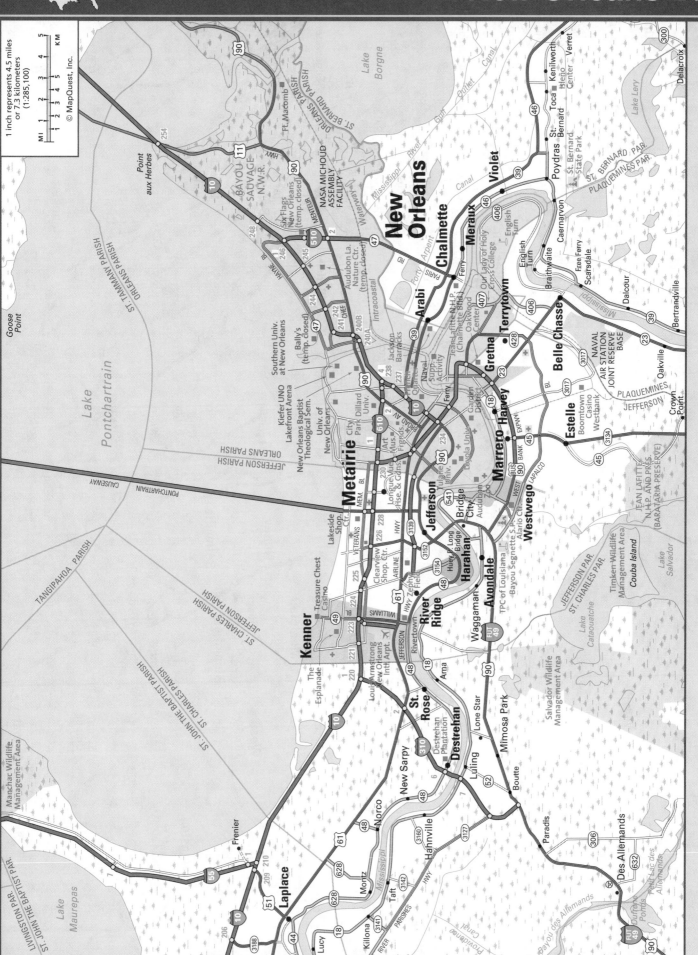

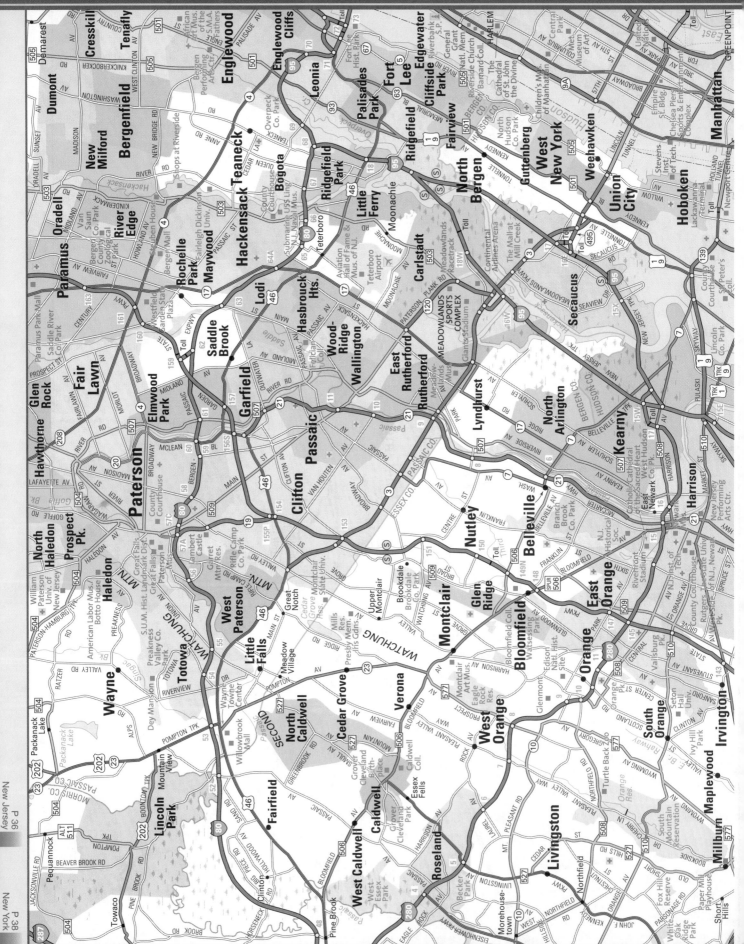

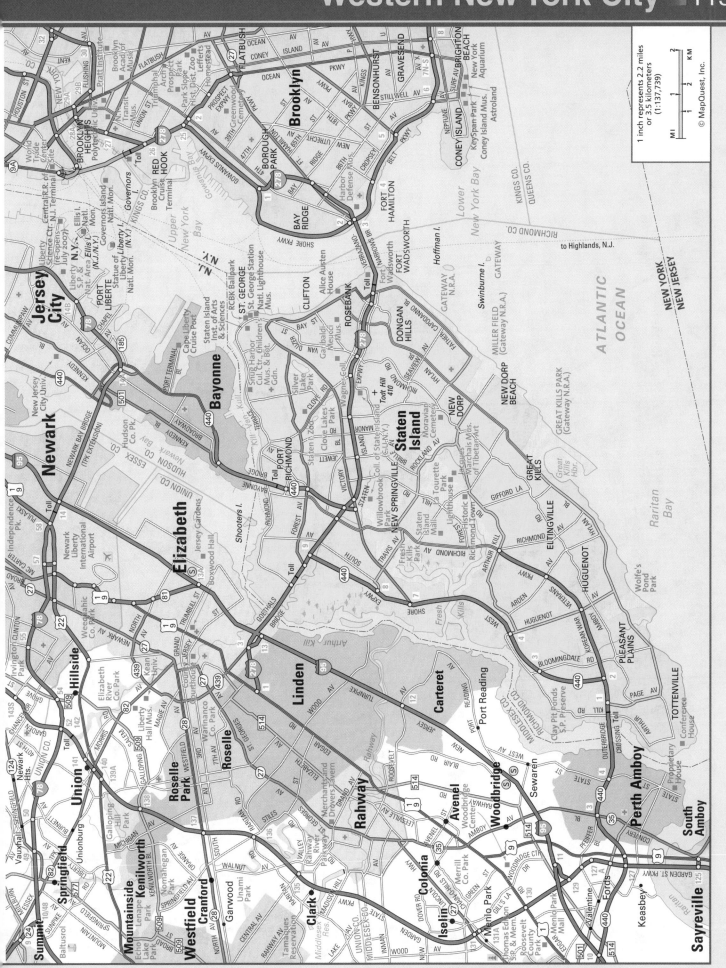

1 inch represents 2.2 miles
or 3.5 kilometers
(1:137,739)

© MapQuest, Inc.

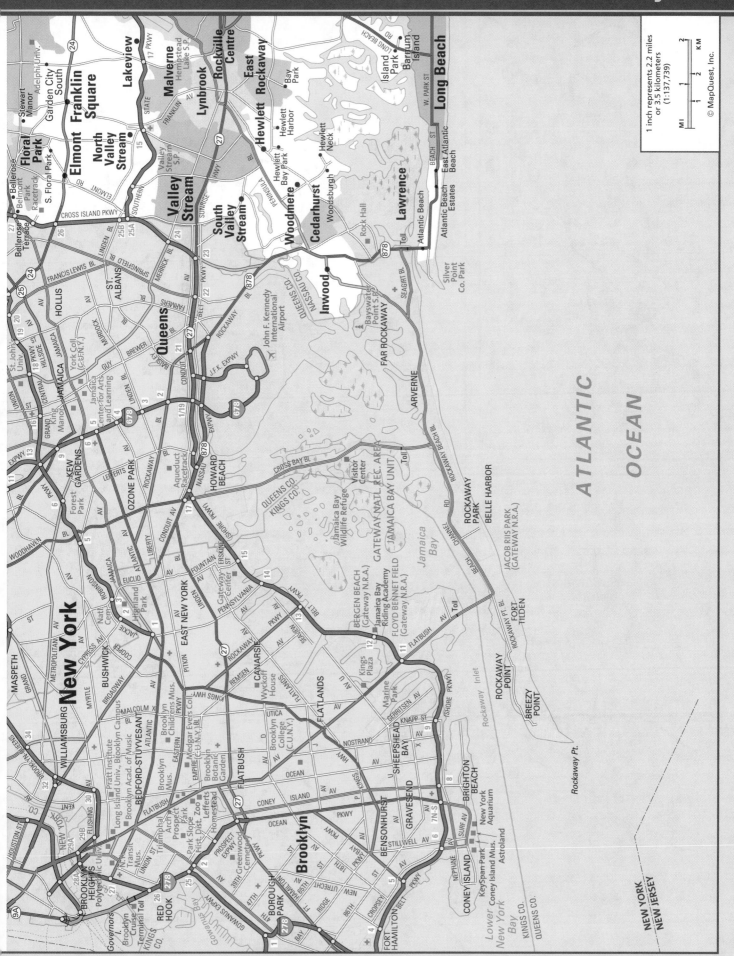

ATLANTIC

OCEAN

New York

Brooklyn

Queens

Long Beach

Rockville Centre

Lynbrook

Malverne

Lakeview

Franklin Square

Elmont

Floral Park

North Valley Stream

Valley Stream

South Valley Stream

Hewlett

East Rockaway

Woodmere

Cedarhurst

Lawrence

Inwood

Far Rockaway

John F. Kennedy International Airport

Howard Beach

Ozone Park

Kew Gardens

Forest Park

East New York

Canarsie

Flatlands

Flatbush

Bedford-Stuyvesant

Bushwick

Williamsburg

Maspeth

Woodhaven

Belle Harbor

Rockaway Park

Breezy Point

Rockaway Point

Sheepshead Bay

Gravesend

Bensonhurst

Brighton Beach

Coney Island

Borough Park

Red Hook

Brooklyn Heights

Gateway Natl. Rec. Area

Jamaica Bay Wildlife Refuge

Jamaica Bay

Atlantic Beach

Hewlett Harbor

Hewlett Neck

Woodsburgh

Rock Hall

NEW YORK
NEW JERSEY

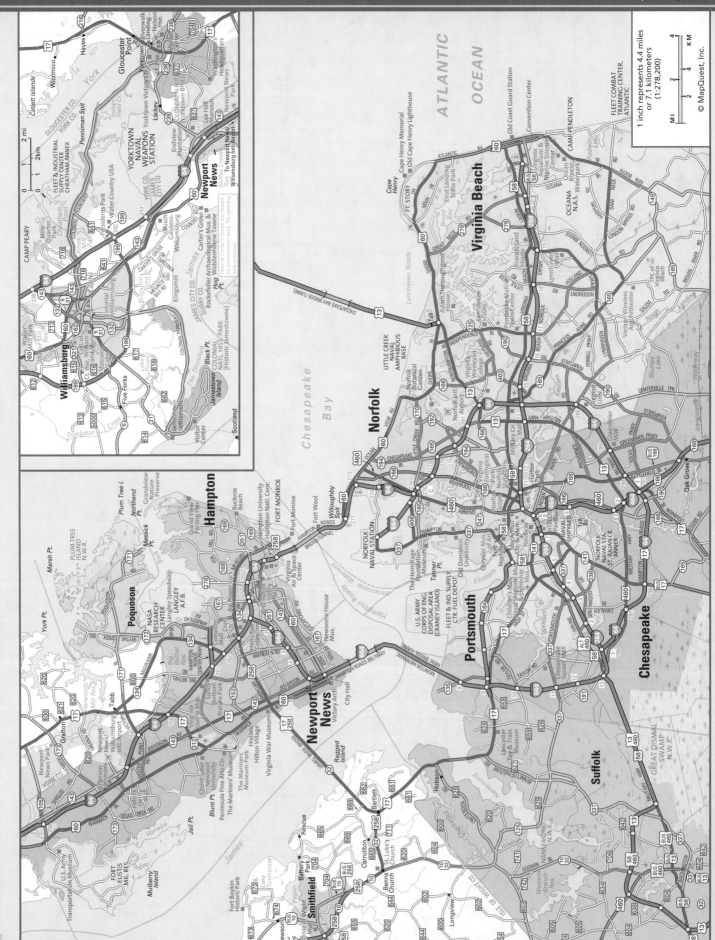

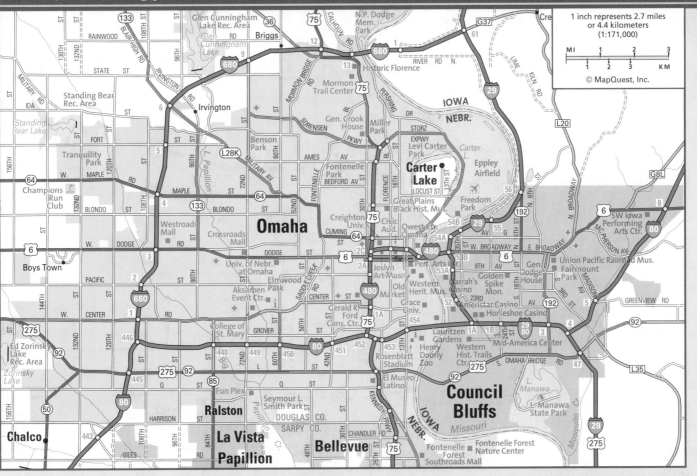

1 inch represents 2.7 miles
or 4.4 kilometers
(1:171,000)

© MapQuest, Inc.

P 33 Nebraska

P 21 Iowa

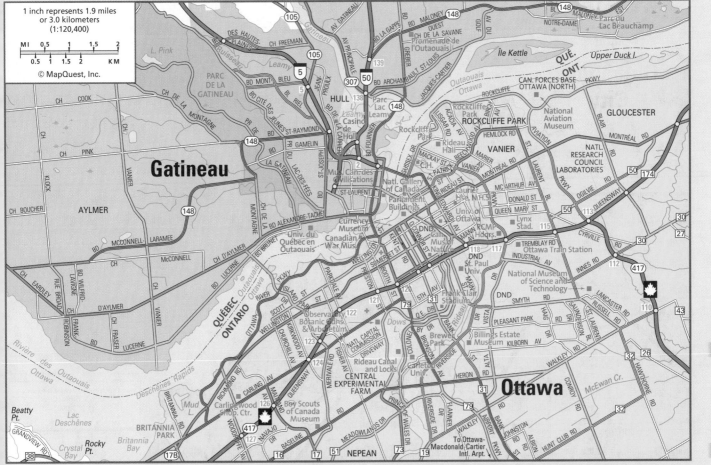

1 inch represents 1.9 miles
or 3.0 kilometers
(1:120,400)

© MapQuest, Inc.

P 64 Québec

P 62 Ontario

Piedmont

Yukon

Mustang

Oklahoma City

Newcastle

Blanchard

Goldsby

Noble

Woodlawn Park

Bethany

Warr Acres

The Village

Nichols Hills

Quail Springs Mall

Martin Park Nature Center

Southern Nazarene Univ.

Will Rogers Park

White Water Bay

Okla. St. Fair Park

Okla. City Univ.

Penn Sq. Mall

Stockyards City

Myriad Bot. Gdns. & Cox Conv. Ctr.

Okla. Heritage Ctr.

Okla. City Natl. Mem.

Overholser Mansion

AT&T Bricktown Ballpark

Ford Center

St. Capitol

Okla. City History Ctr.

Div. Mus. Okla.

45th Infantry

Lincoln Park

Zoo

Natl. Softball Hall of Fame

Firefighters Museum

Remington Park Omniplex

Lake Aluma

Edmond

Univ. of Central Oklahoma

Edmond Hist. Mus.

Arcadia

Arcadia Lake

Okla. Christian Univ.

Frontier City

Jones

Spencer

Nicoma Park

Choctaw

Midwest City

Tinker Air Force Base

Del City

Valley Brook

Crossroads Mall

Smith Village

Heritage Park Mall

Forest Park

Natl. Cowboy and Western Heritage Mus.

Will Rogers World Airport

Mid-America Christian Univ.

Moore

Sooner Mall

Cleveland Co. Fairgrounds

Cleveland Co. Hist. Mus.

UNIV. OF OKLAHOMA Mem. Stadium

Jones Mus. of Art

Oklahoma Mus. of Natural History

Lloyd Noble Ctr.

Norman

Lake Stanley Draper

Lake Thunderbird State Park

Lake Thunderbird

1 inch represents 4.0 miles or 6.4 kilometers
(1:252,000)

© MapQuest, Inc.

N

Philadelphia

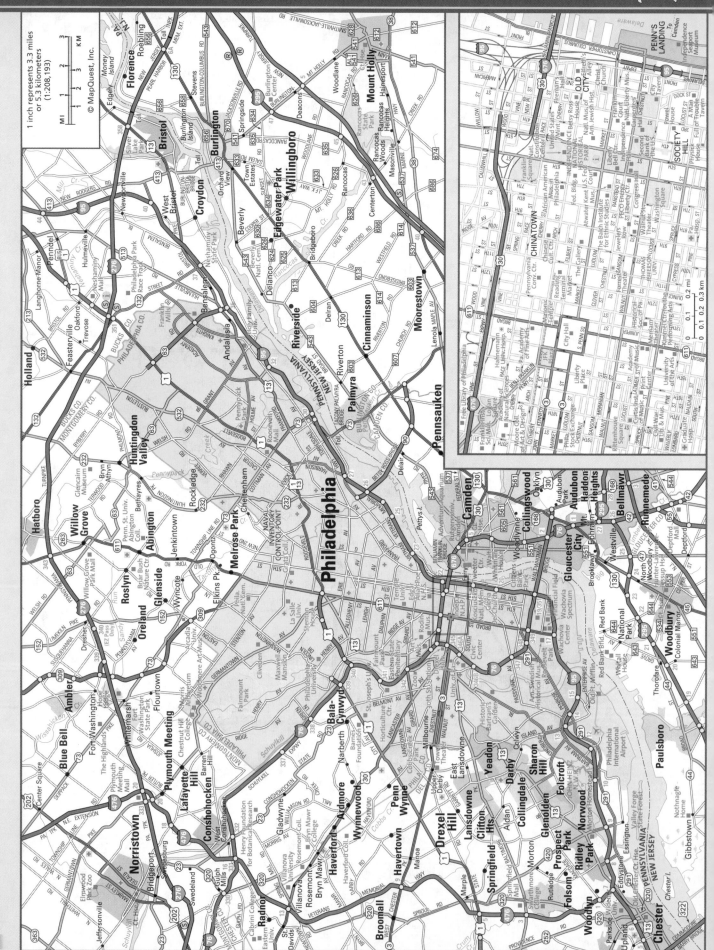

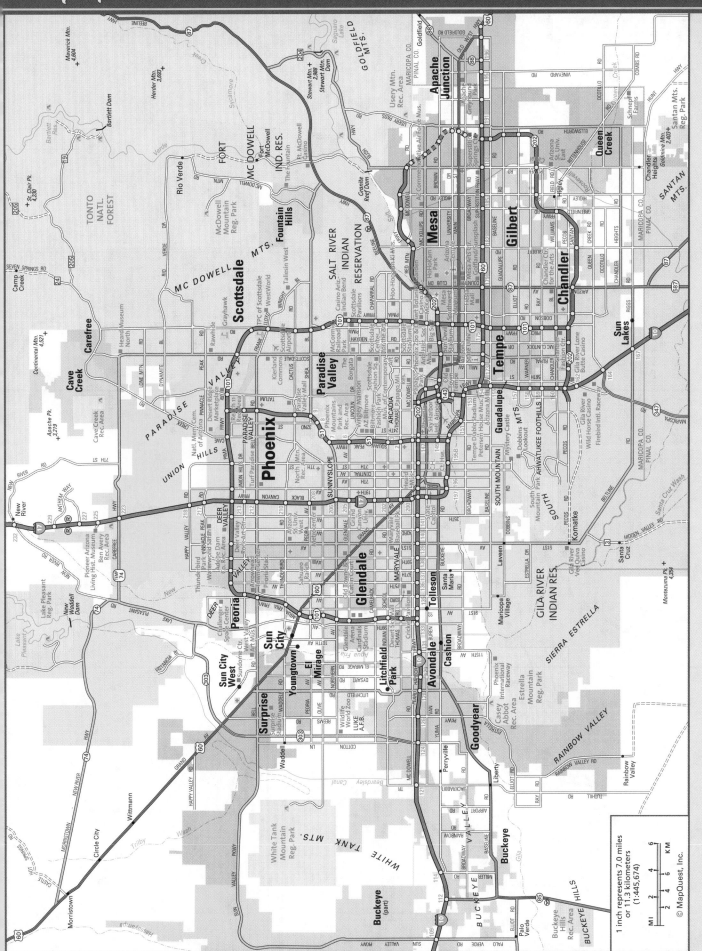

N

Pittsburgh

© MapQuest, Inc.

1 inch represents 2.9 miles
or 4.7 kilometers
(1:186,170)

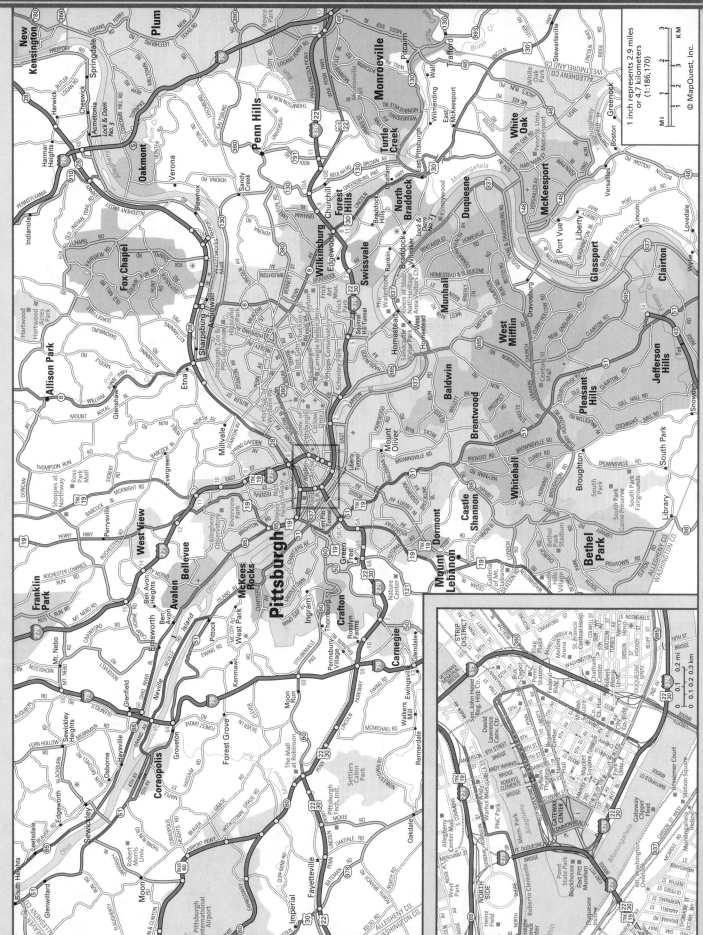

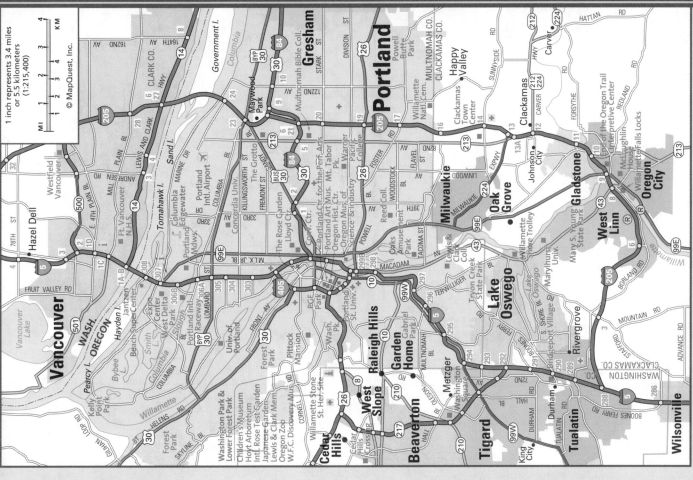

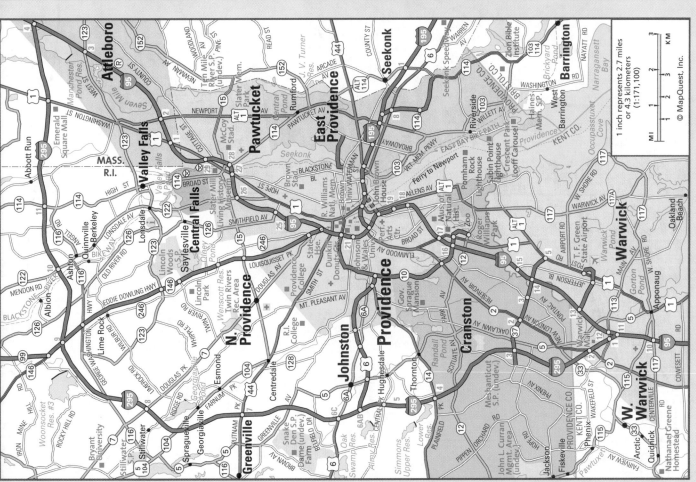

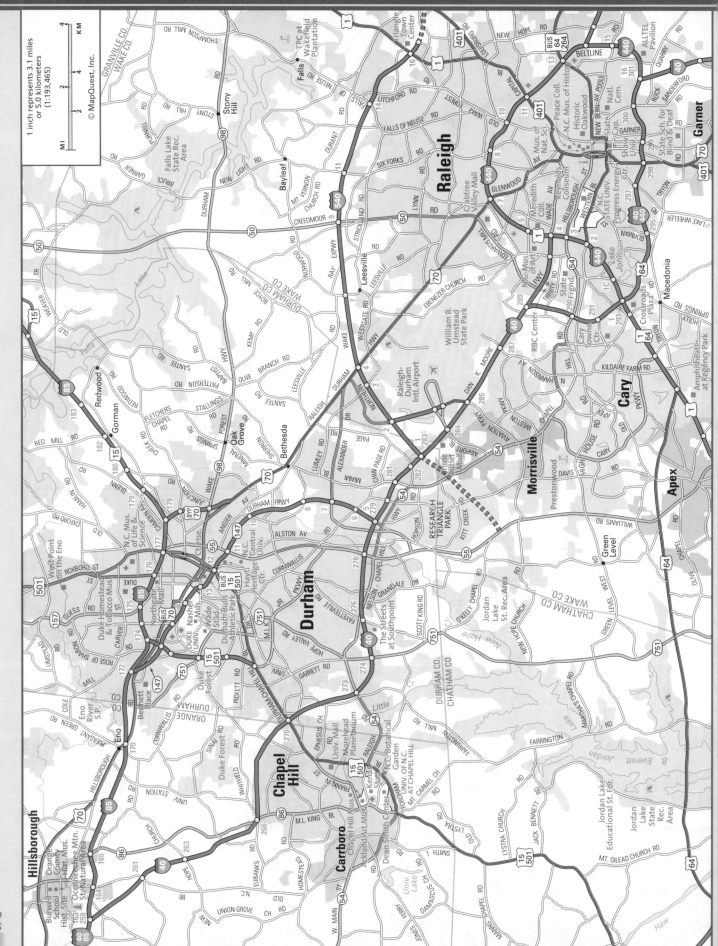

P 52
Virginia

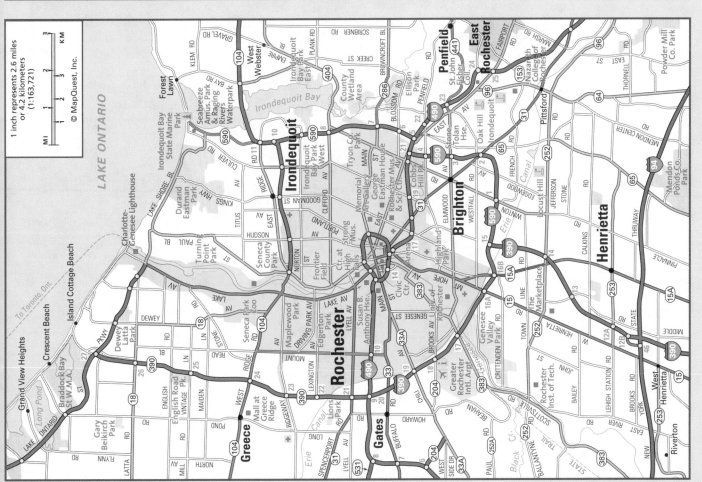

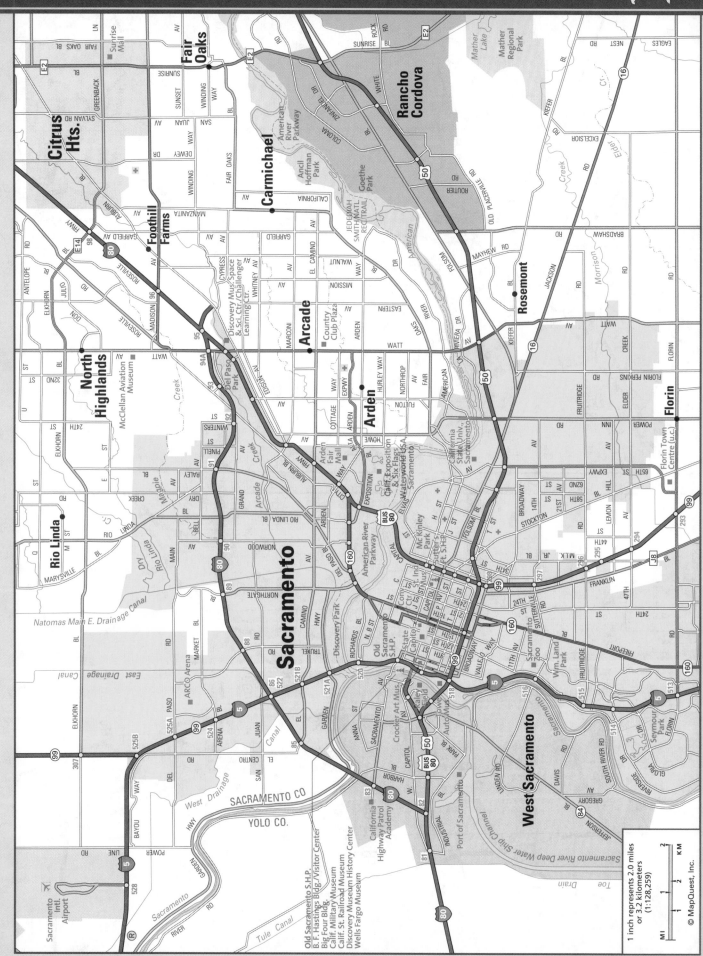

Citrus Hts.

Fair Oaks

Carmichael

Rancho Cordova

Foothill Farms

North Highlands

McClellan Aviation Museum

Arcade

Arden

Rosemont

Florin

Rio Linda

Sacramento

West Sacramento

SACRAMENTO CO
YOLO CO.

Sacramento Intl. Airport

Old Sacramento S.H.P.
B.F. Hastings Bldg./Visitor Center
Big Four Bldg.
Calif. Military Museum
Calif. St. Railroad Museum
Discovery Museum History Center
Wells Fargo Museum

California Highway Patrol Academy

Port of Sacramento

1 inch represents 2.0 miles
or 3.2 kilometers
(1:128,259)

© MapQuest, Inc.

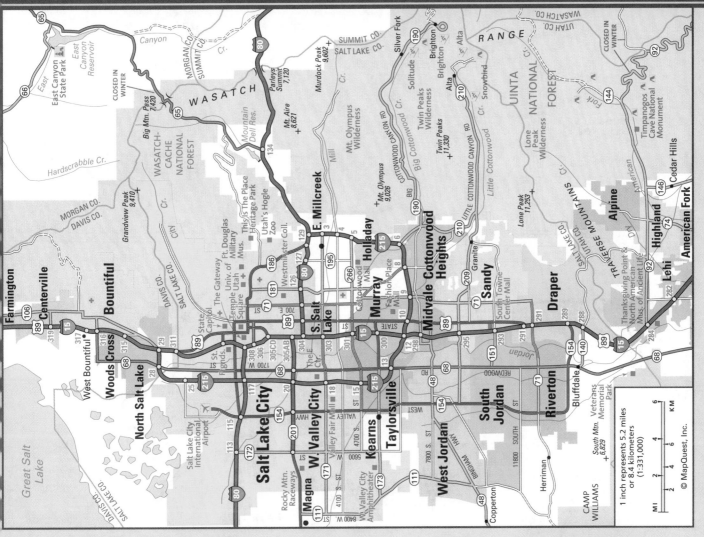

1 inch represents 5.2 miles
or 8.4 kilometers (1:331,000)

© MapQuest, Inc.

P 50
Utah

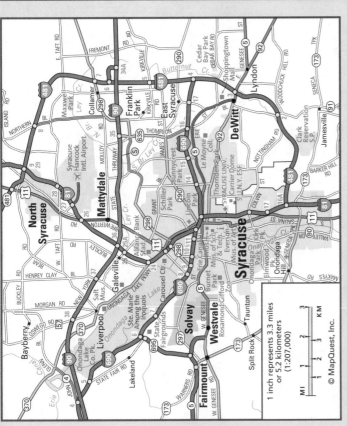

1 inch represents 3.3 miles
or 5.2 kilometers (1:207,000)

© MapQuest, Inc.

P 51
Washington

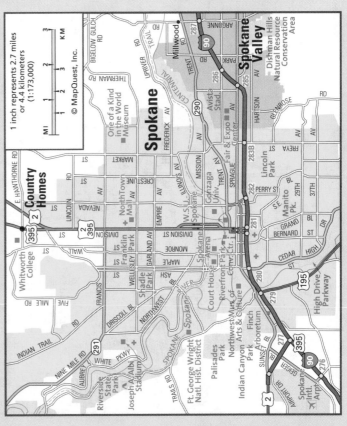

1 inch represents 2.7 miles
or 4.4 kilometers (1:173,000)

© MapQuest, Inc.

P 38
New York

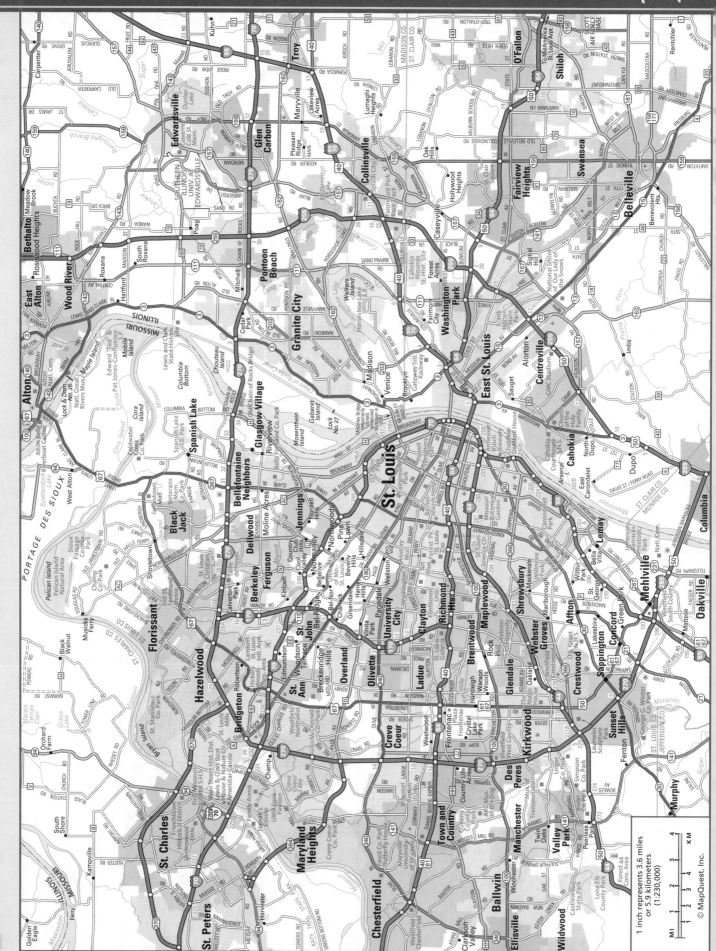

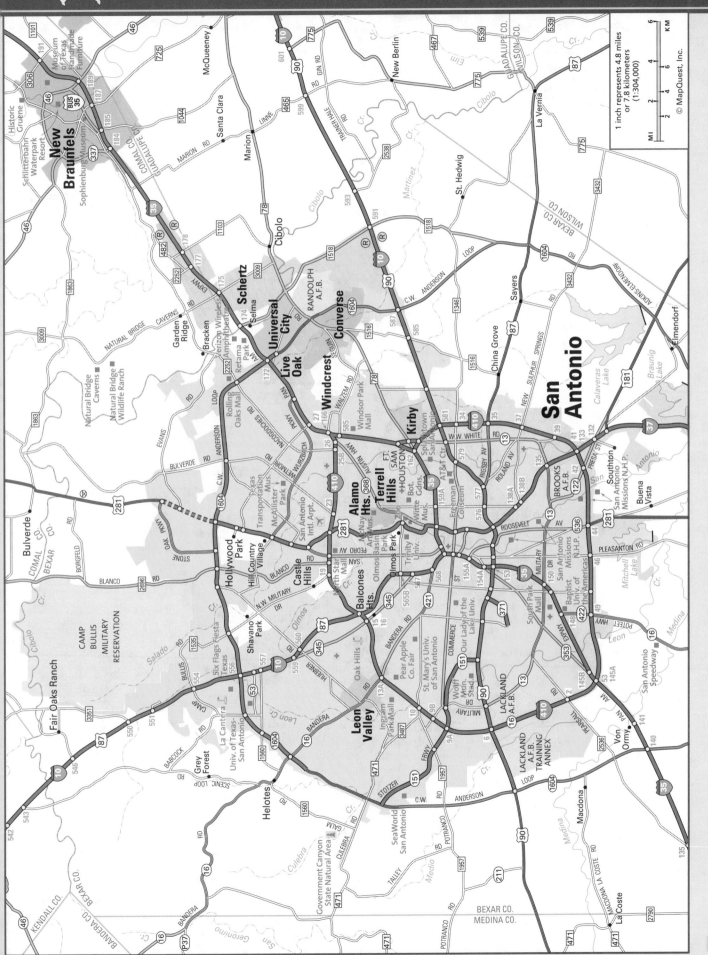

1 inch represents 4.8 miles
or 7.8 kilometers
(1:304,000)

© MapQuest, Inc.

KM

MI

New Braunfels

Museum of Texas Handmade Furniture

Historic Gruene

Schlitterbahn Waterpark Resort

Sophienburg Museum

Natural Bridge Caverns

Natural Bridge Wildlife Ranch

Bulverde

Fair Oaks Ranch

CAMP BULLIS MILITARY RESERVATION

Grey Forest

Helotes

McQueeney

Santa Clara

Marion

Cibolo

Schertz

Universal City

Selma

Garden Ridge

Bracken

Verizon Wireless Amphitheatre

Retama Park

Rolling Oaks Mall

Live Oak

Windcrest

Windsor Park Mall

Texas Transportation Mus.

McAllister Park

San Antonio Intl. Arpt.

Hollywood Park

Hill Country Village

Castle Hills

Balcones Hts.

Shavano Park

North Star Mall

Olmos Park

Trinity Univ.

Witte Mus.

Bot. Gdns.

San Antonio Mus.

Alamo Hts.

Terrell Hills

FT. SAM HOUSTON

Converse

Kirby

Splashtown San Antonio

AT&T Ctr.

Freeman Coliseum

San Antonio

New Berlin

St. Hedwig

China Grove

New Sulphur Springs

La Vernia

Sayers

Calaveras Lake

Braunig Lake

Southton

San Antonio Missions N.H.P.

Buena Vista

Elmendorf

Leon Valley

Ingram Park Mall

Six Flags Fiesta Texas

La Cantera

Univ. of Texas-San Antonio

Oak Hills

Pear Apple Co. Fair

St. Mary's Univ. of San Antonio

Our Lady of the Lake Univ.

Wolff Mun. Stad.

LACKLAND A.F.B.

LACKLAND A.F.B. TRAINING ANNEX

SeaWorld San Antonio

Government Canyon State Natural Area

Univ. of the Americas

San Antonio Missions N.H.P.

Baptist Univ.

South Park Mall

Mitchell Lake

Von Ormy

Macdona

La Coste

BEXAR CO.
MEDINA CO.

BEXAR CO.
WILSON CO.

GUADALUPE CO.
WILSON CO.

COMAL CO.
GUADALUPE CO.

COMAL BEXAR CO.

KENDALL CO.
BEXAR CO.

BANDERA CO.
BEXAR CO.

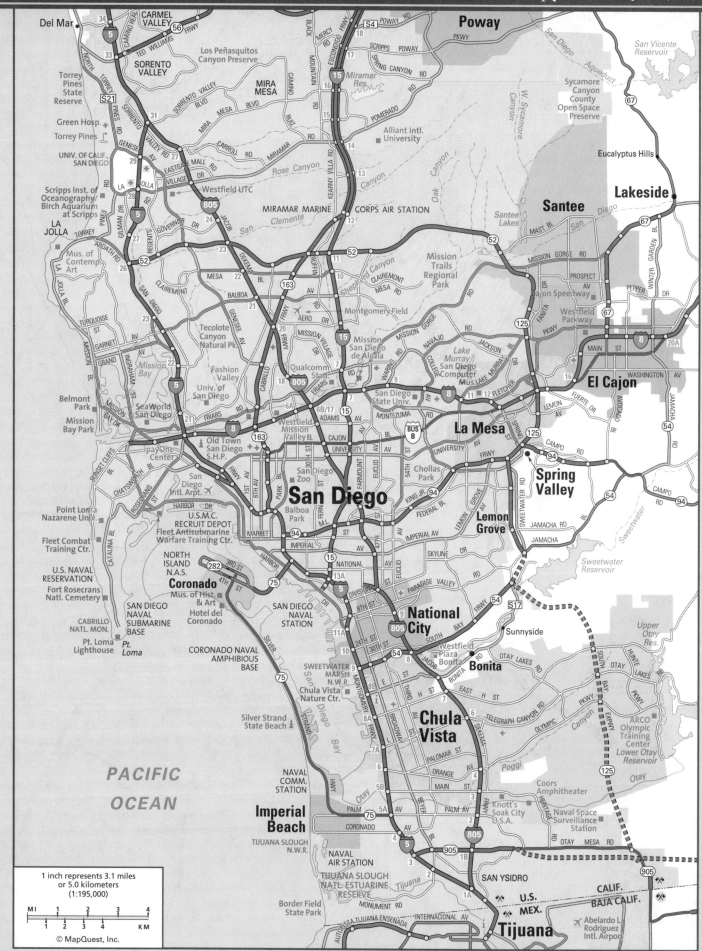

1 inch represents 3.1 miles
or 5.0 kilometers
(1:195,000)

MI   1   2   3   4
KM   1   2   3   4

© MapQuest, Inc.

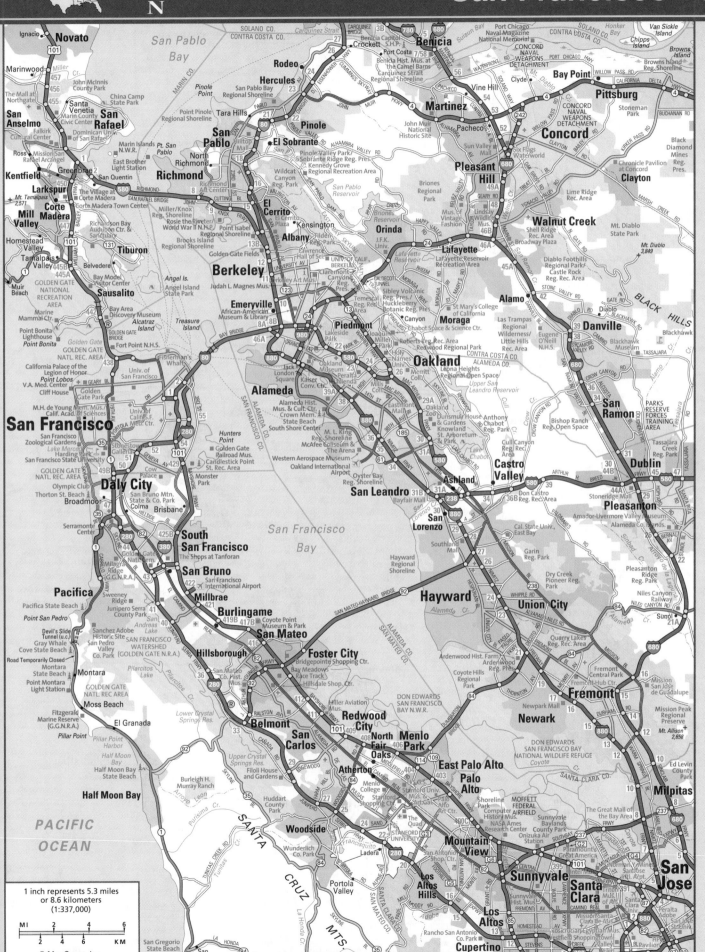

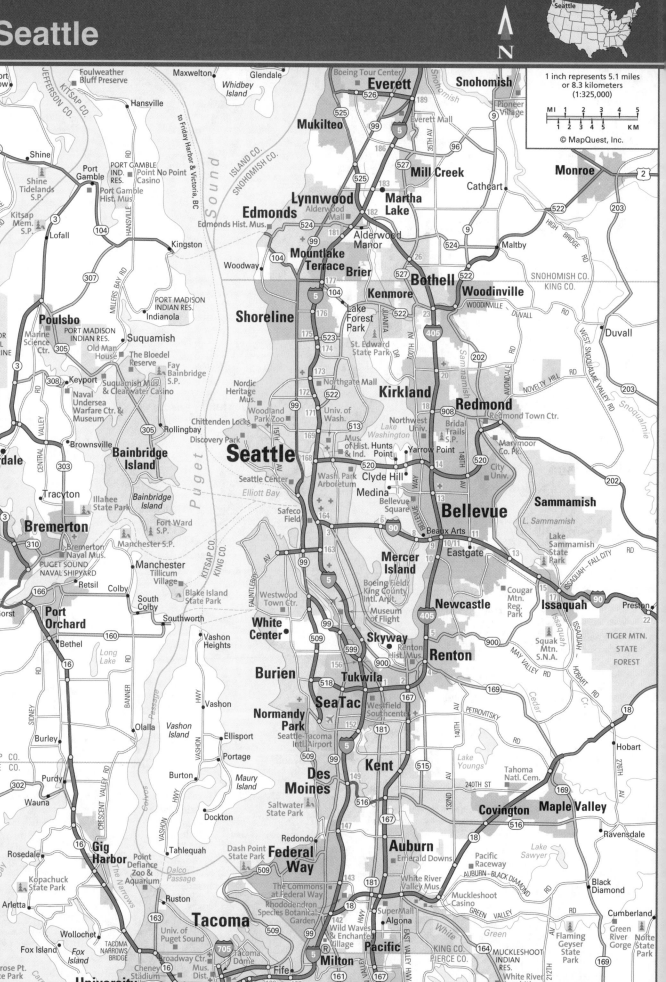

1 inch represents 5.1 miles
or 8.3 kilometers
(1:325,000)

© MapQuest, Inc.

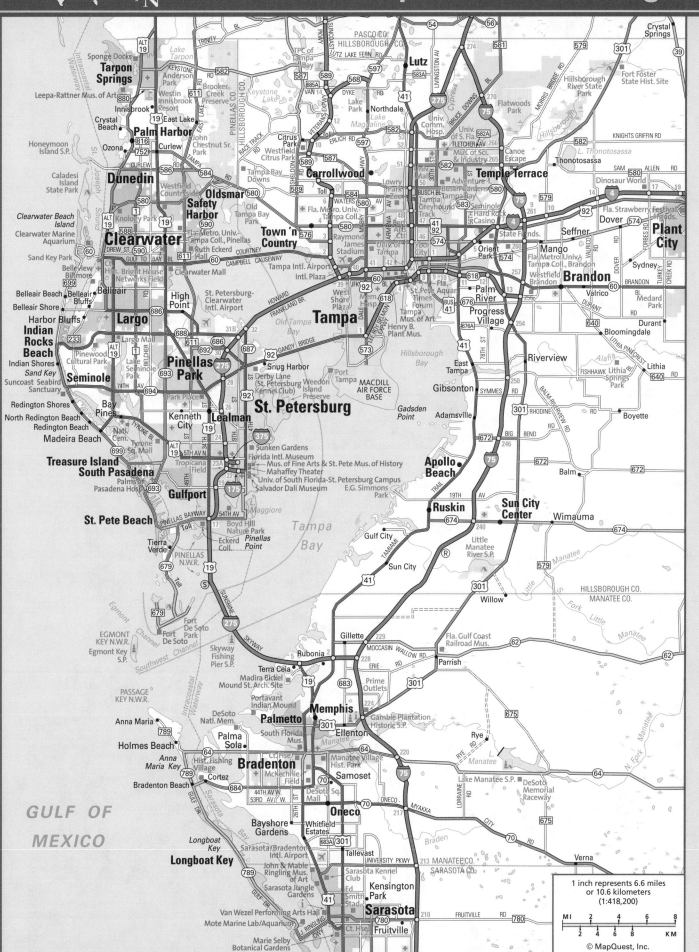

Tampa

St. Petersburg

N

PASCO CO.
HILLSBOROUGH CO.

Sponge Docks
Tarpon Springs
Leepa-Rattner Mus. of Art
Innisbrook
Westin Innisbrook Resort
Crystal Beach
East Lake
Honeymoon Island S.P.
Ozona
Curlew
Caladesi Island State Park
Dunedin
Knology Park
Clearwater Beach Island
Clearwater Marine Aquarium
Sand Key Park
Clearwater
Belleview Biltmore
Belleair Beach
Belleair Bluffs
Belleair
Belleair Shore
Harbor Bluffs
Indian Rocks Beach
Indian Shores
Sand Key
Seminole
Suncoast Seabird Sanctuary
Redington Shores
North Redington Beach
Redington Beach
Madeira Beach
Bay Pines
Kenneth City
Treasure Island
South Pasadena
Palms of Pasadena Hosp.
Gulfport
St. Pete Beach
Tierra Verde
Boyd Hill Nature Park
Eckerd Coll.
Pinellas Point
PINELLAS N.W.R.
EGMONT KEY N.W.R.
Egmont Key S.P.
Fort De Soto Park
Fort De Soto
Skyway Fishing Pier S.P.

Palm Harbor
816
752
Curlew
586
584
580
580
Oldsmar
Safety Harbor
Old Tampa Bay Park
Fla. Metro. Univ.- Tampa Coll.
Town 'n Country
576
580
580
WATERS AV
Fla. Metro. Univ.- Tampa Coll., Pinellas
Ruth Eckerd Hall
Clearwater Mall
Campbell Causeway
Tampa Intl. Airport
Intl. Plaza
St. Petersburg-Clearwater Intl. Airport
High Point
Largo Mall
Largo
Pinewood Cultural Park
Lake Seminole Park
Park Place
Pinellas Park
Snug Harbor
Derby Lane (St. Petersburg Kennel Club)
Weedon Island Preserve
Port Tampa
MACDILL AIR FORCE BASE
Gadsden Point
Tyrone Sq. Mall
Natl. Cem.
Tyrone
5TH AV N
Tropicana Field
Sunken Gardens
Florida Intl. Museum
Mus. of Fine Arts & St. Pete Mus. of History
Mahaffey Theater
Univ. of South Florida-St. Petersburg Campus
Salvador Dali Museum
St. Petersburg
L. Maggiore
Tampa Bay
54TH AV
PINELLAS BAYWAY
Pinellas Point
E.G. Simmons Park
Gulf City

GULF OF MEXICO

PASSAGE KEY N.W.R.

Anna Maria
Holmes Beach
Anna Maria Key
Cortez
Bradenton Beach
Longboat Key
Longboat Key
DeSoto Natl. Mem.
Portavant Indian Mound
Palma Sola
Hist. Fishing Village
Bradenton
McKechnie Field
South Florida Mus.
44TH AV W
53RD AV. W.
DeSoto Sq. Mall
26TH ST
Bayshore Gardens
Whitfield Estates
John & Mable Ringling Mus. of Art
Sarasota/Bradenton Intl. Airport
Sarasota Jungle Gardens
Van Wezel Performing Arts Hall
Mote Marine Lab/Aquarium
Marie Selby Botanical Gardens
Sarasota
Sarasota Kennel Club
Ed. Smith Stad.
Kensington Park
Terra Ceia
Madira Bickel Mound St. Arch. Site
Rubonia
Palmetto
Memphis
Gamble Plantation Historic S.P.
Ellenton
Prime Outlets
Manatee Village Hist. Park
Samoset
Oneco
Tallevast
UNIVERSITY PKWY
Fruitville

Lutz
Lake Fern RD
Lutz
Northdale
Lake Park
Lake Magdaline
Univ. Comm. Hosp.
Univ. of S. Fla.
FLETCHER AV
Mus. of Sci. & Industry
Canoe Escape
Temple Terrace
Busch Gardens Tampa Bay
Tampa Greyhound Track
Hard Rock Casino
Seminole
Carrollwood
Lowry Park Zoo
Raymond James Stadium
Univ. of Tampa
West Shore Plaza
Tampa
Mem. Hosp.
Ybor City
Fla. Aquarium
St. Pete Times Forum
Tampa Mus. of Art
Henry B. Plant Mus.
JFK
Old Tampa Bay
HOWARD FRANKLAND BR.
LEROY SELMON EXPWY
GANDY BRIDGE
West Tampa
East Tampa
Palm River
Progress Village
Hillsborough Bay
Gibsonton
Adamsville
Apollo Beach
Ruskin
Sun City Center
Wimauma
Sun City
Little Manatee River S.P.
Willow
Gillette
Moccasin Wallow RD
ERIE RD
Parrish
Fla. Gulf Coast Railroad Mus.
Rye
Rye RD
L. Manatee
Lake Manatee S.P.
DeSoto Memorial Raceway
Verna
Braden
MANATEE CO.
SARASOTA CO.
FRUITVILLE RD

Plant City
Fla. Strawberry Festival Grnds.
Dover
Seffner
Mango
Valrico
Sydney
Brandon
Fla. Metro Univ.- Brandon
Westfield Brandon
Medard Park
Durant
Bloomingdale
Lithia
Lithia Springs Park
FISHHAWK
Boyette
Balm
Thonotosassa
L. Thonotosassa
KNIGHTS GRIFFIN RD
Dinosaur World
Fort Foster State Hist. Site
Flatwoods Park
Hillsborough River State Park
Canoe Escape
Crystal Springs

P 16
Florida

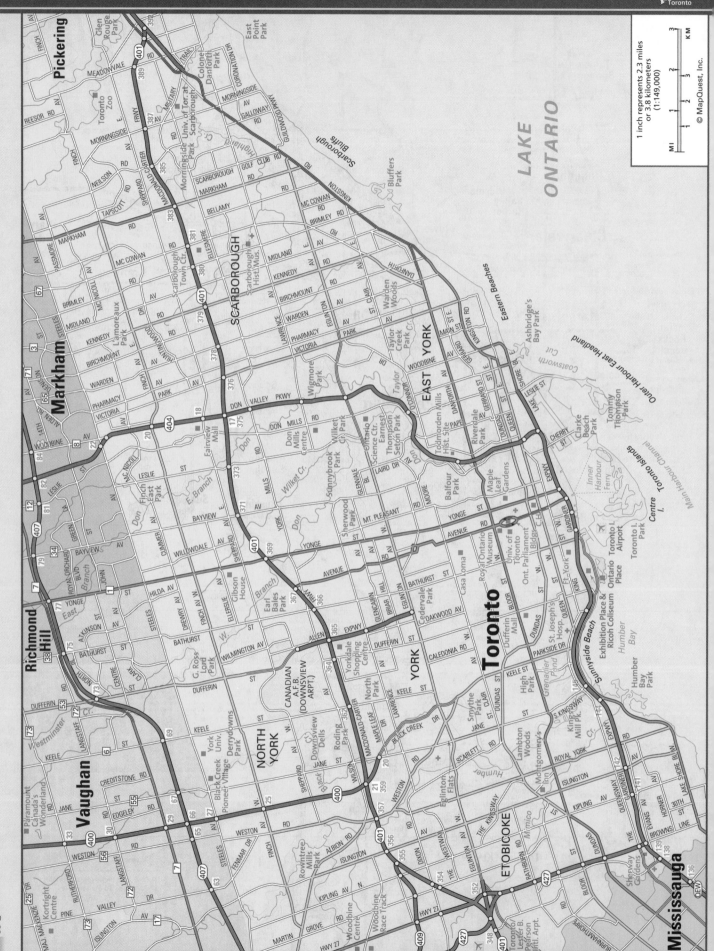

N

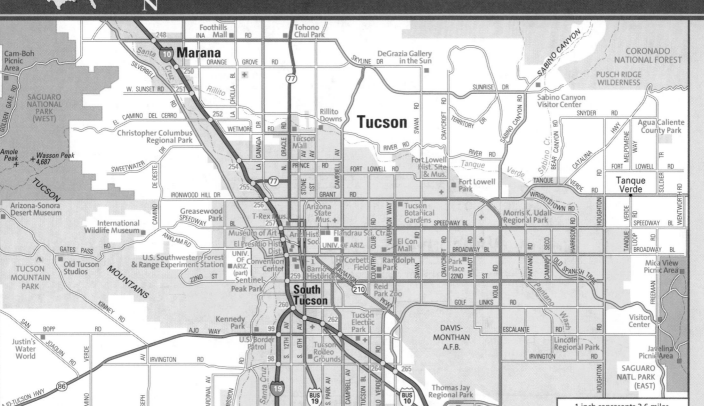

Tucson map detail:

Cam-Boh Picnic Area · Foothills Mall · INA · Tohono Chul Park · DeGrazia Gallery in the Sun · CORONADO NATIONAL FOREST · PUSCH RIDGE WILDERNESS

Santa Cruz · Marana · ORANGE · GROVE RD · SKYLINE DR · Sabino Canyon Visitor Center · Agua Caliente County Park

SILVERBELL · W. SUNSET RD · Rillito · LA CHOLLA BL · N. ORACLE · Tucson · SWAN RD · CRAYCROFT RD · TERRITORY · SNYDER · SUNRISE DR

SAGUARO NATIONAL PARK (WEST) · GOLDEN GATE RD · EL CAMINO DEL CERRO · WETMORE · LA CANADA · Rillito Downs · RIVER RD · RIVER RD · SABINO CANYON · BEAR CANYON RD · CATALINA HWY · FORT LOWELL · MELPOMENE WAY

Amole Peak · Wasson Peak +4,687 · SWEETWATER · DE ANZA · Christopher Columbus Regional Park · IRONWOOD HILL DR · PRINCE · Fort Lowell RD · FORT LOWELL RD · Fort Lowell Hist. Site & Mus. · Fort Lowell Park · Tanque Verde · Tanque Verde · SOLDIER RD · WENTWORTH RD · Tanque Verde

Arizona-Sonora Desert Museum · Greasewood Park · T-Rex Mus. · 256 · Tucson Mall · STONE · CAMPBELL AV · GRANT · RD · Arizona State Mus. · Tucson Botanical Gardens · SPEEDWAY BL · Morris K. Udall Regional Park · HOUGHTON RD · SPEEDWAY · Mica View Picnic Area

International Wildlife Museum · CAMINO · ANKLAM RD · Museum of Art · El Presidio Hist. Dist · Ariz. Hist. Soc. · Flandrau Sci. Ctr. · El Con Mall · BROADWAY BL · SECO · PANTANO · OLD SPANISH TRAIL · TANQUE · LOOP · Broadway · BROADWAY BL

GATES PASS RD · U.S. Southwestern Forest & Range Experiment Station · 22ND ST · UNIV. OF ARIZ. (part) · H. Corbett Field · Randolph Park · Park Place · WILMOT · KOLB · CAMINO · Tucson Mountain Park · Old Tucson Studios · TUCSON · MOUNTAINS · KINNEY RD · Sentinel Peak Park · Barrio Historico · AVIATION · 210 · Reid Park Zoo · 22ND ST · GOLF LINKS RD · Lincoln Regional Park · Javelina Picnic Area · Visitor Center

Justin's Water World · SAN JOAQUIN RD · BOPP RD · VERDE · AJO WAY · Kennedy Park · S 12TH AV · S 6TH AV · 262 · Tucson Electric Park · Tucson Rodeo Grounds · DAVIS-MONTHAN A.F.B. · 264 · 265 · ESCALANTE · IRVINGTON · HOUGHTON · SAGUARO NATL. PARK (EAST)

86 · AJO-TUCSON HWY · IRVINGTON RD · CARDINAL AV · MISSION RD · S PARK AV · S. CAMPBELL AV · TUCSON BL · PALO VERDE · Thomas Jay Regional Park

VALENCIA RD · JOSEPH · CAMINO DE OESTE · BUS 19 · 95 · BUS 10 · VALENCIA RD · 267 · Pima Air & Space Mus. · WILMOT · KOLB

Casino Del Sol · Casino of the Sun · PASCUA YAQUI INDIAN RESERVATION · Mission San Xavier del Bac · Desert Diamond Casino · Tucson Intl. Arpt. · LOS REALES RD · 268 · ALVERNON · SWAN RD · 269 · 10 · 270

TOHONO O'ODHAM (SAN XAVIER) INDIAN RESERVATION · West Branch Santa Cruz · 91

1 inch represents 3.6 miles or 5.7 kilometers (1:226,000)

MI 1 2 3 4 · KM 1 2 3 4

© MapQuest, Inc.

P 8 Arizona

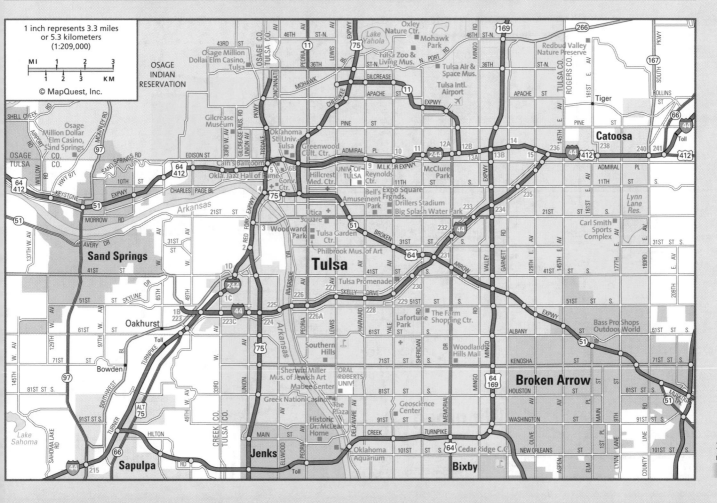

Tulsa map detail:

1 inch represents 3.3 miles or 5.3 kilometers (1:209,000)

MI 1 2 3 · KM 1 2 3

© MapQuest, Inc.

OSAGE INDIAN RESERVATION · Osage Million Dollar Elm Casino, Tulsa · 43RD · 46TH ST-N · Lake Yahola · Oxley Nature Ctr. · Mohawk Park · 36TH ST-N · 169 · 266

OSAGE CO. · TULSA CO. · 36TH · 11 · PEORIA · LEWIS · MOHAWK · GILCREASE EXPWY · 75 · Tulsa Zoo & Living Mus. · N. PORT · MINGO · APACHE · ST · Redbud Valley Nature Preserve · 167

Osage Million Dollar Elm Casino, Sand Springs · 97 · Gilcrease Museum · 33RD W AV · TISDALE · GILCREASE · CHEROKEE · APACHE · PINE · Tulsa Air & Space Mus. · Tulsa Intl. Airport · APACHE ST · 161ST E. AV · ROGERS CO. · TULSA CO. · Tiger · PINE · ROLLINS · 66

OSAGE CO. · TULSA CO. · SHELL CREEK RD · McKINLEY RD · AIRPORT RD · EDISON ST · Oklahoma St. Univ. Tulsa · ADMIRAL PL · 11 · 12A · 12B · 14 · 236 · Catoosa · 238 · 240 · 241 · 412 · 44 Toll

64 412 · SAND SPRINGS RD · Cain's Ballroom · Greenwood Cult. Ctr. · 244 · 13A · 13B · 15 · 44 · 412 · ADMIRAL PL · 11TH · 44

WILLOW · HWY 97 · 10TH ST · CHARLES PAGE BL · Okla. Jazz Hall of Fame · 5 · 6B · 75 · UNIV. OF TULSA · M.L.K. JR EXPWY · McClure Park · 145TH · 161ST E. AV · 177TH · 193RD · 51

KEYSTONE EXPWY · 51 · Arkansas · 21ST ST · 4 · Bell's Expo Square Amusement Park Frgnds. · 233 · 234 · 235 · Drillers Stadium · Big Splash Water Park · Lynn Lane Res.

MORROW RD · AVERY DR · 31ST ST · Utica Square · 3 · Woodward Park · Tulsa Garden Ctr. · BROKEN · 51 · 232 · 44 · 231 · Carl Smith Sports Complex · 31ST ST S.

Sand Springs · 41ST ST · RIVERSIDE DR · Philbrook Mus. of Art · 64 · 230 · ARROW · VALLEY · GARNETT · 129TH · 145TH · 41ST ST S.

RED FORK EXPWY · 244 · 1D · 41ST ST · 226 · Tulsa Promenade · 227 · SKELLY DRIVE · 229 · 51ST ST · SHERIDAN · MEMORIAL · MINGO · 51ST ST S.

51ST ST · SKYLINE AV · 65TH · 49TH · 1C · 225 · Southern Hills · 228 · Lafortune Park · HARVARD · YALE · 51ST ST · The Farm Shopping Ctr. · 51 · ALBANY · Bass Pro Shops Outdoor World · 61ST ST S.

61ST ST · 1B · 223 · 223C · 224 · 226A · LEWIS · PEORIA · 64 · 169 · HOUSTON · Broken Arrow · KENOSHA · 71ST ST S.

Oakhurst · 75 · TURNPIKE · Toll · Sherwin Miller Mus. of Jewish Art · Mabee Center · ORAL ROBERTS UNIV. · Woodland Hills Mall · 81ST ST · MINGO · ALBANY · 81ST ST S.

129TH W AV · 97 · 71ST AV · 49TH · Bowden · Greek Nation Casino · The Plaza · Geoscience Center · WASHINGTON · 91ST ST · 1ST PL · MAIN · LYNN LANE · 91ST ST S.

81ST ST S. · SOUTHWEST BL · UNION · 33RD · DELAWARE · Historic Dr. McLean Home · 101ST ST · NEW ORLEANS · OLIVE · ASPEN · MAIN · 101ST ST S.

SAPULPA LAKE RD · Lake Sahoma · ALT 75 · HILTON · 66 · Jenks · ELWOOD · PEORIA · MAIN · Oklahoma Aquarium · CREEK · TURNPIKE · Toll · 64 · Cedar Ridge C.C. · Bixby · COUNTY LINE

44 · 215 · Sapulpa · CREEK CO. · TULSA CO.

P 44 Oklahoma

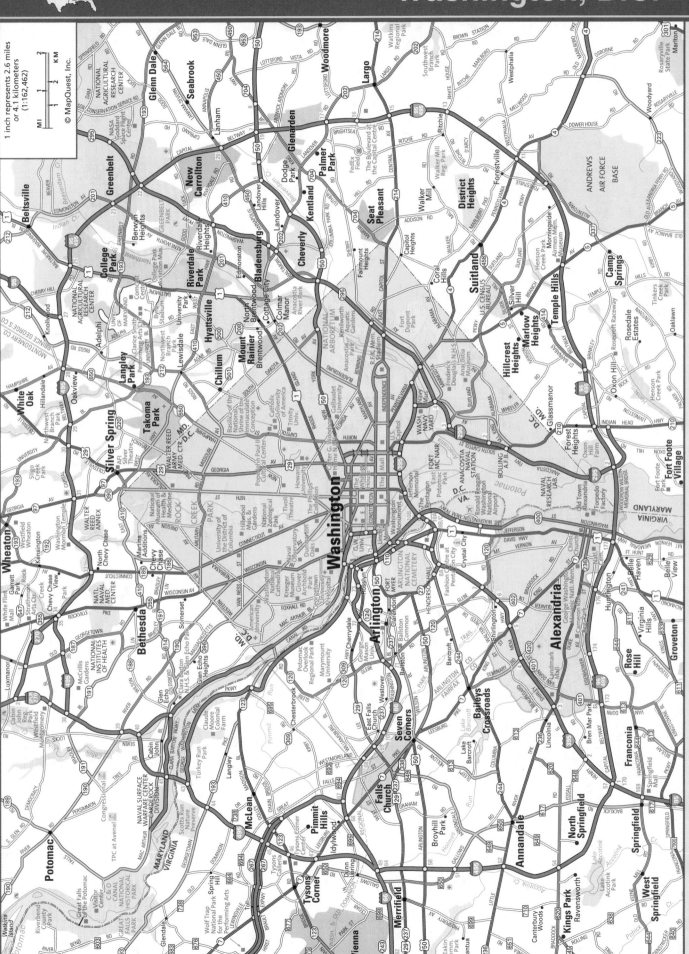

Washington, D.C.

1 inch represents 2.6 miles
or 4.1 kilometers
(1:162,462)

© MapQuest, Inc.

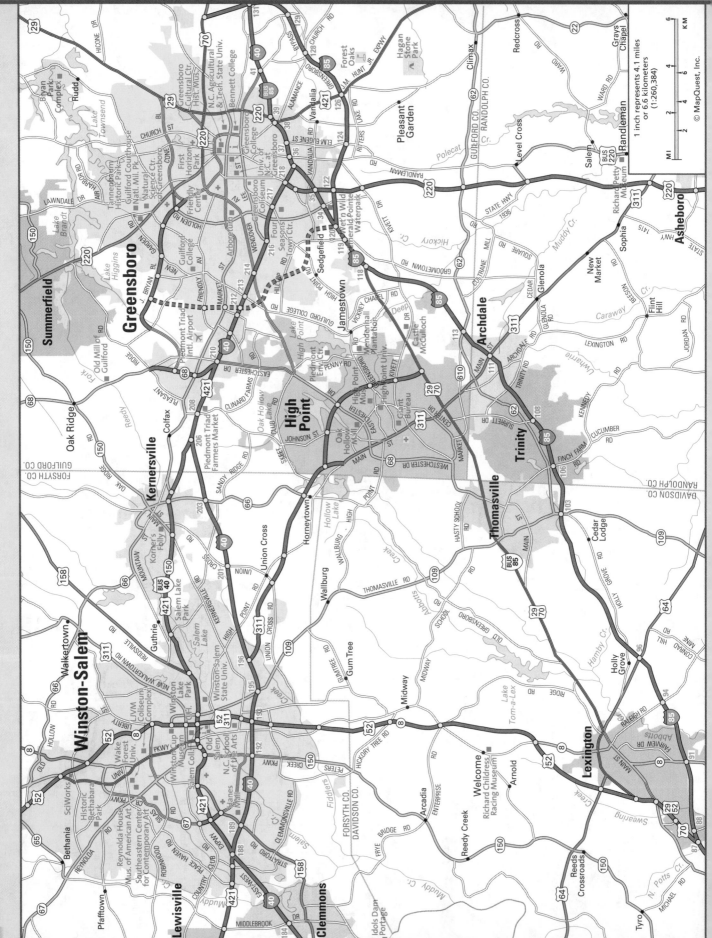

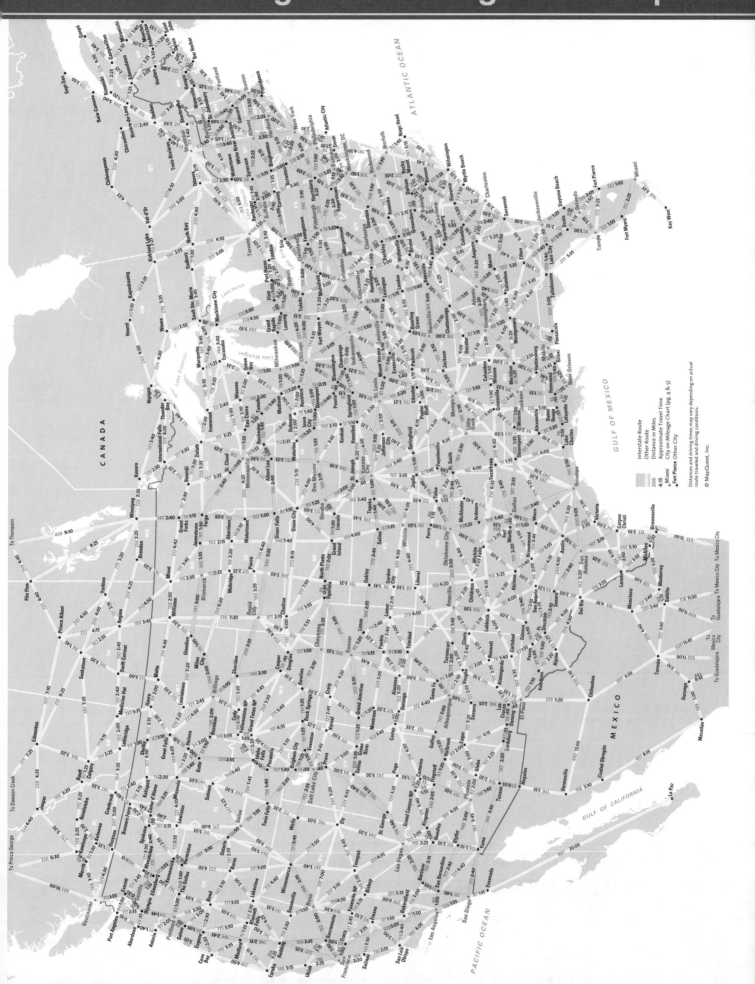